CW01261905

Criminology of Serial Poisoners

Michael Farrell

Criminology of Serial Poisoners

palgrave macmillan

Michael Farrell
Herefordshire, UK

ISBN 978-3-030-01137-6   ISBN 978-3-030-01138-3   (eBook)
https://doi.org/10.1007/978-3-030-01138-3

Library of Congress Control Number: 2018956579

© The Editor(s) (if applicable) and The Author(s), under exclusive licence to Springer Nature Switzerland AG 2018
This work is subject to copyright. All rights are solely and exclusively licensed by the Publisher, whether the whole or part of the material is concerned, specifically the rights of translation, reprinting, reuse of illustrations, recitation, broadcasting, reproduction on microfilms or in any other physical way, and transmission or information storage and retrieval, electronic adaptation, computer software, or by similar or dissimilar methodology now known or hereafter developed.
The use of general descriptive names, registered names, trademarks, service marks, etc. in this publication does not imply, even in the absence of a specific statement, that such names are exempt from the relevant protective laws and regulations and therefore free for general use.
The publisher, the authors and the editors are safe to assume that the advice and information in this book are believed to be true and accurate at the date of publication. Neither the publisher nor the authors or the editors give a warranty, express or implied, with respect to the material contained herein or for any errors or omissions that may have been made. The publisher remains neutral with regard to jurisdictional claims in published maps and institutional affiliations.

Cover credit: Qiang Fu/Getty Images
Cover design: Fatima Jamadar

This Palgrave Macmillan imprint is published by the registered company Springer Nature Switzerland AG
The registered company address is: Gewerbestrasse 11, 6330 Cham, Switzerland

Preface

In writing *Criminology of Serial Poisoners*, I have aimed to set out some key components of criminology of serial poisoning. I hope this will aid academics, researchers, professionals, and others wishing to have an overview of the subject, and that the book provides a structure for further work and development.

I would be happy to receive suggestions to make any future editions of the book more helpful to readers at the following e-mail address: drmjfarrell@bulldog1870.plus.com.

Herefordshire, UK Michael Farrell

Acknowledgements

I am grateful to Dr. Beatrice Yorker, College of Health and Human Services California State University Los Angeles, Los Angeles, CA for kindly clarifying for me aspects of her research.

Contents

1	Introducing Serial Poisoning	1
2	Explanations of Serial Poisoning	21
3	Poisons Used in Serial Poisoning	45
4	Serial Poisoners	69
5	Healthcare Serial Poisoning	93
6	Victims of Serial Poisoners	115
7	Investigating Serial Poisoning	137
8	Summary Note of Serial Poisonings	159
9	Profiles of Selected Serial Poisoning Cases	189
	Index	239

About the Author

Michael Farrell was educated in the UK. After training as a teacher at Bishop Grosseteste College, Lincoln, and obtaining an honours degree from Nottingham University, he gained a M.A. in Education and Psychology from the Institute of Education, London University. Subsequently, he carried out research for an M.Phil. at the Institute of Psychiatry, London, and for a Ph.D. under the auspices of the Medical Research Council Cognitive Development Unit and London University.

Professionally, Michael Farrell held senior posts in schools and units for people with various mental disorders. He managed a UK-wide psychometric project for City University, London and directed a national initial teacher-training project for the UK Government Department of Education. For over a decade, he led teams inspecting mainstream and special schools and units (boarding, day, hospital, psychiatric). Currently, he works as a private consultant with a range of clients and has lectured or provided consultancy services in various countries including China, Japan, the Seychelles, Australia, Peru, Sweden, the Emirates, and the UK.

He has broadcast on UK national radio and has written articles on crime and poisoning in a range of medical, psychological, police, and legal journals. His many books are translated into European and Asian languages.

1

Introducing Serial Poisoning

Preamble

Within a wider context of crime, serial poisoning can be an underestimated issue. Accordingly, I set out the aims of the book, its scope, structure, methodology, and features, and proposed readers. It is also useful to clarify certain terms including criminology, homicide in general, serial homicide, and serial poison homicide. Also important are considerations of the scale of homicide and its different types. Motive is a further potentially slippery term that it is helpful to clarify. After this, we can look ahead to the topics explored by later chapters.

Importance of Serial Poisoning

It is reported that the overall death rate from poisoning homicide is low. In the US, Shepherd and Ferslew (2009) identified 523 homicidal poison deaths between 1999 and 2005, giving an overall rate for the period of 0.26/million/year. However, an analysis of Uniform Crime

Reports 1980s for the US indicated that the unknown offender rate for poisoning cases was 20–30 times higher than that for other homicides (Westveer et al. 1996).

If apparently individual occurrences of poisoning homicide remain unsolved, it is feasible that among them instances of serial poisoning are going undetected.

This is supported by cases of serial poisoning that come to light after many killings. In Germany, in 2017, reports updated previous investigations into the activities of nurse **Niels Högel** [S61, P20] already convicted of murdering patients. Police now believe that Högel committed 36 murders while employed at the Oldenburg Clinic, Lower Saxony, then moved to Delmenhorst near Bremen where he killed a further 48 patients. (The letters in square brackets after a serial poisoner's name refer to glossaries appended to this book, 'S' being a 'summary' of the case and 'P' being a more detailed 'profile', the numbers referring to the order on these lists.)

The combination of likely underestimated prevalence of serial poisoning, and past and recent cases in which more killings than expected have been ultimately detected, make serial poisoning an important topic to study and investigate.

Aims of the Book

A key aim of this book is to provide an outline for developing a criminology of serial poisoning homicide. Drawing on cases of serial poisoning, I suggest parameters of such a study by:

- Defining central terms such as homicide, and motive
- Examining theories and explanations of serial homicide in relation to serial poisoning
- Explaining the features of the substances that have been used in serial poisoning
- Exploring demographic characteristics of serial poisoners and their victims

- Considering healthcare serial poisoning specifically
- Discussing other aspects of investigating serial poisoning, such as seeking an internal structure or logic of some cases.

Scope of the Book

In its scope, this book examines serial homicidal poisonings in the modern era, allowing us to infer implications for contemporary understanding of poisons, poisoners, and investigation. Cases mentioned throughout the book almost invariably concern perpetrators convicted of murder. North America and the UK provide most of the material but there are examples from Europe (France, Germany, Austria, Switzerland, Norway, the Netherlands, Russia, Belgium, Spain); Canada; South America (Argentina); Australia; Japan; India; and Vietnam. Many of the cases raising important issues have been reported in the press, books, articles and internet sites. This chronological, geographical, and well-documented range of cases illustrate points about serial poisoning that inform broader understanding and allow tentative generalisations to be made.

I touch on rare instances of team serial poisoning (involving more than one perpetrator) and mass poisoning (where a group of people are simultaneously poisoned by a perpetrator or perpetrators). Areas of poisoning *not* covered in the book include: poisoning as judicial killing by gas chamber or lethal injection (Farrell 1994), wartime poisoning, corporate homicide, suicide pacts, and political assassinations. The scale, motivations, context, and implications of such poisonings I believe require separate treatment.

Features of the Book

In style, I have tried to be direct and use plain language, avoiding jargon. Where technical terms are used, I explain them. The book comprises chapters on serial poisoning and related matters. In each chapter, the structure is intended to aid the assimilation of its content. Each has an introduction, structured headings and subheadings, a conclusion, suggested activities to encourage reflection and discussion, texts for further reading, and references.

There are two glossaries. The first is a summary list of over sixty serial poisoning cases from the mid-1800s to the present day. These are in broadly chronological sequence according to the year when the perpetrator was sentenced. They illustrate the use of a wide variety of poisons, involving perpetrators worldwide. Where in the body of the book one of these cases is mentioned, it is identified by a letter 'S' (for summary) followed by a number which relates to the sequenced cases. For example, '[S1]' refers to the first case that is summarised in the list. Where a serial poisoner is suspected of deaths other than the ones for which sentenced, I have usually noted this, but tend to concentrate on the homicides for which they were convicted.

The second glossary comprises over 20 profiles (fuller descriptions) of cases selected from the longer list of brief summaries. These describe cases more fully and include 'points of particular interest' and extend from the year 2000 to the present day. Where a case is mentioned in the body of the book which is covered by a fuller profile, this is indicated by the case summary number followed by the profile number.

Methodology Used in the Book

In approaching serial poisoning, I have laid bare the origins of my observations. These are the sixty plus case 'summaries' and the subset of these described more fully in the 'profiles', both towards the end of the book. In turn, the cases are chosen to be broadly representative of a greater number, allowing generalisations that can be tested by future research including that involving other cases.

About twenty countries are represented. A time frame based on the date that the perpetrator was convicted extends from 1850 to the present day, with an emphasis on more recent cases. Referenced sources with internet links where appropriate include books, book chapters, journal articles, national and local press reports, biographies, television news reports, encyclopaedias, judicial reports, public enquiry documents, unpublished research theses, and accounts of court proceedings. Sources in English, French, Spanish, and German have been consulted and referenced. I have tried to balance good sources with availability so that for many references, readers will be able to consult the relevant documents through libraries, book stores, the internet, and elsewhere. Where press reports are used, I have distilled from several what appears to be a reliable and consistent account of the crimes and have given examples of the coverage.

Additionally, in the work underpinning the book, I have sought the advice and views of specialists including homicide officers, lawyers, toxicologists, pathologists, and academics. Researchers and others have exchanged views and clarified points relating to their own publications. The generous response of these colleagues has been greatly encouraging (Farrell 2017).

This information has been used to look at serial poisoners in relation to serial killers in general, comparing demographic features such as gender, age, and ethnicity. All this allows one to trace the contours of serial poisoning and explore reasons for any differences and similarities in relation to serial killing more generally. I have also explored how wider crime and homicide theories apply to serial poisoning.

Proposed Readers

Core readers of the book are likely to be: students of criminology (classes dealing with criminal psychology, and murder investigation); criminal justice professionals: attorneys, homicide detectives, forensic pathologists, forensic and clinical toxicologists, and other forensic investigators. More widely, readers are likely to include others who are interested in poisons and poisoners and the detection of poisoning. Relevant disciplines include: criminology, law and policing, toxicology and forensic science, history of crime and detection, and criminal psychology.

Given the scope of the volume and the worldwide range of examples of poisoning cases, I hope that it will attract readers from many English-speaking parts of the world, especially North America, the UK, India,

Australia, New Zealand, and English-speaking countries of Africa. Other areas where English is widely spoken such as Scandinavia, may also find the book valuable.

Criminology

For Lacey and Zedner (2012) criminology is informed by sociology, social theory, psychology, history, economics, and political science, and concerns 'social and individual antecedents of crime' and 'the nature of crime as a social phenomenon'. It examines 'patterns of criminality and their social construction' and the conditions bringing these about (historical, economic, political or social) (ibid., p. 160). In short, criminology draws on the social sciences, is concerned with the nature of crime, its antecedents, and the conditions that create the social phenomenon of crime.

Rock (2012) views criminology more in terms of its scope than its theoretical assumptions or its attachment to any social science. It is defined, 'principally by its attachment to an empirical area' and it is 'the study of *crime* that gives unity and order to the enterprise' (ibid., p. 70, italics in original). Furthermore, it is in 'the examination of *crime* that psychologists, statisticians, lawyers, economists, social anthropologists, sociologists, social policy analysts, and psychiatrists meet and call themselves criminologists…' (ibid., italics in original).

In the light of such perspectives, criminology is a multidisciplinary area concerning crime, its antecedents, and context, and recognises different theories. If this description begins to define criminology, its scope is suggested by textbook coverage.

The fifth edition of, *The Oxford Handbook of Criminology* (Maguire et al. 2012) comprises five parts. These cover respectively, 'criminology: history and theory', 'social constructions of crime and crime control', 'dimensions of crime' (such as gender, ethnicity, and victims), 'forms of crime' (e.g. violent crime, white-collar crime and terrorism), and 'reactions to crime' (including prevention, policing, and sentencing).

A single-authored *Textbook on Criminology* (Williams 2012) looks at political, theoretical, philosophical, and practical elements of the subject. Key questions include how crime is defined, why crime is committed, and how society should respond to criminals. Also pertinent is the changing nature of crime, and society's response, for example, the modern implications of terrorism.

In brief, the scope of criminology is wide, embracing history and modern trends, theory, social perspectives of crime and responses to it, practicalities, demographics, and classifications of crime.

Homicide and Types of Homicide

Conceptions of Homicide

A wide view of homicide includes its social and cultural context, and changes in homicide over time. Its forms can be variously categorised, for example, relating to victim ('infanticide') or motive ('sexual homicide') (Brookman et al. 2017).

While initial considerations of the term 'homicide' may equate it with unlawful killing, it can have much wider application. Indeed, the concept can include sanctioned killings such as state-administered execution. Understandings of the term can vary according to social and historical context. Social conceptions and therefore social responses to homicide may be different in different countries and in the same country over different time periods. Mainstream and social media depictions and discussions contribute to views of homicides and the differing responses to them.

Legal Frameworks for Homicide

Law in England and Wales relating to homicide is reflected in approaches common to many other countries. Under common law and its derivatives, 'actus reus' referring to the 'guilty act' and 'mens rea' concerning 'guilty mind' are both considered in judging criminal liability. Homicide covers the offences of murder and of manslaughter. Also included are other instances of a person causing (or being involved in) the death of another where the 'actus reus' is the same, but where causation is problematic (Croner 2008, p. 37).

An offence of murder under common law is committed when 'a person unlawfully kills another human being under the Queen's Peace, with malice aforethought' (Croner 2008, p. 37). 'Unlawful killing' includes, as well as actively causing another's death, failing to act after creating a situation of danger. If there is 'malice aforethought' there is an intention to kill or to cause 'grievous bodily harm' (ibid., p. 38).

Rather than a conviction of murder, certain 'special defences' namely diminished responsibility (impaired mental responsibility), provocation, and a suicide pact, allow for a conviction of 'voluntary manslaughter' (Croner 2008, p. 39). By contrast in, 'involuntary manslaughter' a defendant causes the death of another person but is not shown to have the required 'mens rea' for murder. They may have killed another person by, 'an unlawful act which was likely to cause bodily harm; or by gross negligence' (ibid., p. 41).

Furthermore, an organisation is guilty of an offence if 'the way in which its activities are managed and organised (a) causes a person's death, and (b) amounts to a gross breach of a relevant duty of care owed by the organisation to the deceased' (*Corporate Manslaughter and Corporate Homicide Act* 2007 Act, Section 1).

Further Categorisations of Homicide

As well as the categorisations of murder, manslaughter, and corporate homicide, there are other designations relating to the perpetrator (e.g. 'male perpetrated homicide'), victims (e.g. 'infanticide'), or circumstances and location (e.g. 'school killings'). Another way of parsing homicide is according to the mode of killing (e.g. 'strangling', 'shooting' or 'stabbing').

Hough and McCorkle (2017, passim) discuss among other areas 'intimate partner' homicide, 'confrontational' homicide, family killings, school killings, 'workplace mass killings', terrorism, and 'cults and gangs'. Such groupings indicate the diversity of homicide. Different types of homicide may be attributed to different apparent causes. A further distinction may be made of 'multiple homicide' and it is to this that we now turn.

Multiple Homicide: Mass and Serial Killing

Multiple homicides can be further designated as 'mass' and 'serial'. In mass homicide 'multiple victims are killed in a single episode and in the same geographic location' (Brookman 2005, p. 211). An example is the mass shooting at a nightclub in Orlando, Florida in June 2016 when Omar Mateen killed 49 people (*New York Times* 2016).

Regarding serial murder, there has been extensive discussion about its definition. One area of contention has been the 'required' number of killings involved and the intervals between them. Contemporary understandings tend to view serial homicides as ones that, 'occur repetitively over an extended period' (Brookman 2005, p. 211). Holmes and Holmes (2010) suggest a minimum period of more than 30 days but the homicides may continue for longer. Unlike mass homicide, serial killing involves 'cooling off' periods (ibid., pp. 5–6). Some researchers argue for a minimum of four killings in a series to constitute serial murder (Levin and Fox 2017, p. 252). However, Hickey (2010) notes, 'Most researchers now agree that serial killers have a minimum of two victims' (ibid., p. 27). Succinctly, serial homicide is, 'the unlawful killing of two or more victims by the same perpetrator(s), in separate incidents comprising a series' (Behavioural Analysis Unit 2005, pp. 8–9). For example, Jeffrey Dahmer murdered 17 men and boys between 1978 and 1971, often dismembering the bodies and eating body parts (Daniszewska 2017, pp. 52–57). Peter Sutcliffe the 'Yorkshire Ripper' murdered 13 women between 1975 and 1980 (Yallop [1981] 2014). Sometimes, serial killers work in a pair as 'team killers'. They may be male-male, female-female, or male-female pairs (Holmes and Holmes 2010, pp. 46–48). An example of team serial killers is Fred and Rosemary West in the UK (Bennett 2005).

Multiple Poison Homicide: Mass and Serial Poisoning

Mass poisoning involves more than one victim being poisoned in a single episode, and in the same location. Large scale atrocities have occurred in wartime (Fitzgerald 2008; Holocaust Education and Archive Research Team 2007). Suicide pacts have sometimes involved mass poisoning (Guinn 2017, passim) as have terrorist attacks (Pletcher 2017). Outside such major examples, the 'simultaneous poisoning' of several people at the same time occasionally arises (Farrell 2017, p. 104). Arthur Ford the manager of a pharmaceutical supply firm, doctored sweets (candy) with cantharides, mistakenly thinking it was an aphrodisiac and killing two secretaries (Farrell 1992, pp. 91–92). Arthur Devereaux simultaneously poisoned his wife Beatrice and twin sons (Browne and Tullett 1951). Richard Brinkley intending to poison a potential witness to forgery Reginald Parker, inadvertently killed Parker's visiting landlord and the landlord's wife (Oddie 1941). In a bank in Japan, pretending to be an official issuing precautionary medication, Sadamichi Hirasawa poisoned several bank tellers with cyanide (Morikawa 1977).

Among well-known instances of serial poison murder, perhaps the most notorious are the killings of **Dr. Harold Shipman** [S41, P1] an English physician convicted of 15 murders but likely responsible for about 250 killings of his patients mainly using morphine-based drugs (*The Shipman Inquiry* 2002–2005). Norwegian **Arnfinn Nesset** [S30] over several years killed 21 of his nursing home residents with succinylcholine chloride. In the US, **Nannie Doss** [S24] by some accounts confessed to poisoning four husbands and is suspected of murdering other family members. Many other examples are discussed throughout this book.

Perhaps less well known are some of the poisonings in non-English-speaking countries. **Chisako Kakehi** [S63, P22], in Kyoto, Japan poisoned her husband and two common law partners with cyanide and was sentenced to death in 2017. In central Russia, **Viacheslav Soloviev** [S56, P15] used thallium to kill several family members, as well a police officer investigating a disturbance involving Soloviev. Also, historical cases may be less familiar to some readers. **Marie Jeanneret** [S4] illustrates what we today would call healthcare serial poisoning but being convicted in 1868 may not be well known.

Challenges in Determining the Scale of Homicide

The Scale of Homicide Generally

There are challenges to establishing the scale of homicides in general. Indications of the numbers of homicides (e.g. instances of murder and manslaughter) are given by police statistics but may not provide a full picture. From time to time during police investigations an unrelated discovery of a body is made, bringing to light a previously unsuspected murder. Each year many people go missing and it is sometimes later discovered that they were murdered. It is difficult to estimate what proportion of untraced missing persons have also met a similar end. Brookman (2005, pp. 20–23) further discusses this 'dark figure' of homicide.

The Scale of Serial Homicide

As with homicides generally, it is difficult to form a complete picture of the number of serial homicides. Connections between several apparently different and separate unsolved murders may go unrecognised. Only when a perpetrator is apprehended, may it emerge that they have committed many previously unreported or unsolved murders. In 1994 following a tip-off, police discovered several bodies buried in the garden of the home of Fred and Rosemary West in Cromwell Street, Gloucester, England. Further digging at properties previously owned by Fred West unearthed more corpses. In all, the bodies of 12 women were found, some having been buried for twenty years. Fred West hanged himself in his prison cell while awaiting trial. His wife Rosemary was found guilty of murdering ten young women and girls including her daughter and her stepdaughter between 1971 and 1994 (Sounes 1995).

Daniszewska (2017) suggests that the number of serial killers and victims may have declined. Early estimates of 200 serial murders in the US fell to 100 at the beginning of the twenty-first century. This may relate to improvements in DNA research and fingerprint matching with specimens in computer databases (ibid., p. 13). However, Daniszewska (2017) recognises the difficulties of establishing the extent of serial murder. As she states, 'The problem arises when it is unclear as to whether a given murder can be deemed as an isolated crime or as part of a series. For these reasons, many serial murders remain a dark figure, namely one which is undisclosed, undiscovered, or invisible in police or prosecutor's statistics' (ibid.).

The Scale of Serial Poison Homicide

Similar problems to those involved in trying to determine the number of serial homicides, arise when attempting to grasp the scale of serial poison homicides. Many instances of poisoning appear to go unsolved (Westveer et al. 1996) and within these, there may be undetected examples of serial poisoning. Also, consider the cases already mentioned of **Dr. Harold Shipman** [S41, P1], **Arnfinn Nesset** [S30] and **Nannie Doss** [S24]. Had not their 'final' killing come to light, numerous of their poisonings could have remained undetected.

Motive

The Complexity of the Term 'Motive'

In the present context, the term 'motive' concerns the reasons why something is done. Motive in relation to homicide is an attempt to state why the killing took place. It may not always be possible to assign a motive, and where one can be discerned, it may be highly speculative. To further complicate matters, there may be several possible motives that interact, and which might be assigned differing weight or priority by different people.

Levels of Description Regarding Motive

A general motive for a homicide might be financial gain if the victim's life was insured and the perpetrator benefitted from the death. Or it might be to gain sexual freedom to be with a lover, if the victim was a spouse or long-term partner. Other motives might be jealousy, revenge or sadism. The motive may be quite speculative as with the murders perpetrated by **Niels Högel** [S61, P22], a German nurse. When he was convicted in 2015 of the poison murder of two intensive care patients and the attempted murder of three others, it was suggested that he was driven by compulsively seeking thrills and the elation of resuscitating patients.

Also, it is possible to speak of the motive or motives for various features or events within a homicide. For what reason was the murder weapon chosen? Was it an obvious weapon such as a blunt instrument that lay to hand when a violent altercation took place? If poison was used, the perpetrator may have calculated that it reduced the chances of being caught because, unlike shooting or stabbing, poisoning may be mistaken for death by natural causes. Perhaps the perpetrator(s) disposed of the body of their poison victim rather than trying to convey that death was from natural causes. In this unusual scenario, what could have been the motivation?

Motive Relating to Personality Traits and Behaviour

Supposed personality traits of poisoners may be suggested, which can overlap with motive. Some traits are comparatively straightforward to describe and recognise. If someone maintains that poisoners tend to be 'calculating' one can quickly recognise that while being calculating is not a motive for poison homicide, the trait might help in carrying out a poison murder. A calculating person is not likely to express explosive violence as in some homicides but will tend to plan and use more subtle means. A trait of 'avariciousness' can be associated with some poison killings (Trestrail 2007, pp. 50–52) and this too can be related to motive. The perpetrator may kill to gain financially from a Will or life insurance. Such a motive of financial gain can be described, driven by the trait of avariciousness.

Demonstrating motive is likely to involve identifying examples of behaviour that may indicate the underlying volition. Jealousy as a motive could be inferred where a perpetrator had expressed jealous sentiments to others or to the victim. These might have been conveyed verbally (face to face or by telephone), or in texts, e-mails or letters. **Hélèna Jégado** [S1], a French domestic servant, poisoned fellow workers and servants with arsenic from apparent jealousy which she had confided to others. Prosecutors attributed a motivation of sadism to **Graham Young** [S27], a store worker at a photographic supplier, who used thallium to poison co-workers. Evidence of this proposed motive included that the poison was administered in tiny doses over a prolonged period to extend suffering, and that Young apparently took pleasure in keeping a diary of the doses and effects of his poisonings.

Subsequent Chapters

Following the present chapter, the next one (Chapter 2, 'Explanations of Serial Poisoning') concerns theories and explanations of serial homicide in general and serial poisoning particularly. A common way of distilling extensive information is to classify and group it. Accordingly, we start by looking at typologies of serial killing which include attempts to group and understand motives and other features. In briefly outlining theories of serial killing, we further distinguish groupings of biological, psychological and social factors. Theories relating to serial poisoning are examined. (These are broader theories of crime applicable to poisoning homicide in general and relevant to serial poisoning.) The chapter discusses theories such as moral reasoning theory, rational choice theory, and labelling theory. I examine the problem of trying to explain repeated killing. Finally, I suggest that chronic poisoning of the same person can be understood as a form of serial poisoning.

Chapter 3, 'Poisons Used in Serial Poisoning' discusses different groupings of these substances, while recognising that no one system of classification subsumes every disparate poison. Some well-known poisons can legitimately be allocated to more than one grouping—morphine is a plant poison and is also used as a drug. I restrict myself to grouping the poisons that have been used by serial poisoners referenced in this book. One group of poisons is plant poisons such as aconite (*Aconitum napelus*) which is also known as wolf's bane or monk's hood. Regarding animal poisons, it is rare to hear of deliberate poisoning using a live snake or spider and I have come across no such examples of serial poisoning. However, I include insulin as an animal poison because it is derived from the pancreas. The use of bacterial poisons includes diphtheria and of tuberculosis. A large grouping is that of drugs used as poisons. These are further divided according to being essentially heart drugs such as lidocaine, muscle relaxants like mivacurium, analgesics such as pethidine, or diabetic medication for example glyburide. Another substantial classification is elements and their compounds and derivatives, embracing well-known poisons such as arsenic and less familiar ones like organic phosphorus compound E605. Finally, where poisons do not seem to fit elsewhere, I have designated a small group of 'other poisons' including anti-freeze. For each of these substances, I provide information such as their appearance and how they act on the body and refer to cases where serial poisoners have used the substance.

'Serial Poisoners' (Chapter 4) moves the focus from poisons to perpetrators, making comparisons between serial killers in general and their poisoning counterparts. Where feasible we look at collated information and statistics. There are difficulties in gathering meaningful information about such features as serial killers' age and ethnicity because any sample may not be representative of the wider population of serial killers, many of whom will be uncaught and unknown. Regarding serial poisoners, while reliable and extensive statistics are not available, individual cases can be examined and several can be compared to provide insights. Accordingly, the chapter compares where possible serial killers and serial poisoners according to gender, age, ethnicity, social background and occupation, personal history of violent criminal or abnormal behaviour, location, methods of killing, and motives.

Team serial poisoners are almost unheard of so are only briefly discussed. Finally, I consider, in relation to poison serial murder, a typology of serial murder in general which concerns motivation, location of killing, and other factors.

Turning to Chapter 5 ('Healthcare Serial Poisoning') attention moves to a subgroup of offenders. Healthcare Serial Poisoners are defined as perpetrators who kill in their healthcare role and in healthcare or related settings. This excludes therefore killers who are physicians, nurses or other healthcare professionals who kill for example their spouse outside of any healthcare 'patient' relationship. Although the scale of healthcare serial poisoning is not reliably known, enough cases have been reported to arouse public and professional disquiet. We look at a study of serial healthcare killing (that includes poisoning and other methods) and relate the findings to serial healthcare poisoning. Where motives can be discerned, those for health care serial poisoning tend to be different from those of other serial poisoners. Possible drivers are: power and control, sadism, seeking excitement, and factitious disorder imposed on another. Attention has also been paid to the behaviour and personality of health care workers including attempts to identify features that might require further investigation. Suggestions have been made for improving staff background checks, monitoring patients' outcomes and other factors, and communicating worries or suspicions. As efforts to improve accountability have gained traction, attention has turned to occasions when healthcare workers may have been unjustly accused, raising questions about possible miscarriages of justice.

In Chapter 6 ('Victims of Serial Poisoners') I first consider the victims of serial killers in general. There are various sources and statistics for such victims and, as with perpetrators, the accuracy of information can be questioned. Data on serial poison victims is even more sketchy, but individual cases can be considered, and some tentative generalisation drawn. The number of victims, their gender, age, ethnicity, social background, and occupation can be reviewed. Any relationship between perpetrator and victim can be examined as can the location of the killing. Also informative is interaction between such relationships and location and demographic information. A useful source of information can be the victim's recent contacts, and their routines and preferences.

Bringing together the various factors can suggest why a victim might have been selected. While team serial killing in general represents a considerable proportion of all serial killing, team serial poisoning and consequently victims are rare.

Chapter 7 ('Investigating Serial Poisoning') brings together aspects of police investigation and its relationships to prosecution at trial. I introduce the notion of 'case logic' which concerns an examination of cases to seek consistencies and inconsistencies that might clarify accounts. Murders associated with Nannie Doss a US serial poisoner are reviewed. I examine the contribution of profiling in relation to serial poison murder including distinctions between 'signature' and modus operandi (method of operating). The chapter considers the potential use of demographics to inform investigations. Effective and unsuccessful police investigations are briefly contrasted.

After these main chapters is the summary list of poisoners and details of their crimes. This is followed by a more detailed coverage of recent cases presented as 'profiles'.

Conclusion

I set out the justification of the book, its aims, scope, structure, methodology, features, and proposed readers. Criminology was briefly defined. The concept of homicide, legal frameworks, and types of homicide were discussed. Multiple homicide (serial and mass killing) and multiple poison homicide were described. I discussed the scale of homicide, serial homicide and serial poisoning. The evasive issue of motive was considered. Finally, I gave a brief outline of the content of the remainder of the book.

Suggested Activities

Consider and discuss with others several difficulties that arise in estimating the scale of serial poison homicide.

Reflect on whether estimating the scale of serial poisoning homicide could be harder in certain countries and jurisdictions than others. If you consider that there are place-specific difficulties, identify and reflect on possible reasons.

Examine some cases from previous centuries and contemporary cases and consider whether estimating the scale of serial poisoning was harder in the past than in the present time and if so why.

Key Texts

Brookman, F., Maguire, E. R., & Maguire, M. (Eds.). (2017). *The Handbook of Homicide* (Wiley Handbooks in Criminology and Criminal Justice). Chichester, UK: Wiley.

This book discusses the broad context of homicide including trends. Different forms of homicide are considered such as 'infanticide' and 'sexual homicide' and including 'Multiple homicide' which covers serial and mass murder. Homicide in different countries is examined.

The authors also cover the investigation and prevention of homicide.

Hough, R. M., & McCorckle, K. D. (2017). *American Homicide*. Thousand Oaks, CA: Sage.

This textbook systematically and engagingly covers key aspects of individual, mass and serial homicide. Included is the scale of homicide, offender and victim demographics, and theories and explanations of homicide. The authors discuss types of homicides including 'intimate partner homicide', terrorism, and serial homicide.

References

Behavioural Analysis Unit. (2005). *Serial Murders: Multi-disciplinary Perspectives for Investigators*. Washington, DC: National Center for the Analysis of Violent Crime, US Department of Justice.

Bennett, J. (2005). *The Cromwell Street Murders: The Detective's Story*. Gloucester: The History Press.

Brookman, F. (2005). *Understanding Homicide*. London and Los Angeles: Sage.

Brookman, F., Maguire, E. R., & Maguire, M. (Eds.). (2017). *The Handbook of Homicide* (Wiley Handbooks in Criminology and Criminal Justice). Chichester, UK: Wiley.

Browne, D. G., & Tullett, E. V. (1951). *Sir Bernard Spilsbury: His Life and Cases.* London: George G. Harrap.

Corporate Manslaughter and Corporate Homicide Act 2007 Act, Chapter 19, Section 1, 'The Offence' http://www.legislation.gov.uk/ukpga/2007/19/contents.

Croner, P. (2008). *Blackstone's Police Manual 2009: Volume 1—Crime* (11th ed.). Oxford and New York: Oxford University Press.

Daniszewska, A. (2017). *Serial Homicide: Profiling of Victims and Offenders for Policing.* New York: Springer.

Farrell, M. (1992). *Poisons and Poisoners: An Encyclopaedia of Homicidal Poisoning.* London: Robert Hale.

Farrell, M. (1994). Execution by Poison Gas and Lethal Injection. *The Criminologist, 18*(4), 201–204.

Farrell, M. (2017). *Criminology of Homicidal Poisoning: Offenders, Victims and Detection.* London and New York: Springer.

Fitzgerald, G. J. (2008, April). Chemical Warfare and Medical Response During World War I. *American Journal of Public Health, 98*(4), 611–625. https://www.ncbi.nlm.nih.gov/pmc/articles/PMC2376985/.

Guinn, J. (2017). *The Road to Jonestown: Jim Jones and the People's Temple.* New York, NY: Simon & Schuster.

Hickey, E. W. (2010). *Serial Murderers and Their Victims.* Belmont, CA: Wadsworth and Cengage Learning.

Holmes, R. M., & Holmes, S. T. (2010). *Serial Murder* (3rd ed.). Los Angeles and London: Sage.

Holocaust Education and Archive Research Team. (2007). *Auschwitz Concentration Camp—The Gas Chambers and Crematoria—Mass Extermination.* H. E. A. R. T. http://www.holocaustresearchproject.org/othercamps/auschwitzgaschambers.html.

Hough, R. M., & McCorckle, K. D. (2017). *American Homicide.* Thousand Oaks, CA: Sage.

Lacey, N., & Zedner, L. (2012). Legal Constructions of Crime. In M. Maguire, R. Morgan, & R. Reiner (Eds.), *The Oxford Handbook of Criminology* (5th ed.). Oxford: Oxford University Press.

Levin, J., & Fox, J. A. (2017). Multiple Homicide: Understanding Serial and Mass Murder. In F. Brookman, E. R. Maguire, & M. Maguire (Eds.), *The*

Handbook of Homicide (Wiley Handbooks in Criminology and Criminal Justice). Chichester, UK: Wiley.

Maguire, M., Morgan, R., & Reiner, R. (Eds.). (2012). *The Oxford Handbook of Criminology* (5th ed.). Oxford: Oxford University Press.

Morikawa, T. (1977). *The Truth About the Teigin Incident.* Tokyo: Kodansha.

New York Times. (2016). www.nytimes.com/news-event/2016-orlando-shooting.

Oddie, S. I. (1941). *Inquest.* London: Hutchinson.

Pletcher, K. (2017). Tokyo Subway Attack of 1995—Terrorist Attack, Japan. *Encyclopaedia Britannica.* https://www.britannica.com/event/Tokyo-subway-attack-of-1995.

Rock, P. (2012). Sociological Theories of Crime. In M. Maguire, R. Morgan, & R. Reiner (Eds.), *The Oxford Handbook of Criminology* (5th ed., pp. 39–80). Oxford: Oxford University Press.

Shepherd, G., & Ferslew, B. C. (2009). Homicidal Poisoning Deaths in the United States 1999–2005. *Clinical Toxicology, 47*(4), 342–347.

Sounes, H. (1995). *Fred and Rose: The Full Story of Fred and Rose West and the Gloucester House of Horrors.* London: Sphere.

The Shipman Inquiry. (2002–2005). http://webarchive.nationalarchives.gov.uk/20090808154959/http://www.the-shipman-inquiry.org.uk/fr_page.asp.

First Report. (2002, July). *Volume 1—Death Disguised; Volume 2—Decisions Todmorden; Volumes 3–6—Decisions Hyde.*

Second Report. (2003, July). *The Police Investigation of March 1998.* Cm 5853.

Third Report. (2003, July). *Death Certification and the Investigation of Deaths by Coroners.*

Fourth Report. (2004, July). *The Regulation of Controlled Drugs in the Community.*

Fifth Report. (2004, December). *Safeguarding Patients: Lessons from the Part—Proposals for the Future.*

Sixth Report. (2005, January). *Shipman: The Final Report.*

Trestrail, J. H. (2007). *Criminal Poisoning: Investigational Guide for Law Enforcement, Toxicologists, Forensic Scientists and Attorneys* (2nd ed.). Totowa, NJ: Humana Press.

Westveer, A. E., Trestrail, J. H., & Pinizotto, J. (1996). Homicidal Poisonings in the United States—An Analysis of the Uniform Crime Reports from 1980 Through 1989. *American Journal of Forensic Medicine and Pathology, 17*(4), 282–288.

Williams, K. (2012). *Textbook on Criminology* (7th ed.). Oxford: Oxford University Press.

Yallop, D. ([1981] 2014). *Deliver Us From Evil.* London: Constable.

2

Explanations of Serial Poisoning

Introduction

Factors relating to serial poison homicide can be compared with explanations of wider serial killing. Particularly interesting are typologies of serial murder and the extent to which similar frameworks of serial poisoning might be developed. Turning to broader theory, for serial killing generally, biological, psychological, and social factors are implicated. Regarding serial poisoning, various perspectives contribute. We look at moral reasoning theory, rational choice theory, strain theory, differential reinforcement theory, control theory, and labelling theory. Chronic poisoning of an individual is explainable as a form of serial poisoning of the same person.

Typologies of Serial Homicide and Their Relevance to Serial Poisoning

Typologies of Serial Killing

In approaching complex phenomena, classification can aid understanding. For serial homicide, several typologies have been suggested. Fox et al. (2018) examine the broad phenomenon of 'extreme killing' or multiple homicide considering both mass and serial murder. They distinguish serial killers as driven by power, revenge, loyalty, benefit, or terror.

Typologies, as well as conveying likely motivations and other features of serial killing, can support wider explanations. Mitchell (1997), drawing on various typologies, developed an integrated model of serial murder. This model attempts to relate pathological foundations (e.g. interacting biological, family, and socio-cultural factors) and developmental consequences (e.g. possible sexual fantasies/dysfunction).

Holmes and Holmes (2010) propose a categorisation of serial killers as: 'visionary', 'missionary', 'power/control' and 'hedonistic', while recognising that the types can overlap. 'Visionary' serial killers are regarded as psychotic in experiencing breaks with reality. They may hear voices or see visions. Sex is not an integral motivating factor for these killers. The motivation is intrinsic to the killer, while the anticipated gain is psychological. Their victims are of a non-specific type, are randomly selected, and are strangers to the killer. Method of killing is swift and focused on the act of killing, not the process. It is spontaneous and disorganised. Regarding location, the killings tend to be concentrated in one area (ibid., pp. 76–78). Finally, the killer is usually male (ibid., p. 89). Joseph Kallinger, a US serial killer stated that he was forced to kill by a disembodied floating head called Charlie although some commentators believe that Kallinger invented these claims to mitigate his own responsibility (McPadden 2017).

'Missionary' serial killers, are generally psychopathic (pathologically lacking fellow feeling) and consider that they have a mission to rid the world of certain people or perceived types of people. Their motivation may be intrinsic, for example, the satisfaction of getting rid of undesirables; and they anticipate the gains of self-reward for, as they see it, doing the right thing. Their victims are specific 'types' (e.g. members of a particular racial group or occupation) but are strangers and otherwise randomly selected. Method of killing is focused on the act rather than the process and is planned and organised. Location tends to be a specific area (Holmes and Holmes 2010, p. 101, Table 6.1). Peter Sutcliffe, a UK serial killer, murdered prostitutes (or supposed prostitutes) apparently from a missionary motive (Home Office 2006).

A 'power/control' serial killer, is motivated by psychological reasons, in that the motivation is intrinsic to the killer's personality. It involves complete power over the destiny of the victim. The killer tends to select and stalk specific victims who are otherwise strangers. Method of killing is focused on the process rather than the outcome and is planned and organised. The locations may be dispersed (Holmes and Holmes 2010, p. 159, Table 10.2). US serial killer Ted Bundy's crimes included control through rape, and necrophilia (Sullivan 2009).

Hedonistic serial killers are sub categorised as killing for 'lust', 'thrill' or 'comfort'. *Lust* killers experience fantasies and a compulsion for sexual satisfaction which may include necrophilia. Their expected gain is psychological. Victims, although strangers, are of a specific type and are selected non-randomly. Method of killing is planned and organised and focused on process rather than outcome. Location is likely to be one area. Jerry Brudos a US serial killer is an example (Holmes and Holmes 2010, pp. 112–113, Table 7.2).

Thrill hedonistic killers have strong fantasies and find thrills in the act of killing so that it tends to involve long drawn out death and torture, but not necrophilia. Victims are stalked and of a specific type but are never the less strangers. Method of killing is process focused and organised. Location tends to be dispersed. Holmes and Holmes (2010) provide a case study of a killer whom they call 'Randy' as an example (ibid., p. 129, Table 8.1).

Comfort hedonistic killers tend to be female and kill for material or financial gain. Victims are non-specific but not random and may be affiliates (such as a spouse or co-worker) or strangers (as in the victim of a contract killer). Method of killing is focused on the act rather than the process and is planned and organised. Location of the killings is concentrated in specific areas. Richard Kuklinski thought to have killed around 100 men and women is of this type (ibid., p. 143, Table 9.1).

Relevance of the Holmes and Holmes Typology to Serial Poisoning

Aspects of Holmes and Holmes' (2010) typology apply to some serial poisoners. This is further discussed in a later chapter on healthcare serial poisoners, but a few general points can also be made here. It is hard to envisage serial poisoners as 'visionary' serial killers because the planning and foresight associated with poisoning seems incompatible with sustained psychotic behaviour. Serial poisoners sometimes seem to be exercising 'power/control' over victims especially where the poisoning is chronic and purposely prolonged. Yet this does not fit exactly with the general serial killer typology where control and power are exerted actively and aggressively over an individual. Turning to the 'hedonistic lust' type, serial poisoners are rarely driven by direct overpowering motivation of sexual gratification over the victim, although there can be ultimately sexual motives in shedding a partner to take on a lover. Sometimes a poisoner seems attracted by the thrill and excitement of killing but this rarely manifests itself in ensuring long drawn out deaths and torture as is the case with the 'hedonistic thrill' type.

However, the 'hedonistic comfort' pattern can certainly be found among serial poisoners. **Nannie Doss** [S24] in the US is said to have confessed to poisoning four husbands and was suspected of killing other family members where financial gain was a factor. Strangers (or barely known acquaintances) can also be poisoned for gain as when **K. D. Kempanna** [S58, P17] killed and robbed temple worshipers in India. Finally, a serial poisoner might sometimes reflect a 'missionary' type. **Dr. Neil Cream** [S9] is a possible example as he killed prostitutes in London (Farrell 2017) although there is no clear evidence that he did this to somehow cleanse the world. It may be that prostitutes were simply easily available as victims.

Typologies of Serial Poisoning

Trestrail (2007) suggests a typology of poisoners according to the perpetrator's motivation and selected victim. This recognises that some poisoners might select a certain familiar victim such as a spouse or business partner, while others will choose a random victim whom they do not know. Trestrail proposes that the motivation for each type of offender is different. A further factor is the speed of planning, whether it is 'slow' (carefully planned and with a selected poison) or 'quick' (quickly planned and using a poison coincidentally at hand).

These elements can be coded. S/S refers to a 'specific victim' and 'slow planning' with a selected poison; while S/Q concerns a 'specific victim' and 'quick planning' with a poison to hand. For both S/S and S/Q poisonings the motive tends to be money, elimination, revenge, or political ambition. R/S refers to a 'random victim' and 'slow planning'; and R/Q conveys a 'random victim' and 'quick planning'. For both R/S and R/Q poisoning, the motive tends to be ego, product tampering, boredom, or sadism. This typology concerns poisoning generally, including serial poisoning, so, to what extent does it convincingly describe possible types of serial poisoner?

Regarding '*specific/slow*' cases, an example is **Chisako Kakehi** [S63, P22] of Japan who was sentenced in 2017 for poisoning her husband, and two common law partners. With these specific victims, chosen because of their wealth, she planned and carried out cyanide poisoning in supposed health cocktail drinks. Her motive was to acquire money to clear her debts. Teacher **Mohan Kumar** [S54, P13] in India gave cyanide tablets as supposed birth control pills to several women victims after having had sex with them and having promised them marriage. He then stole their possessions. Many healthcare serial poisonings are specific/slow' in that they are planned and directed at known specific patients. Nurse **Elizabeth Wettlaufer** [S62, P21] of Ontario, Canada was sentenced in 2017 for killing long-term care home patients (using insulin injections). Nurse **Niels Högel** [S61, P20] in Germany was convicted of killing intensive care patients and attempting to murder others. He used overdose injections of substances including ajmaline, sotalol (Sotalex), lidocaine, amiodarone, and potassium chloride. Many serial poisonings can be characterised as 'specific/slow'.

Turning to a '*specific/quick*' types, it is possible to find single poison murders such as Susan Barber's killing of her husband in the UK. He had beaten her and her lover earlier on the day of his murder having found them naked together. Susan took a quantity of paraquat which was to hand (quick planning), adding it to her husband's next meal. The motive was revenge (Farrell 2017, pp. 138, 192). However, as this instance illustrates, 'specific/quick' poisoning, does not lend itself to repeated killing, but is more of a 'one off' spur of the moment phenomenon. One cannot envisage Susan Barber, had she escaped detection in killing her husband, going on to repeatedly kill others whom she knew, spontaneously with any poison to hand. Serial poisoning of victims known to the offender lends itself much more to careful planning to avoid detection.

What about '*random' victim/'slow' planning*? An example might be a perpetrator who carefully chooses a poison (slow planning) and adds it to foods or medication on display in stores, intending to blackmail the company concerned. Because the offender cannot know who the victims will be, they are in this sense random. While the offence is 'tampering', the motive is likely to be (contrary to Trestrail's motivational suggestions) essentially financial. **Stella Nickell** [S35] in the US killed her husband with cyanide added to Excedrin capsules. She then replaced local shop stock with poisoned capsules ('product tampering') killing bank manager Susan Snow randomly. Her motive was financial gain as her husband's life insurance paid more for accidental death than for expected death. As Trestrail (2007, p. 49) points out, this is also an example of a specific poisoning (that of Nickell's husband) disguised as a random one (an example of supposed contaminated medication). A further instance might be nurse **Victorino Chua** [S60, P19], charged with the murder of hospital patients in 2015. He introduced insulin into saline bags which was subsequently unwittingly administered to patients by other nurses. Here the planning was careful ('slow') and the victims were random in the sense that seemingly Chua would not know which ones would be killed. However, the victims were not entirely random as they were from a limited population of patients in the wards where Chua worked. In line with Trestrail's (2007) typology, the motive was likely sadistic.

Regarding '*random victim/quick planning*' Trestrail (2007, p. 49) gives an example of a poisoner upset with their employer, say a food company, who impetuously (quick planning) adds some poison that is to hand to contaminate the food product and harm the company. Because the poisoner cannot know in advance who will consume the contaminated product, the victims are random. While the action is 'tampering', the motive is probably revenge on the company. There are definitional difficulties here. The crime is a single act of introducing poison. Even if several victims were killed over a period, the crime would not constitute a serial killing as usually defined. This is because there is a single act with no extended period between killings. Indeed, the deaths would emerge randomly, beyond the offender's control. An example of '*random victim/quick planning*' is the Chicago Tylenol murders in 1982. Seven people died because of product tampering when an offender added cyanide to over-the-counter Tylenol branded capsules. No perpetrator was convicted (Wolnik et al. 1984).

In brief, Trestrail's (2007) typology draws attention to the important features of perpetrator planning and victim selection. It has widest application to serial poisoning for 'specific victim/slow planning' cases, but less for 'specific victim/quick planning' types. 'Random victim/slow planning' describes several cases while 'random victim/quick planning' raises definitional problems for serial poisoning.

Other categorisations of serial poisoning have been suggested not entailing a comprehensive typology, but which can still usefully identify common features. One emerging in recent years is, 'healthcare serial killer'. Ramsland (2007) discusses this topic extensively. Holmes and Holmes (2010) consider, 'healthcare professionals and serial murder' (ibid., pp. 203–214). Hickey (2010) also looks at 'healthcare killers' (ibid., pp. 168–182). As we will see in a later chapter of the present volume, a related but more limited designation 'healthcare serial poisoner' allows observations to be made about the motives of such killers, and the special opportunities that they have for murder. These 'opportunities' include knowledge of drugs and their effects, and access to vulnerable people as patients.

Theory Relating to Serial Killing

Biological Factors and Serial Murder

Holmes and Holmes (2010) review theories of serial killing with reference to biological, psychological, and sociological factors. They conclude that there is currently no evidence to indicate the influence of biological factors on serial murder. The authors state that, '…no scientific statement can be made concerning the exact role of biology as a determining factor of a serial killer personality' (ibid., pp. 55–56).

If biological factors are securely identified in the future, it is likely that they will be combined in explanations featuring psychological and social variables. Considering the highly complex nature of criminal behaviour including that of serial killing it stretches credibility to envisage a direct link to biological features. More likely, biological factors may be found that increase the likelihood of developing certain psychological traits which in turn along with social influences might predispose an individual to deviance/violence, including homicide.

Psychosocial Factors and Serial Murder

Regarding psychological explanations of serial killing, Holmes and Holmes (2010) cite 'psychopathic personality' or 'sociopathic personality' as seemingly attracting 'the most attention of contemporary academics' (ibid., p. 56). Current psychiatric terminology refers to 'anti-social personality disorder' (American Psychiatric Association 2013, pp. 659–663). Its essential feature is a 'pervasive pattern of disregard for, and violation of, the rights of others'. This starts in childhood or in early adolescence and extends into adulthood (ibid., p. 659). Among the diagnostic criteria for personality disorder is 'failure to conform to social norms' regarding lawful behaviour, a failure that is manifested by the individual 'repeatedly performing acts that are grounds for arrest' (Criteria A, 1). Aggressiveness is indicated by 'repeated physical fights or assaults' (Criteria A, 4). There is a 'lack of remorse' indicated by being 'indifferent to or rationalising' having hurt or mistreated another person (Criteria A, 7) (ibid., p. 663).

As suggested by the typology of a 'visionary' serial killer (Holmes and Holmes 2010, p. 41), psychosis is a factor in some killings. Key features of psychotic disorders are: delusions, hallucinations, disorganised speech, grossly disorganised or catatonic behaviour, and negative symptoms (American Psychiatric Association 2013, p. 99). Especially relevant here are delusions and hallucinations. Delusions are rigid beliefs 'not amenable to change in the light of conflicting evidence' (ibid., p. 87). An example is 'thought insertion' in which the individual believes that alien thoughts have been inserted in their mind; and 'delusions of control' in which it is held that one's body or actions are being operated by an outside force (ibid.). Hallucinations are involuntary 'perception-like experiences' but they occur without an external stimulus (ibid.). The most usual in schizophrenia are auditory hallucinations, usually voices which are perceived as 'distinct from' the individuals' own thoughts (ibid.). *DSM-5* (American Psychiatric Association 2013) provides diagnostic criteria for disorders in which psychosis is integral including: 'schizophrenia', 'delusional disorder', and 'brief psychotic disorder' (ibid., pp. 87–122).

Holmes and Holmes (2010) suggest an interaction between frustration and fantasy might contribute to serial murder. Fantasy provides the 'rationale, ritual, motivation, anticipated gain, victim selectivity and satisfaction' (ibid., p. 58). Should the killing not be completed, the fantasy is frustrated, which drives action. If the killing is continually frustrated, the individual will commit more murders and 'the character and extent of violence may change and grow' (ibid.).

Hale (1993) links psychological drives with (usually) early learned experiences to suggest how serial murder might be understood. He argues that serial murder can be seen, not so much as the actions of a 'deranged or irrational individual', but someone responding to a 'perceived wrong'. Part of the process is a sort of 'internalised humiliation' (e.g. maternal rejection) which contributes to the motivation towards violence. An early humiliation is turned into a quest for power. Hale (1993) describes the process of the response to humiliation behaviourally so that ultimately serial murder is presented as a learned response. 'Cues' from the humiliating situation become associated with the humiliation itself. The humiliation is considered a 'non-reward' situation in that a reward did not occur in a context formerly associated with one. This produces an unconditioned frustration response. Cues present during the humiliation become conditioned to produce an 'anticipatory frustration response'. The response also produces a 'distinctive internal stimuli'. This motivates the individual to avoid future potentially humiliating situations as indicated by similar cues. For various reasons proposed by Hale, the individual is unable to visit the violence of his frustration on the person who caused it, so channels it towards others.

Holmes and Holmes (2010) refer to instances where serial murder may relate to rejection and abuse by parents (ibid., p. 66). Early trauma seems to have been associated with later violence. Yet they recognise the limitations of such part explanations. They accept that it is not known to what extent environmental, psychological and biological factors might play a part, and how they might interact (ibid., p. 69).

Theory and Serial Poisoning

Theories Relevant to Poisoning Including Serial Poisoning

Among theories of crime that appear relevant to poisoning homicide in general and may apply to serial poisoning, several stand out. These are: moral reasoning theory, rational choice theory, strain theory, differential reinforcement theory, control theory, and labelling theory (Farrell 2017, pp. 29–42).

Moral Reasoning Theory

Moral reasoning theory (Kohlberg 1978) proposes that such reasoning develops sequentially with maturity and involves three levels, each associated with two stages.

- Level 1 is that of premorality having one stage characterised by punishment and obedience; and another associated with a hedonistic concern with one's own needs.
- Level 2 relates to conventional conformity. It involves a stage of interpersonal concordance (associated with social approval) and a 'law and order' stage involving a commitment to law and order for its own sake.
- Level 3 concerns autonomous principles. Its two stages involve social contract and universal ethical principles.

As the person matures, the stages pass from the concrete to the more abstract. For Kohlberg (1978), offending is associated with delays in the development of moral reasoning. So, when opportunity to offend presents itself, an individual lacks reasoning power to stand up to the temptation. Unsurprisingly, therefore moral reasoning has been associated with criminal conduct (Palmer 2003).

How might this have relevance to serial poisoning? Clearly, poisoning often involves calculated planning and reasoning in one sense. However, in moral development, the perpetrator may lack the reasoning to resist the temptation towards criminal conduct. Temptations of financial gain or the desire to escape an unwanted relationship may overpower any other considerations, leading to poisoning. If that act was successful once, it could lead to serial poisoning. In short, a serial poisoner shows a repeated and persistent lack of moral constraint.

One can see cases in which a serial poisoner has moral understanding but ignores it or rationalises it when offending. In other instances, the poisoner seemingly lacks a grasp of basic moral reasoning such as equitability between perceived wrong and justifiable retaliation. This might show itself vividly in the poisoner's attempts to explain their actions and motivation. Jackson and Pittman (2015) quote a confession given to a police stenographer by **Nannie Doss** [S24], the US serial poisoner. They state that, 'in her confession, Doss said she killed Samuel (Doss) "because he got on my nerves". She said he wouldn't let her read *True Detective* magazines, have a radio or visit neighbours to watch television' (ibid.).

Rational Choice Theory

Rational choice theory operates at the sociological level in that it concerns opportunities for crime according to environmental variables. It also has a psychological element in viewing individuals as able to reason and to calculate risks. Rational choice theory proposes that people make reasoned decisions about committing crime rather as they make other life choices, by taking account of opportunity and risk. Accordingly, the crime rate reflects factors influencing such decisions. Clarke (1992) delineates groups of factors that make it harder to commit the crime, or make it riskier to do so, or that reduce the rewards of crime (ibid., p. 13, paraphrased). Included in the first group of factors making it harder to commit the offence is 'controlling facilitators' such as gun restrictions which would be expected to reduce firearm crime.

Examples of 'controlling facilitators' relevant to criminal poisoning are limiting the sale and purchase of poisons; and tightening rules for death certification to deter poisoning by physicians. This may be relevant to serial poisoning in a general sense. Controlling facilitators may have deterred potential poisoners and perhaps potential serial poisoners from carrying out the killings. Where a poisoning had been committed and gone undetected, the perpetrator's awareness of controlling factors may have deterred them if they intended to commit further poisonings.

Instances of serial poisoning where perpetrators weighed costs and benefits include ones offering financial gain. **K. D. Kempanna** [S58, P17] used cyanide to kill women worshipers at various temples, then robbed them. Her planning to lure victims to remote temples and her judgements of the value of the possessions they carried seemingly weighed potential financial benefits against risks of being apprehended.

Strain Theory

Before considering strain theory, it is necessary to examine 'anomie' or 'normlessness' as influenced by French sociologist Emile Durkheim ([1893] 1964, [1897] 1952). For some, anomie suggests that crime thrives when social disorganisation is such that society approaches collapse. Anomie could seem disillusioning and debilitating to such an extent that people could be led to 'commit suicide and homicide' (Lukes 1967, p. 139). Another implication is that crime develops owing to flawed social regulation which provides limited restraint or moral direction.

Merton (1938) argued that crime emerges from tension between society's cultural goals and structural social limitations. In the US, individuals had been encouraged to pursue financial success, but those in the lower class were often prevented from reaching such goals via education or employment. In response to the ensuing strain and frustration, some individuals would continue to conform to ideals of monetary success despite not performing well, but others would respond with deviance. One response, 'innovation' tends to be associated with crime: the individual continues to pursue wealth but does so by adopting deviant means such as robbery (ibid.). At its most extreme, anomie can involve the collapse of a social order and high levels of violence (Rock 2012, personal communication 2017).

These implications of anomie contributed to 'strain theory' (Farrell 1991). Adaptations of strain theory have maintained that crime could be precipitated through tensions, not just of unfulfilled goals of wealth but also of frustrations in not achieving status and self-reliance (Agnew 2001). Extending strain theory in this way widens its applicability so that it aids understanding of homicide (Brookman 2005, pp. 103–104).

This may partly explain some serial poisonings. **Hélèna Jégado** [S1] of Brittany, France, was a domestic worker. She poisoned fellow hotel workers and domestic servants using arsenic administered in food and drink. This was apparently driven by frustrated motives of jealousy if Jégado sensed that others were preferred to her (Heppenstall 1970). **Yiya Murano** [S33] of Argentina killed relatives and a friend for financial gain (to avoid paying promissory notes) using cyanide concealed in confections. By some accounts, she resented her lack of education and tenuous financial position and liked to present herself as wealthier than she was.

Differential Reinforcement Theory

Prior to differential *reinforcement* theory, differential *association* theory (Sutherland 1947) took account of social factors defining crime and the environment in which it most frequently occurs, maintaining that criminal behaviour is learned in a social context. Taking up the implications of learned behaviour, Jeffrey (1965) developed differential reinforcement theory. This drew on the phenomenon of 'operant conditioning' concerning the effects of reward, punishment, and the avoidance of unpleasant circumstances on the frequency of the occurrence of behaviour (Skinner 1938).

In differential reinforcement theory, criminal behaviour is 'operant' behaviour, determined by the consequences that it created. A successful property crime rewarding the perpetrator is likely to 'positively reinforce' the criminal behaviour so that is will be repeated. For someone in poverty, acquiring property through crime enables escape in a scenario of 'negative reinforcement', also increasing the likelihood of the criminal behaviour recurring. Risks of being caught and the consequences of punishment (a fine or imprisonment) act to reduce the likelihood of the crime being repeated. As well as such physical or material consequences, social and personal repercussions also act as encouragements or deterrents. Although this is a theory of crime in the broad sense, it might apply to crimes of violence where violent behaviour goes unpunished or is even rewarded from the perpetrator's viewpoint.

Also, the theory could apply to serial poisoning. Where a perpetrator is not caught yet gains financially or otherwise from the death of their victim, this might 'reinforce' the crime. Second attempts at poisoning where an earlier one has 'succeeded' could be explained similarly. **Lynn Turner** [S49, P8] gained financially from poisoning to death her former husband. She later killed her boyfriend using an almost identical modus operandi and was apprehended for the second murder.

Control Theory

Control theory implies that many people would commit crimes if there were no inducements to comply with social rules. Hirschi (1969) suggested four inducements to rule compliance: attachment, commitment, involvement, and belief. To take just one example, attachment concerns the extent to which some individual responds to the opinions of others.

In one application of control theory, Laub and Sampson (2003) focused on the life course of men over many years, looking at how the subjects resisted or accepted delinquency. They examined how social bonds (e.g. friends, family, military service, and employment) act as informal controls, filtering influences existing in the wider social structure. Certain situations arise contrary to the theory's expectations. For example, sometimes military personnel whom one might expect to have social bonds that encourage conformity, commit crimes including illegal homicide (Beevor 2002).

Control theory may aid understanding of a 'career' of serial poisoning involving minimal adherence to social rules. Over time, refinements are made to the modus operandi, making the perpetrator increasingly adept at avoiding detection. Where murder remains undetected, the perpetrator may feel no social pressure because others would be ignorant of the wrongdoing.

Controls would be diminished. Another factor diminishing potential control might be self-justifications as when healthcare serial killers claim to be acting mercifully towards suffering patients. Nurse **Stephan Letter** [S55, P14] of Germany killed patients with drugs including the muscle relaxant succinylcholine chloride (as lysthenon). Although Letter purported to be acting to end suffering, some patients were in a stable condition when killed. **Charles Cullen** [S52, P11] of New Jersey, US confessed to murdering thirty patients in hospitals in Pennsylvania and New Jersey over a sixteen-year period, using injections of digitoxin. Cullen said that he was easing suffering, but contrary to this, some victims were not terminally ill. French nurse **Christine Malèvre** [S48] was found guilty of killing by administering lethal doses of morphine, potassium, and other drugs to seriously ill patients at François Quesnay Hospital, Paris. Malèvre claimed that the deaths were mercy killings, but families of the deceased rejected this.

Labelling Theory

Two contributions to labelling theory are phenomenology and symbolic interactionism. Phenomenology is philosophical perspective which includes the transcendental phenomenology of Husserl ([1913]

1980, [1913] 1982, [1913] 1989). He maintains that although one can question the independent existence of things, one cannot doubt how things appear to us immediately in consciousness. Therefore, knowledge should be based on these phenomenal experiences (see also Farrell 2012, pp. 49–53). Symbolic interactionism, a sociological perspective of self and society, sees people as living in a symbolic environment. The meaning of symbols (social objects derived from culture) is shared and developed in interaction with others. Language allows symbols to be the means of constructing reality, largely as a social product. A sense of self, society, and culture emerge from symbolic interactions, being dependent on symbolic interaction for their existence. One's physical environment is interpreted through symbolic systems in the way that it is made relevant to human behaviour (ibid., pp. 145–148).

These ideas suggest how deviant acts and identities are constructed, interpreted, evaluated, and controlled over time. In the process of developing a 'career' of deviance, the importance of language is central to labelling theory. Labelling within the criminal justice system accrues power and authority. An individual commits an initial delinquent act ('primary deviance'), experiences the reactions of others identifying them as deviant, and responds in a deviant role perhaps as a means of defence or attack. In such circumstances, the deviance becomes, 'secondary', incorporating the knowledge, stereotypes, and experience of others in shaping identity and future behaviour (Becker 1963).

An adaptation of labelling theory might apply to serial poisoning. In this scenario, a serial poisoner may witness accounts of their crimes in the mass media, and gradually shape their offending according to these depictions. Such individuals are not directly confronted by others' views and reactions but experience them secretively through the media and through what others around them say unsuspectingly.

In such a way, someone such as Russian **Viacheslav Soloviev** [S56, P15] might come to see themselves as 'a poisoner' encouraging this deviant identity. Soloviev used thallium rat poison, administered in food to kill six victims including his wife Olga. One of his victims was the police investigator of a brawl involving Soloviev. It appears that the offender had an obsessive fascination with poisons which he administered over extended periods, an activity which seems to have been central to his identity.

The Question of Repeated Killing

Serial Homicide

Intrinsic to understanding serial killing, is to try to explain why killing is repeated. With serial killing in general it is suggested that some personality traits may be pertinent. Very severe 'anti-social personality disorder' (American Psychiatric Association 2013, pp. 659–663) may be thought to lead to a person killing once; and given that the trait persists can lead to further killings. With examples of serial killing involving psychotic disorder (American Psychiatric Association 2013, p. 99) a similar explanation could be offered. A person driven to kill by supposed voices or visions, where these persist, could kill more than once. Repeated killing here is 'explained' by the *persistence* of a disorder.

Holmes and Holmes (2010) suggest an interaction between frustration and fantasy might contribute to serial murder. If the killing is not completed, the fantasy is frustrated. If the killing is continually frustrated, it is hypothesised that the individual will commit more murders. This notion that frustration drives action suggests a driving force that could lead not to just a single killing but to repeated killing over time. Frustration can be eased but may well return and require further appeasement. Hale (1993) too links psychological drives with early learned experiences to suggest how serial murder might be understood. Expressed in behavioural terms, the driving force is related to 'frustration'. Unable to visit the violence of his frustration on the person who caused it, the individual channels it towards others. In short, a supposed emotional driving force propels repeated killing.

Serial Poisoning

Turning to serial poisoning, the repetition of killing can sometimes be attributed to a severe 'anti-social personality disorder'. Occasionally it may be claimed that a serial poisoner had a psychotic disorder, but a tenuous contact with reality sits uneasily with the careful planning frequently associated with poisoning.

Fantasy and frustration suggested by Holmes and Holmes (2010) may well describe some perhaps sexually driven serial killings but again seems less relevant to poisoning. Frustration as a driver envisaged by Hale (1993) is diffuse and removed from its supposed source. It does not convincingly explain repeated poisoning calculatedly and precisely directed at victims for clear reasons (financial gain, sexual freedom).

Moral reasoning theory implies that poor moral development can sustain repeated poisoning, for example, with supposed reasons or justifications that would not satisfy usual moral demands. With rational choice theory, a poisoner may make the apparent rational choice to kill several times. Strain theory providing a context for jealousy, revenge, and other powerful emotions could explain repeated poison homicides. It better explains a more down to earth frustration than does the hypothesis of fantasy (Holmes and Holmes 2010) or displaced frustration (Hale 1993). In differential reinforcement theory, if behavioural reinforcement can lead to one poisoning, it can contribute to several so long as the 'reward' is available. With control theory, lack of controls that lead to one poisoning can lead to several, perhaps helped by self-justification as with claimed mercy killing. Labelling theory again can suggest contributing to an identity built in secret that can feed one poisoning or several.

Serially Poisoning the Same Person: Chronic Poisoning

Acute poisoning aims to murder the victim quickly, while chronic poisoning kills slowly over a longer period. Poisons associated with acute action include cyanide which can elicit symptoms within a few minutes, and strychnine which often produces violent symptoms shortly after being consumed. With poisons such as arsenic the effect is more dependent on the dose than is the case with some other poisons as arsenic can kill quickly or slowly.

Chronic poisoning has been used by serial poisoners, for example, **Graham Young** [S27], who slowly killed co-workers with thallium. In one sense, the chronic poisoning of one victim may be understood as serial poisoning because it involves repeated acts over a period leading to death. There may even be a parallel to the 'cooling off' period associated with serial killing generally, as the poisoner anticipates the next opportunity to act. Chronic poisoning may be deployed to suggest that the victim has been unwell for a long time so that their death, when it comes, is expected. It is said that Major Herbert Armstrong administered arsenic to his wife Katherine until she was admitted to a sanatorium where she began to recover. When she was discharged, he continued the poisoning until she died (Young 1927). In Perth, Australia, Martha Rendell swabbed the mouth of her stepson 14-year-old Arthur Morris with hydrochloric acid over an extended period (as a supposed treatment for sore throat) leading to his lingering death (Skehan, n.d.).

To the extent that chronic poisoning of an individual victim is like the serial poisoning of several victims (whether by acute or chronic means) similar explanations and theories may apply. For example, differential reinforcement theory can help explain serial poisoning where a perpetrator evades suspicion once and uses the same or similar modus operandi for a subsequent killing. It can also apply to a single poisoner who anxiously gives an initial small dose to the victim. Seeing that suspicion is not aroused, the offender continues administering small doses of poison (as did Herbert Armstrong). Each 'successful' administration reinforces the act until eventually the victim's death is accomplished.

Conclusion

Typologies of serial killing and typologies specific to poisoning can have relevance to serial poisoning. For serial killing in general we looked at various theories and factors (biological, psychological, and social). Similarly, with serial poisoning, theory was examined. We looked at moral reasoning theory, rational choice theory, strain theory, differential reinforcement theory, control theory, and labelling theory. The possible drivers for *repeated* killing were touched on. Chronic poisoning of an individual seen as a form of serial poisoning is open to similar explanations.

Suggested Activities

Consider the typology of serial killing developed by Holmes and Holmes (2010). Discuss to what extent this informs understanding of serial poisoning.

Reviewing the theories that seem relevant to serial poisoning, discuss which you find most convincing and why.

Key Texts

Dobrin, A. (2016). *Homicide Data Sources: An Interdisciplinary Overview for Researchers* (Springer Briefs in Criminology). New York: Springer.

A useful guide to interpreting homicide data.

Holmes, R. M., & Holmes, S. T. (2010). *Serial Murder* (3rd ed.). Los Angeles and London: Sage.

Many of the chapters of the book elaborate on a suggested typology of serial killing, such as 'Hedonistic—comfort type' and 'Power/control'. There is also a chapter on 'Healthcare Professionals and Serial Murder'.

References

Agnew, R. (2001). Strain Theory. In E. McLaughlin & J. Muncie (Eds.), *The Sage Dictionary of Criminology*. London: Sage.
American Psychiatric Association. (2013). *Diagnostic and Statistical Manual of Mental Disorders Fifth Edition (DSM5)*. Washington, DC: APA.
Becker, H. ([1963] 2008). *Outsiders: Studies in the Sociology of Deviance*. New York: Free Press.
Beevor, A. (2002). *Berlin: The Downfall 1945*. New York and London: Viking Press and Penguin.
Brookman, F. (2005). *Understanding Homicide*. London and Los Angeles: Sage.
Clarke, R. V. (Ed.). (1992). *Situational Crime Prevention: Successful Case Studies*. New York: Harrow and Heston.

Dobrin, A. (2016). *Homicide Data Sources: An Interdisciplinary Overview for Researchers* (Springer Briefs in Criminology). New York: Springer.

Durkheim, E. ([1893] 1964). *The Division of Labour in Society.* New York: Free Press.

Durkheim, E. ([1897] 1952). *Suicide.* London and New York: Routledge & Keegan Paul.

Farrell, M. (1991). Strain Theory. *The Criminologist, 15*(2), 107–108.

Farrell, M. (2012). *New Perspectives in Special Education: Contemporary Philosophical Debates.* New York and London: Routledge.

Farrell, M. (2017). *Criminology of Homicidal Poisoning: Offenders, Victims and Detection.* London and New York: Springer.

Fox, J. A, Levin, J., & Fridel, E. E. (2018). *Extreme Killing: Understanding Serial and Mass Murder* (4th ed.). Thousand Oaks, CA: Corwin Press.

Hale, R. L. (1993). The Application of Learning Theory to Serial Murder, or "You Too Can Be a Serial Killer". *American Journal of Criminal Justice, 17*(2), 37–46. https://www.slideshare.net/nyinmaw/application-of-learning-theory-to-serial-murder.

Heppenstall, R. (1970). *French Crime in the Romantic Age.* London: Hamish Hamilton.

Hickey, E. W. (2010). *Serial Murderers and Their Victims.* Belmont, CA: Wadsworth and Cengage Learning.

Hirschi, T. (1969). *The Causes of Delinquency.* Berkley: University of California Press.

Holmes, R. M., & Holmes, S. T. (2010). *Serial Murder* (3rd ed.). London: Sage.

Home Office. (2006, June 1). *Sir Lawrence Byford Report into the Police Handling of the Yorkshire Ripper Case.* London: Home Office. https://www.gov.uk/government/publications/sir-lawrence-byford-report-into-the-police-handling-of-the-yorkshire-ripper-case.

Husserl, E. ([1913] 1980). *Ideas Pertaining to a Pure Phenomenology and to a Phenomenological Philosophy, Third Book: Phenomenology and the Foundations of Science* (R. Rojcewitz & A. Schuwer, Trans. from the German). Dordrecht: Kluwer.

Husserl, E. ([1913] 1982). *Ideas Pertaining to a Pure Phenomenology and to a Phenomenological Philosophy, First Book: General Introduction to a Pure Phenomenology* (R. Rojcewitz & A. Schuwer, Trans. from the German). Dordrecht: Kluwer.

Husserl, E. ([1913] 1989). *Ideas Pertaining to a Pure Phenomenology and to a Phenomenological Philosophy, Second Book: Studies in the Phenomenology of Constitution* (R. Rojcewitz & A. Schuwer, Trans. from the German). Dordrecht: Kluwer.

Jackson, D., & Pittman, H. (2015, August 27). Throwback Tulsa: Charming, Friendly Nannie Doss Poisoned Four Husbands. *Tulsa World*.

Jeffrey, C. R. (1965). Criminal Behaviour and Learning Theory. *Journal of Criminal Law, Criminology and Police Science, 56*, 294–300.

Kohlberg, L. (1978). Revisions in the Theory and Practice of Mental Development. In W. Damon (Ed.), *New Directions in Child Development: Moral Development*. San Francisco, CA: Jessey-Bass.

Laub, J., & Sampson, R. (2003). *Shared Beginnings Divergent Lives: Delinquent Boys to Age 70*. Cambridge, MA: Harvard University Press.

Lukes, S. (1967). Alienation and Anomie. In P. Laslett & W. Runciman (Eds.), *Philosophy, Politics and Society*. Oxford: Blackwell.

McPadden, M. (2017, October 13). Joseph Kallinger: The Shoemaker Who Teamed with His Teen Son to Rape, Torture and Kill. *Crimefeed*. http://crimefeed.com/2017/10/joseph-kallinger-the-shoemaker-who-teamed-with-his-teen-son-to-rape-torture-kill/.

Merton, R. K. (1938). Social Structure and Anomie. *American Sociological Review, 3*, 672–682.

Michell, E. W. (1997). *The Aetiology of Serial Murder: Towards an Integrated Model* (Unpublished master's dissertation in Psychology). University of Cambridge.

Palmer, E. J. (2003). *Offending Behaviour: Moral Reasoning, Criminal Conduct and Rehabilitation of Offenders*. Cullompton: Devon, Willan Publishing.

Ramsland, K. (2007). *Inside the Minds of Healthcare Serial Killers: Why They Kill*. Westport, CT: Praeger.

Rock, P. (2012). Sociological Theories of Crime. In M. Maguire, R. Morgan, & R. Reiner (5th ed., pp. 39–80), *The Oxford Handbook of Criminology*. Oxford: Oxford University Press.

Skehan, P. (n.d.). Western Australia Police Historical Society.

Skinner, B. F. (1938). *The Behaviour of Organisms: An Experimental Analysis*. New York: Appleton-Century-Crofts.

Sullivan, K. M. (2009). *The Bundy Murders: A Comprehensive History Jefferson*. Jefferson, NC: McFarland.

Sutherland, E. H. (1947). *Principles of Criminology* (2nd ed.). Philadelphia, PA: Lippincott.

Trestrail, J. H. (2007). *Criminal Poisoning: Investigational Guide for Law Enforcement, Toxicologists, Forensic Scientists and Attorneys* (2nd ed.). Totowa, NJ: Humana Press.

Wolnik, K. A., Fricke, F. L., Bonnin, E., Gaston, C. M., Satzger, R. D. (1984, March). The Tylenol Tampering Incident—Tracing the Source. *Analytical Chemistry, 56*(3), 466–470.

Young, F. (Ed.). (1927). *The Trial of Herbert Rowse Armstrong* (Notable British Trials Series). Edinburgh: William Hodge.

3

Poisons Used in Serial Poisoning

Introduction

Elsewhere can be found fuller details about the nature of poisons such as how poison is defined, and the ways that fatal dosage is represented (Farrell 2017, pp. 47–61). Here the focus is on basic information about poisons that have been used by serial poisoners, and how they work.

When talking about the toxicity of poisons, the number of grams or milligrams (thousandths of a gram) that are likely fatal is often mentioned. As a rough reminder, a gram of salt is about 1/6 of a teaspoonful and a gram of sugar approximately 1/4 of a teaspoonful. Roughly a fatal dose of copper sulphate is relatively large at around 10 grams while a lethal dose of strychnine is only about 100 mg.

Plant Poisons

Digitalis

Foxglove is a purple plant with a finger (digit) shape, hence its Latin name *Digitalis purpurea*. Digitalis the poison is extracted from foxglove leaves. Long used as a herbal tea remedy for 'dropsy', in which excessive fluid accumulates under the skin, digitalis acted by causing the excretion of copious quantities of urine. More recently, digitalis was used to treat heart conditions characterised by rapid and irregular heartbeat.

Digitalis increases muscular tissue activity especially of the heart and arterioles (small blood vessels). Therapeutically, it strengthens each heartbeat and lengthens, 'rest' beats. Increased blood flow encourages the kidneys to produce more urine, decreasing 'dropsy' where it relates to heart problems. Toxic amounts cause nausea, vomiting, blurred vision, irregular heartbeat and laboured breathing. Convulsions and unconsciousness may occur before death ensues.

Marie Alexandrine Becker [S17] of Liege, Belgium, was charged with the murders of her first and second husbands, a lover, and an elderly customer of her dress shop. She added digitalis to their food or drink.

Atropine (Belladonna)

Belladonna (*Atropa belladonna*) is a plant commonly called deadly nightshade. Atropine is an alkaloid extracted from the plant. It is absorbed by the gastrointestinal tract and can also be administered intravenously. Partly oxidised in the liver, atropine is excreted in urine. Death has been reported after doses of less than 10 mg for children and 100 mg for adults.

Atropine, affects the parasympathetic nervous system which (among other things) inhibits heart action and encourages digestive action. By blocking the effect of the neurotransmitter acetylcholine, atropine antagonises the parasympathetic nervous system so that heart action is augmented, and digestive action is discouraged. Tiny doses relieve spasm by paralysing the muscles of digestion, and raising heart rate. Atropine's excitor effect is followed by a depressant influence on the brain's motor areas. When someone experiences atropine poisoning, their mouth and throat become very dry, eye pupils dilate, and heart rate increases. They become excited and delirious yet at the same time feel weak. Later, they suffer cerebral depression, paralysis, coma, and the gradual cessation of breathing and heartbeat.

Swiss nurse **Marie Jeanneret** [S4] was convicted in 1868 of the murder of seven of her patients with belladonna.

Aconite

Aconite (*Aconitum napelus*) is a plant known in the countryside as wolf's bane or monk's hood. A poisonous alkaloid extracted from the plant as a white crystalline powder is also called aconite (or aconitine). If someone swallows aconite, they feel a warm sensation or tingling in their mouth, throat, stomach and skin. Later their skin feels cold, and they become giddy, and restless. They experience vomiting and diarrhoea, convulsions, and increasing breathing problems as the muscles controlling respiration become paralysed. Death ensues from about eight minutes to four hours after the poison is taken. Aconite can kill in a dose as little as 1 mg, or 5–10 ml of tincture.

British Royal Navy surgeon **Dr. Edward Pritchard** [S2] killed his mother-in-law and his wife with aconite (and antimony).

Strychnine

Obtained from plants of the genus *Strychnos*, strychnine is a vegetable alkaloid having an extremely bitter taste. If swallowed, strychnine is quickly absorbed by the intestine but excreted only slowly in urine. A fatal dose is about 100 mg.

Strychnine stimulates the central nervous system, and inhibits the nerves of the spinal cord from counteracting over stimulation. Consequently, overdoses cause twitching and then convulsions. Central nervous system stimulation is followed by a period of depression.

In poisoning, convulsions cause the body to arch back with arms and legs extended, while facial muscles contract producing a sardonic grin. As this wave of convulsions occurs, the senses are heightened and the diaphragm and related muscles contract, preventing breathing during spasms. Typically, convulsions last for a minute or two with ten or fifteen minutes respite, usually proving fatal after the second to the fifth seizure. Strychnine affects the respiratory muscles, so causing asphyxiation. A massive dose of strychnine can kill suddenly without convulsions (Farrell 1993).

Mary Ann Britland [S7], in the UK, poisoned several family members with strychnine pest exterminator. **Dr. Neill Cream** [S9], killed four prostitutes in London, UK using strychnine. Nurse **Jane Toppan** [S10], killed both patients and relatives including using strychnine to poison her foster sister. In Canada, **Sukhwinder Singh Dhillon** [S44, P4], used the poison to kill his wife and a business partner.

Morphine

Raw opium is extracted from the poppy (*Papaver somniferum*). It contains many alkaloids, the most prominent being morphine. As an alkaloid derived from opium, morphine (also known as morphia) is essentially the same regarding absorption, distribution, excretion, action, and symptoms.

Morphine induces euphoria in the dying and eases anxiety in conditions such as shock or cardiac arrest. Absorbed by the alimentary tract when taken by mouth, morphine is taken up more quickly when injected under the skin. Detoxicated in the liver, it is excreted in urine. The drug acts as a cerebral depressant although at the same time, it stimulates other aspects of the central nervous system, causing eye pupils to contract, and inducing vomiting. In its main depressant role morphine dampens down aspects of the central nervous system so disrupting concentration and inducing lethargy and sleep. It depresses the cough reflex and respiration which can lead to coma and death.

Elisabeth Wiese [S11] of Hamburg, Germany, banned from continuing as a midwife for illegally carrying out abortions, offered care for children, and poisoned several with morphine. **Dorothea Waddingham**

[S18] killed two of her nursing home patients with morphine for financial gain. **Dr. Harold Shipman** [S41, P1] killed some 250 of his patients, often using overdoses of morphine-based drugs.

Cyanide

Cyanides are poisonous salts of hydrocyanic acid (also known as prussic acid). Sodium and potassium salts of hydrogen cyanide are inert, but water or gastric acid immediately hydrolyses them (breaks them down) into hydrogen cyanide. Consequently, if cyanide salts are swallowed, hydrogen cyanide is produced. It is then absorbed by the gastrointestinal tract and inhaled into air passages. A minimum lethal dose lies between 0.7 and 3.5 mg per kilo of body weight. A tiny dose of 50 mg constitutes about ten cyanide molecules to each body cell.

Cyanide inhibits the bodily enzyme cytochrome oxidase, preventing the body from using oxygen, even though it is present. Lack of oxygen damages the nerve cells of the respiratory centre of the brain and affects the muscle walls of the heart leading to death by respiratory failure. Once cyanide is administered, symptoms appear rapidly including giddiness, limb weakness, and blue discoloration of the lips and face. Heart action slows and becomes irregular and after a few minutes, convulsions may occur before breathing and heartbeat cease. Exposure to hydrogen cyanide gas can cause unconsciousness in seconds and death in a minute owing to complications affecting control of the heartbeat.

During the Second World War German occupation of France, physician **Dr. Marcel Petiot** [S20] pretended to be part of the French Resistance aiding anyone wishing to flee the country. Unsuspecting victims would visit his surgery at night with their money and possessions. Purporting to vaccinate them against diseases prevalent in their desired country of destination, Petiot injected victims with cyanide. In 1946 he was guillotined for murdering twenty-four people.

In the US, **Stella Nickell** [S35] poisoned her husband with cyanide for life insurance. Stella reported that her husband had died after having taken Excedrin™ capsules. Knowing that accidental demise paid more than death from natural causes, Stella then doctored similar capsules in local stores to imply that the pill manufacture was at fault. As a result, Susan Snow, a local bank manager, died after taking such capsules. Eventually the truth emerged, and Nickell was charged with product tampering and given a lengthy prison term.

Cyanide poisoning was one of the methods used by serial killer **Donald Harvey** [S34] who murdered patients mainly at hospitals in Kentucky and Cincinnati. In India, **K. D. Kempanna** [S58, P17] poisoned six women temple worshipers with cyanide. Posing as a pious devotee, she befriended the wealthy women and visited temples with them. Then suggesting a visit to an out of the way temple, on arrival there she would dose the victim's food with cyanide and rob them. In Vietnam, **Lê Thanh Vân** [S47, P7], trained in the army medical corps, confessed to 13 killings including his mother-in-law, brother-in-law, foster mother, lovers, and acquaintances. He used cyanide administered in food and drinks. **Chisako Kakehi** [S63, P22] of Japan killed her husband and two common law partners with cyanide administered in a health cocktail drink. She murdered to gain money from inheritances to pay off her debts.

For further information on plant poisons, readers may also consult Nelson et al. (2007), *Handbook of Poisonous and Injurious Plants*.

Animal Poisons (Zootoxins)

In nature, animal poisoning tends to occur when an individual is stung or bitten by a venomous snake, insect, spider, or fish (White et al. 2008). But the use of animal poisons in homicides is rare and examples involve not 'natural' venom but other animal-derived poisons such as insulin. Because insulin is also a widely recognised drug, I consider it as such later in the chapter.

Bacterial Poisons: Diphtheria and Tuberculosis

Bacteria cause disease by producing toxins harmful to bodily tissues. Diphtheria is caused by *Corynebacterium diphtheriae* bacteria. Symptoms may include severe throat inflammation, a thick grey membrane covering the throat, swollen neck glands (Lymph nodes), nasal discharge, and difficulty breathing or rapid breathing (Barlow et al. 2016, Chapter 11). Tuberculosis is caused by *Mycobacterium tuberculosis* and sometimes by *Mycobacterium bovis* or *Mycobacterium africanum*. Being a facultative intracellular organism, the bacterium can invade cells and can be grown in a laboratory. Mainly affecting the lungs, it can also act on other parts of the body. Symptoms may include a persistent blood producing cough, fever, fatigue, and lack of appetite (Kumar and Clark 2016, pp. 86–87).

US dentist and bacteriologist **Dr. Arthur Waite** [S14] poisoned his mother in law with diphtheria and tuberculosis bacteria (and murdered his father-in-law with arsenic) for which he was executed in 1917.

Drugs Used as Poisons

Heart Drugs

Digitoxin and Digoxin

The drugs digitoxin and digoxin are powerful extracts of digitalis and their action reflects that of their original source. A lethal dose of digitoxin is 3–5 mg, that of digoxin is rather more, while that of most digitalis preparations is much greater (about 2.5 gm).

Digitoxin injections were administered by US nurse **Charles Cullen** [S52, P11], who confessed to murdering thirty patients in hospitals in Pennsylvania and New Jersey over a sixteen-year period.

Lidocaine

Lidocaine (also known as xylocaine) is used to treat certain heart conditions. It has other medical uses including as a local anaesthetic 'numbing agent'. Overdoses can adversely affect heart function and can be fatal.

Robert Diaz [S29], a US coronary care nurse, killed patients at several hospitals with injections of Lidocaine when he worked as a temporary nurse on night shifts. Autopsies revealed that the bodies contained many times the legal dose.

Potassium Chloride

Potassium is a metallic chemical element which was first isolated from potash (the ashes of plants) hence its name. The chemical compound potassium chloride is odourless and either white or colourless. Easily dissolved in water, it has a salty taste. Medicinally, potassium chloride has been used since the 1950s. It helps to treat and prevent low blood potassium which can occur owing to vomiting and diarrhoea. It can be administered orally or (slowly) intravenously. If injected too quickly into a vein, it can cause heart problems. Indeed, its ability to cause cardiac arrest is recognised in its inclusion in a cocktail of three drugs used in judicial lethal injections in some US states.

US nurse **Orville Lynn Majors** [S40] killed patients at Vermillion County Hospital using potassium chloride and epinephrine seemingly because she hated elderly people. **Christine Malèvre** [S48], a French nurse, was found guilty of killing patients by administering lethal doses of potassium, morphine, and other drugs.

Epinephrine

Epinephrine, also known as adrenaline, is a hormone and a neurotransmitter produced by the adrenal glands and some neurons. Binding to alpha and beta receptors, it contributes to the so-called fight-flight reaction including by increasing the heart output, and accelerating blood flow to muscles. Epinephrine was first isolated in the late 1800s. Medically, epinephrine is a heart stimulant used for treating various conditions including cardiac arrest and anaphylaxis (an acute allergic reaction to an antigen such as a bee sting). It is administered by inhalation or by injection into muscle or skin. Possible side effects include fast heart rate, abnormal heart rhythm, and high blood pressure.

In the US, **Kristen Gilbert** [S45, P5] was convicted of killing patients using epinephrine injections. One of her motives appeared to be self-aggrandisement by inducing cardiac arrest then demonstrating supposed nursing skills by trying to save victims.

Ajmaline

Ajmaline (trade names include Gilurytmal) is an alkaloid first isolated from the roots of Indian snake root (Rauwolfia serpentina) and named after an Unani medicine practitioner. Therapeutically, the drug is used to treat certain heart conditions characterised by irregular or abnormal heart rhythm.

Amiodarone

An antiarrhythmic drug, amiodarone (Cordarex) works partly by increasing the time before a heart cell can contract again. It is used to treat various conditions associated with irregular heartbeat including ventricular arrhythmias. Amiodarone can be administered in various ways including intravenously. It can have serious side effects, including causing problems with the liver and with vision, and can be fatal.

Sotalol

Discovered in 1960, solatol (also known as solatex) became used as a drug for treating abnormal heart rhythms in the 1980s. It is prescribed for serious abnormal rhythms because it poses a small risk to life. Solatol prolongs the so-called QT interval. This interval is a measure of the time between two waves of the heart's electrical cycle—the Q wave and the T wave. The interval represents the electrical polarisation and depolarisation of the heart ventricles. A lengthened QT interval can indicate potential ventricular tachyarrhythmias (heart rate greater than the normal resting rate) which can cause sudden death. In prolonging the QT interval sotalol acts as an antiarrhythmic drug.

German serial poisoner nurse **Niels Högel** [S61, P20] killed patients using drugs including potassium chloride, lidocaine, ajmaline, amiodarone, and sotalol. When administered as an overdose these can cause cardiac arrhythmia and lowered blood pressure which can be fatal.

Muscle Relaxant Drugs

Mivacurium Chloride Injection

Mivacurium chloride injection (also known as Mivacron) is a nondepolarising skeletal muscle relaxant, administered intravenously. It is used to relax muscles during surgery or when a patient is on a breathing machine.

In 2006, vocational nurse **Vickie Dawn Jackson** [S53, P12], was found guilty of killing ten patients by administering mivacurium chloride (as Mivacron). All died of respiratory arrest. It seems that Jackson became vengeful to patients when other nurses were compassionate towards them.

Pancuroneum

Pancuroneum (tradename Pavulon) is a muscle relaxant and neuromuscular blocking agent (aminosteroid). The drug is used in anaesthetics during surgery to relax muscles and to allow ventilation or intubation (putting a tube into the patient's windpipe to keep the airway open). Side effects include respiratory depression. In euthanasia, following a drug to induce coma, pancuroneum is used to stop breathing. It is one of the three drugs used in judicial lethal injections in some US states.

Nurse **Richard Angelo** [S37] of New York was convicted of murdering several patients, by injecting Pavulon (and succinylcholine chloride) into their IV tubes. It appears that he wanted to create patient respiratory problems, so that he could intervene and demonstrate competence. Respiratory therapist **Efren Saldivar** [S46, P6] was sentenced to six consecutive life sentences without parole for killing patients.

He injected victims with drugs causing respiratory arrest or cardiac failure. These included Panuronium (and possibly morphine and suxamethonium chloride).

Vecuronium

Vecuronium (also known as Norcuron) is a non-depolarising neuromuscular blocker. It may be used in general anaesthesia to relax muscles during surgery or when a patient is on a breathing machine.

UK nurse **Benjamin Geen** [S50, P9], was convicted of murdering two patients at a hospital in Oxfordshire, UK. He was said to have used several drugs including vecuronium (and midazolam) possibly by injection or through drips.

Succinylcholine Chloride

Succinylcholine chloride (also known as Anectine, lysthenon, and suxamethonium chloride, 'sux') is a synthetic muscle relaxant. A whitish crystalline powder, it has little odour, a salty taste, and is water soluble. The drug is used intravenously in anaesthetics, for example in brief operations requiring a tube to be passed down the trachea to aid breathing. A neuromuscular blocking agent, small doses of the drug briefly paralyse the muscles through depolarisation, preventing muscle–nerve 'communication'. Overdose can cause irregular heart action: slow beats, extra contracting as opposed to resting phases, and heart failure. This appears to relate to extra stimulation of the vagal nerve supplying branches to the heart and other organs. In treating succinylcholine chloride poisoning, blood transfusion can help replace the nerve transmitting agent cholinesterase rendered inactive by the drug.

US paediatric nurse **Genene Jones** [S32] used succinylcholine to kill 15-month-old Chelsea McClellan, and heparin (a blood thinning drug) to murder another child, Rolando Santos. Norwegian nursing home manager **Arnfinn Nesset** [S30] was found guilty in 1982 of twenty-one charges of poisoning residents of his nursing home with succinylcholine chloride. Nurse **Stephan Letter** [S55, P14] of Westphalia,

Germany was found guilty of 16 counts of murdering patients at a hospital in Sonthofen, Bavaria. He used drugs including succinylcholine chloride (as lysthenon).

Analgesic (Pain Relieving) Drugs

Pethidine

Pethidine is also known as meperidine (trade names include Demerol). It is an opioid-based synthetic analgesic (pain reliever). Synthesised in the late 1930s, it was later recognised as a potential analgesic. It can be administered as tablets, syrup, or by injection (intravenous, subcutaneous, or intramuscular) and is considered safer and more effective than morphine.

Brian Rosenfeld [S38], a US nurse, pleaded guilty to murdering three patients with overdoses of pethidine (as Demerol).

Acetaminophen

Acetaminophen (trade name Tylenol) is used to relieve pain and to reduce fever. It has been used to treat headache, arthritis, and muscle pains. Care is taken if a second medication containing acetaminophen (perhaps with a different name) is also being used, so that overdose is avoided. Following early signs of nausea, vomiting, and confusion, overdose can be fatal.

US nurses' aide and later care-home manager **Dorothea Puente** [S39] was convicted of killing three patients using overdoses of drugs including acetaminophen (as Tylenol) to gain from cashing her victims' security checks.

Diabetic Drugs

Insulin

Insulin is a bodily hormone produced by the pancreas, helping to maintain normal blood sugar levels. With increased blood glucose, the pancreatic 'Beta cells' are signalled to secrete insulin. The insulin attaches to cells, signalling them to absorb blood sugar to be used for energy. In the condition of diabetes mellitus, blood sugar levels are too high because the body produces insufficient insulin. When insulin is depleted, blood glucose concentration increases, and glucose is passed out in the urine. Injections of insulin (increasingly made available through genetic engineering) enable blood sugar to be fully used. Where too much insulin is taken, blood sugar levels can be reduced too much (hypoglycaemia). An insulin overdose can be treated by dextrose or ordinary sugar to restore the balance. Because glucose is an important source of energy for the brain, a deficiency can damage the central nervous system, leading to convulsions, coma, and death (Kumar and Clarke 2016).

In England, in 2015, nurse **Victorino Chua** [S60, P19] was found guilty of murdering two patients with overdoses of insulin. Similarly, nurse **Colin Norris** [S57, P16] was sentenced for the murder of several patients at hospitals in Leeds, UK. Canadian nurse **Elizabeth Wettlaufer** [S62, P21] was charged with murder of eight patients using insulin injections. The victims were at a long-term care home and at another facility in Ontario. US nurse **Bobby Sue Dudley-Terrell** [S36] was charged with four counts of murder and following plea bargaining admitted guilt to second-degree murder. She administered insulin injection overdoses killing four elderly patients at a centre in Florida. (For discussion of further cases, please also see Marks and Richmond 2007.)

Glyburide

Glyburide (also known as Euglucon) is a drug which lowers blood sugar levels and is used to treat high blood sugar levels in people with type 2 diabetes.

For financial gain, Austrian **Elfriede Blauensteiner** [S43, P3] killed her third husband, a male companion, and a neighbour including by administering glyburide (as Euglucon) and the anti-depressant clomipramine (as Anafranil).

Elements, Their Compounds and Derivatives

Arsenic

Elemental arsenic is a semi metal whose compounds may be classed as organic or inorganic.

Organic arsenicals were so called owing to the erroneous supposition that organic materials contained a life force lacking in inorganic ones. Inorganic arsenicals are either trivalent (having three electrons available for bonding with other substances) or pentavalent (with five electrons for bonding). Among trivalent arsenicals, arsenic trioxide (white arsenic) when widely available was a common choice for homicidal poisoning, being almost tasteless. Pentavalent forms include potassium arsenate and lead arsenate which are used in paint manufacture (Farrell 1990).

Some arsenicals such as arsenic trioxide dissolve only slowly in water, so that bodily absorption is dependent on how finely they are powdered. Coarse powder is less toxic because it can be excreted in faeces before dissolving. More soluble arsenates such as potassium arsenate are better absorbed. Bodily distribution of arsenic is affected by the arsenical administered and the dosage period. Arsenic is predominantly stored in heart, lung, liver and kidney tissue. High concentrations gather in hair, nails, bones, and teeth because natural keratin found in these body parts, contains a high proportion of sulphur atoms to which arsenic particularly binds. Within hours of being administered, arsenic begins to accumulate in the hair, where signs of it can remain for years. Arsenic is excreted mainly in urine. Trivalent arsenicals primarily bind to sulphur atoms in the body's enzymes. They inhibit suphydril containing enzyme systems essential to normal cellular metabolism. Pentavalent arsenicals compete in the cells for inorganic phosphate. Substituting themselves for phosphate, they combine with an organic compound to form a quickly broken-down derivative.

Acute arsenic poisoning can quickly cause burning lips, throat constriction, and difficulty swallowing. Severe gastric pains, violent vomiting, and excessive watery diarrhoea follow. Kidneys become inflamed, and proteins and blood appear in depleted urine. The individual develops a raging thirst and muscular cramps. As body fluid is lost, symptoms of 'shock' appear followed by coma and death. Where poisoning is very severe, death can occur in an hour but more commonly severe poisoning kills in about 24 hours. With *chronic* arsenic poisoning, excessive fluid accumulates beneath the skin especially the eyelids and face. Other signs are loss of appetite, nausea, vomiting, and diarrhoea. The eye conjunctiva and nasal mucus membranes become inflamed and itchy, and the mouth becomes sore. Later symptoms include anaemia and cirrhosis of the liver. Jaundice appears as bile pigment is deposited in the deep layers of the skin, turning its surface yellow. Peripheral neuritis (nerve inflammation) develops. Numbness and tingling affect the limbs, especially the feet. A dose of arsenic small enough to be held on the tip of a knife blade can be lethal.

In the nineteenth century, **Hélèna Jégado** [S1], a French domestic servant, administered arsenic in food and drink to kill colleagues mainly out of jealousy. Laundrywoman **Maria Swanenberg** [S6] of the Netherlands was found guilty of three poisonings using arsenic administered in food and drink. **Sarah Whiteling** [S8] in the US used arsenic rat poison to kill her husband, her daughter, and her son to benefit from their life insurance.

In the twentieth century, **Madame Popova** [S12] of Russia, was executed by firing squad in St Petersburg, for killing the husbands of various unhappy wives. Arsenic administered in food and drink, and other methods were used. **Bertha Gifford** [S16] of Missouri, US was tried for the murders of two husbands with arsenic administered in their food and drink and found not guilty 'by reason of insanity'. **Nannie Doss** [S24] of Alabama, US, confessed to killing members of her family with arsenic over many years although the exact number of murders is disputed. **Anjette Lylles** [S26] of Georgia, US also used arsenic to kill family members for insurance money. **Janie Lou Gibbs** [S28] of Georgia, US killed family members in a similar way. **Dr. Michael Swango** [S42, P2], was sentenced in 2000 for the arsenic poisoning of several patients.

Antimony

A brittle, bluish-white semi-metal, antimony has a flaky, crystalline texture. Organic antimony compounds may be trivalent (with three electrons available for bonding) or pentavalent (having five electrons available for bonding). Trivalent antimony compounds include antimony potassium tartrate comprising colourless crystals or white powder which is sweet tasting but odourless. Pentavalent antimony compounds include sodium antimony gluconate (see also Emsley 2005, pp. 198–217).

Absorbed slowly from the gastrointestinal tract, antimony is distributed to concentrate in the liver and thyroid. It is excreted mainly in urine. Trivalent antimony compounds are more toxic than pentavalent ones. Trivalent antimony links itself to sulfhydryl groups of atoms in bodily cells to form 'thioantimonates' and binds itself to red blood cells, breaking down key elements of cell structure. Tiny doses of antimony act as an expectorant, clearing secretions from air passages by stimulating the salivary and bronchial glands. Antimony poisoning produces symptoms like those of arsenic and lead. Antimony still in the stomach can be precipitated (turned into a deposit) by calcium hydroxide or magnesium oxide.

English physician **Dr. Edward Pritchard** [S2], used antimony (and aconite) to poison his mother-in-law and his wife, possibly to allow him to continue an affair with a housemaid. **Martha Grinder** [S3] of Pennsylvania, US killed two women in 1865, using arsenic and antimony.

Copper Sulphate

Copper, as an 'essential' element exists in all organisms. It is necessary for blood formation, is contained in several enzymes, and is present in all bodily tissue especially brain, heart, liver, kidney, and hair. Copper sulphate if taken orally is absorbed by the gastrointestinal tract. It is not one of the most toxic poisons, a relatively large dose of 10 grams likely being lethal. Symptoms of copper sulphate poisoning include cramps, convulsions, coma, and eventually death (Farrell 1992, pp. 63–64).

Using copper sulphate, Parisian pharmacist **Pierre Moreau** [S5] poisoned his first and second wives, for which he was guillotined.

Phosphorus and Organic Phosphorus Compound E605

A white, waxy non-metallic element, phosphorus turns yellow when exposed to light. At normal temperatures, it combusts slowly, becoming luminous. Red phosphorus is benign. Yellow (white) phosphorus is fatal in a tiny dose (50 mg). While tasting unpleasant and emitting a sulphurous odour, it has been used as a poison disguised in spirits and strong coffee. Although barely soluble in water, the substance is more soluble in alcohol or in organic fluids like olive oil. Taken by mouth, phosphorus is absorbed by the intestinal tract and distributed to internal organs where it particularly damages the liver. Initially it acts as an irritant while later, as a protoplasmic poison, it breaks up cells in the liver and other internal organs. Acute poisoning produces a garlic smelling breath, vomit and faeces which may be luminescent, burning pains in the stomach, convulsions, and coma. After a day or two, symptoms seem quiescent before the delayed effects of the poison emerge as jaundice, collapse, coma, and eventually death.

Mary Wilson [S25] was convicted of murdering Oliver Leonard (her second husband) and Ernest Wilson (her third husband) with elemental phosphorus as a constituent of rat and beetle poison.

German chemist Gerhard Schroeder developed organic phosphorus compounds E605 which were used as insecticides. E605 (Parathion) has the chemical label diethyl p-nitrophenyl phosphorothionate. It inhibits the acetylcholinesterase enzyme from breaking down acetylcholine, so increasing the action of the neurotransmitter acetylcholine (and its duration). German chemists devised tests to detect E605 in the early 1950s. Symptoms of E605 poisoning are like those for hydrogen cyanide: convulsions, and paralysis of the respiratory centres. Other symptoms include constriction of the eye pupils, slowed heartbeat, and excessive salivation.

German chemical factory worker **Christa Lehmann** [S23] used E605 to kill her husband and her father-in-law, while also unintentionally poisoning friend Annie Hamann. **Maria Velten** [S31], in Germany, confessed to killing her father, an aunt, two husbands, and a lover with E605 from herbicide administered in food. She was sentenced to life imprisonment in 1983.

Thallium

Thallium is a soft, white metallic element, having various forms including thallium sulphate, and salts of thallium. Thallous salts are readily absorbed from the mucous membranes of the mouth and gastrointestinal tract, as well as from the skin. The metal accumulates in the muscles, kidneys and spleen, and less so in hair and skin. Thallium is excreted in urine for up to two months after administration. One of the most toxic of metals, thallium is odourless, tasteless and colourless. It has been detected in the remains of a homicide victim even after cremation. For an adult, the minimum lethal dose is about 800 mg. of thallium sulphate. In its action, thallium competes with the body's potassium at enzyme active centres. It can resemble poisoning by arsenic, lead, mercury, or carbon monoxide (see also Emsley 2005, pp. 321–335).

Acute symptoms include waves of severe abdominal pain, vomiting, diarrhoea, and haemorrhage. Proteins are passed in depleted urine. Bodily extremities become very painful. Delirium, convulsions, and coma follow. Circulatory collapse and respiratory failure may occur twenty to forty hours after initial symptoms. With *chronic* poisoning, nerves serving the hands and feet become inflamed. Power over movement is lost, and facial paralysis and squinting develops. Eye pupils dilate, skin eruptions appear, and the palms of the hands and soles of the feet become horn-like. Hair loss becomes noticeable about twenty days after the initial dose. The person losses appetite, and develops vomiting, and stomach pains.

Austrian **Martha Marek** [S19] killed her husband Emil, her daughter, a relative Susanne Lowenstein, and a lodger using thallium for which in 1938, she was guillotined. Australian **Yvonne Fletcher** [S21], poisoned two husbands with thallium rat poison. Also of Australia, **Caroline Grills** [S22] used thallium rat poison to kill several relatives. In England, 23-year-old **Graham Young** [S27] murdered two work colleagues with thallium having previously been released from a secure hospital where he had been detained for poisoning (but not killing) his stepmother. Russian **Viacheslav Soloviev** [S56, P15] was found guilty of using thallium as a constituent of rat poison to kill several relatives (including his wife) and a police investigator.

Other Poisons

Sodium Hypochlorite

Sodium hypochlorite is a chemical compound. As a solution (bleach) it is perhaps best known as a disinfectant and bleaching agent.

Kimberley Clark Saenz [S59, P18], a licenced practical/vocational nurse, poisoned patients at a clinic in Texas. On one occasion it was reported that she was seen injecting bleach from a cleaning bucket into the dialysis lines of patients who later died. (A dialysis line is a central venous catheter connected to a dialysis machine to enable blood to be circulated to the machine and back to the patient's body.)

Methanol Anti-freeze and Ethylene Glycol Anti-freeze

Methanol is colourless, smells of alcohol, is soluble in water, and has a burning taste. It is used in windshield cleaning solution, paint remover, and gas-line antifreeze for vehicles. A fatal dose is about 20–150 gm. In the body, methanol is oxidised to form the more toxic formaldehyde, which is further oxidised into formic acid. After a few hours the individual may appear drunk and may experience stomach pains. After 30 hours, symptoms may include excessive production of body acid, visual disturbances, blindness, seizures, and coma, and eventually death (Trestrail 2007, pp. 111–114).

Ethylene glycol (1,2 ethanol) is a viscous liquid that is odourless, sweet tasting and highly soluble in water. The compound is used in radiator anti-freeze and in anti-freeze products for heating and cooling systems. The fatal dose of 95% ethylene glycol is about 1.5 mL per kg of body weight. In the body, the compound is oxidised into the more toxic oxalic acid which then combines with blood calcium to form crystals of calcium oxalate which can be found in the kidneys and in urine. Early symptoms are apparent drunkenness and possible gastritis and vomiting. After 4–12 hours the individual experiences acidosis, hyperventilation, convulsion, heartbeat disturbances and coma, and often kidney failure (Trestrail 2007, pp. 111–114).

In 2001 the boyfriend of **Lynn Turner** [S49, P8] died. Police investigations into the similar death of her former husband Glenn Turner convinced them that she had killed both with ethylene glycol antifreeze. Found guilty in 2004 of her husband's murder, and in 2007 of her boyfriend's murder, Julia Lynn Turner died in prison in 2010.

Chloroform

Chloroform, a compound of chlorine, carbon and hydrogen, was discovered in 1831. A volatile, heavy, colourless liquid with a pungent slightly sweet odour, chloroform mixes with alcohol or ether. Medicinally, drops of chloroform were used for sea sickness, and as a skin liniment it eased rheumatic pain. Small doses of chloroform vapour induce drowsiness, while larger amount causes unconsciousness. First employed as an anaesthetic by Sir James Young Simpson in 1847, later, chloroform was administered to ease pain in childbirth and to induce unconsciousness in surgery, although it is now used for neither purpose.

Taken by mouth, chloroform is absorbed by the gastrointestinal tract. As a vapour, it is absorbed by the lungs and distributed into the bloodstream. Sometimes, a very small dose of chloroform can kill quickly and suddenly by stopping the heart. It makes the heart highly sensitive to the bodily hormone adrenalin, so that too much chloroform can precipitate heart failure brought about by the body's own adrenalin secretion.

It can also cause respiratory arrest. Death can sometimes occur several days after taking chloroform owing to damage to the liver, heart, and kidneys.

Frederick Mors [S13], confessed to killing residents in a nursing home in New York, and was found criminally insane. Initially using arsenic and later chloroform, he poisoned eight elderly patients.

Calcium Cyanamide

Calcium cyanamide ('nitrolime') is an inorganic compound used as a mineral fertiliser. Among the deleterious effects of direct exposure are respiratory tract irritation, low blood pressure, and rapid heart rate.

Francisca Ballesteros [S51, P10], living in Melilla, Spain confessed murdering family members with calcium cyanamide administered over an extended period in food and drink. Victims were her daughter aged 6 months, her husband and her older daughter.

Poisoners' Decisions

Given the wide range of poisons available to varying degrees, a (serial) poisoner must make certain decisions. An early one is what poison will be used. Will it be a 'benign' poison such as morphine or will it be a 'violent' one such as strychnine (where some of the symptoms might be passed off as epilepsy, especially if they are reported to but not directly witnessed by an attending physician). Also, will the poison be administered over time as a chronic poison usually to mimic a wasting illness, or will it be administered in a single fatal dose?

A further consideration is access to the poison. This is easier with poisons that are routinely available such as anti-freeze. Access is available to some poisoners owing to their work, as with medical personnel. It requires more planning where the poison is not normally to hand as when the Indian serial poisoner **Mohan Kumar** [S54, P13] purported to be a jewellery maker to obtain cyanide from a supplier.

How the poison is to be administered is also a consideration, often determined by the initial choice of poison. Is it to be given by mouth, or injected (usually associated with medical murders), or administered in some other way? Related to this decision is the choice of how the poison will be conveyed. If it is given orally, which food or drink will be used to convey it?

These and other considerations are involved in serial poisoning, and it is to serial poisoners themselves that we turn in the next chapter.

Conclusion

Poisons that have been used in serial poisoning were described grouped as: plant poisons, animal poisons, bacterial poisons, drugs used as poisons (heart drugs, muscle relaxant, analgesics, and diabetic drugs), elements their compounds and derivatives, and 'other poisons'. Examples of poisoners who had used the various substances were given. Some of the considerations that a serial poisoner must consider, point towards the next chapter dealing with the poisoners themselves.

Suggested Activities

Consider the relative use of different types of poisons in different time periods (eighteenth, nineteenth, twentieth, and twenty-first centuries) and reflect on the reasons for changes in poison preferences. Consider plants, animal, bacterial, drug, and elemental poisons in this way.

Reflect on the use of drugs as poisons and consider whether heart drugs and muscle relaxants are preferred poisons and if so, why.

Key Texts

United States Pharmacopeial Convention. (2015). *United States Pharmacopeia [US Pharmacopeia National Formulary]*. Rockville, MD: United States Pharmacopeial Convention.

Many countries have their pharmacopeia or national formulary. The US version is published annually and provides details of drugs including the ones discussed in the present chapter.

Holstege, C. P., Neer, T. M., Saathoff, G. B., & Furbe, B. (2010). *Criminal Poisoning: Clinical and Forensic Perspectives*. Sudbury, MA: Jones and Bartlett Publishers.

This edited medical textbook covers different poisons each in a separate chapter (Chapters 4 through 25 of the 28-Chapter book), focusing on the main medical diagnostic challenges that are associated with detecting and prosecuting.

References

Barlow, G., Irving, W. L., & Moss, P. J. (2016). Infectious Disease. In P. Kumar & M. Clark (Eds.), *Clinical Medicine* (9th ed.). Philadelphia, PA: Elsevier Saunders.

Emsley, J. (2005). *The Elements of Murder: A History of Poison*. Oxford: Oxford University Press.

Farrell, M. (1990). Arsenic Queen of Poisons. *The Criminologist, 14*(4), 188–189.

Farrell, M. (1992). *Poisons and Poisoners: An Encyclopaedia of Homicidal Poisonings*. London: Robert Hale.

Farrell, M. (1993, March 19). What's Your Poison? *Solicitors' Journal*, 254.

Farrell, M. (2017). *Criminology of Homicidal Poisoning: Offenders, Victims and Detection*. London and New York: Springer.

Holstege, C. P., Neer, T. M., Saathoff, G. B., & Furbe, B. (2010). *Criminal Poisoning: Clinical and Forensic Perspectives*. Sudbury, MA: Jones and Bartlett Publishers.

Kumar, P., & Clark, M. (Eds.). (2016). *Clinical Medicine* (9th ed.). Philadelphia, PA: Elsevier Saunders.

Marks, V., & Richmond, C. (2007). *Insulin Murders: True Life Cases*. London: Royal Society of Medicine Press.

Nelson, L. S., Richard, D. S., & Balick, M. J. (2007). *Handbook of Poisonous and Injurious Plants* (2nd ed.). New York: Springer.

Trestrail, J. H. (2007). *Criminal Poisoning: Investigational Guide for Law Enforcement, Toxicologists, Forensic Scientists and Attorneys* (2nd ed.). Totowa, NJ: Humana Press.

United States Pharmacopeial Convention. (2015). *United States Pharmacopeia [US Pharmacopeia National Formulary]*. Rockville, MD: United States Pharmacopeial Convention.

White, J., Meier, J., & Warrell, D. A. (Eds.). (2008). *Handbook of Clinical Toxicology of Animal Venoms and Poisons* (2nd ed.). New York and London: CRC Press.

4

Serial Poisoners

Introduction

Gathering reliable information of the demographics of serial killers and serial poisoners is challenging. Recognising this, one can tentatively compare serial killers generally and serial poisoners in relation to various demographic categories such as gender and age. Also pertinent are the location of the murder, the methods used to kill, and the motivation of the perpetrator. Comparing serial team killers generally with serial team poisoners is problematic because of the rarity of team serial poisoning.

Sources and Reliability of Information on Serial Murderers

Hickey's US Data

Hickey (2010) collated US data based on 'biographical case study analysis of serial murderers and their victims' from 1800 to 2008 (ibid., p. 34). Sources included 'newspapers, journals, bibliographies, biographies, computer searches and social science abstracts' and a few interviews with serial killers. In the cases, convictions were reported of two or more victims with substantial periods between killings (ibid.). Although Hickey (2010) identifies 'nearly 500 serial killers' these represent fewer cases (400) because some involved team killers implicating more than one offender (ibid., p. 35). Sometimes, Hickey (2010) refers to a shorter timeframe of 1850–2004 giving a smaller sample, for example citing his '2004 study' comprising 431 *serial killers* representing 367 *cases* of serial murder (ibid., p. 278, italics added).

Holmes and Holmes' Case Studies

Case studies presented by Holmes and Holmes (2010) provide illustrations of many serial killings. From these and other information, the authors developed a typology of different serial murders. (I discuss this in other chapters.) Case studies include those of Joseph Kallinger (as a 'visionary' type serial killer), Manuel Pardo ('mission'), Jerry Brudos ('hedonistic—lust'), 'Randy' ('hedonistic—thrill'), Richard Kuklinski ('hedonistic—comfort'), and Ted Bundy ('power/control').

Reliability and Validity of Data on Serial Killers

Hickey (2010) recognises the usefulness as well as the limitations of information on serial killers. He notes difficulties in securing credibility when case records report hundreds of victims from the nineteenth century and record keeping was not always 'accurate or efficient' (ibid., p. 36). Additionally, these sources are not always consistent. Indeed, the 'data on victims may have been exaggerated because of the sensational nature of the crimes' (ibid.). Hickey (2010) excludes such cases from his study, yet the challenge of gathering accurate information remains. For example, estimates of victim numbers still vary widely from 3000 to 4600 homicides. This is in part because 'a few serial murderers killed so many people that only close approximations of the actual numbers can be ascertained' (ibid., pp. 35–36).

Sources and Reliability of Information on Serial Poisoners

Trestrail's Database

Trestrail (2007) collated a database of 1026 cases (including serial poisoners) in which the offender was convicted of homicidal poisoning. Most cases were from either the US (404) or the UK (255) with the remainder from many different regions (ibid., pp. 56–57). Dates span from 339 B.C.E. to 2007 and are mainly from the twentieth century (Trestrail, personal communication, November 2016).

Cases Considered in the Present Book

As described more fully in Chapter 1, the discussion in this volume largely draws on over 60 case summaries of serial poisoners, with more than 20 of these being described more fully as profiles. These represent countries worldwide but focus especially on the US and UK. In all cases, references are cited allowing readers to pursue the examples in further detail.

Reliability and Validity of Data on Serial Poisoners

Challenges in ascertaining demographic data on serial killers apply also to serial poisoners. Indeed, the difficulties are greater. Serial poisoning may be numerous and may have gone unsuspected for long periods. UK physician **Dr. Harold Shipman** [S41, P1] killed around 250 patients over decades. Although a judge-led enquiry thoroughly evaluated the causes of death, as one goes back in time or when information is patchy, uncertainty increases. Undoubtedly, instances of serial poisoning remain undetected and unknown. Consequently, one can see only a partial picture from which inferences must be tentative.

Scale of Serial Homicide

Scale of Serial Homicide

Hickey (2010, p. 187, Chart 7.1) identifies increasing numbers of male serial killers in the US each quarter century as follows: 1900–1924 = 16; 1925–1949 = 26; 1950–1974 = 118; and 1975–2004 = 177. Similarly, of the 64 female offenders he identifies, only 10% were found between 1826 and 1899 while the other 90% were identified since 1900 (ibid., p. 257).

Scale of Serial Poisoning

Trestrail (2007) drawing on a historical and present-day database of 1026 cases in which the offender was convicted of homicidal poisoning, found that 59% of cases involve one victim but in the remaining 41% of cases, there were 'multiple victims' (ibid., p. 59). It is unclear in how many of these multiple victims result from mass poisoning or serial poisoning.

Gender

Gender of Serial Killers

As Holmes and Holmes (2010) point out, the exact number of female serial killers is unknown, although estimated to be about 5–8% of all serial killers (ibid., pp. 49–50). In 1800 and 2008 timeframe Hickey (2010) identifies 'nearly 500 serial killers'. In total, 'nearly 70 female offenders and over 400 male offenders in the United States' are represented (ibid., p. 35). From the period 1826 and 2004, Hickey (2010) finds 61 *cases* of female serial murderers, representing 15% of the total cases. These involved 64 female *offenders* who between them had killed between 410 and 628 victims (ibid., pp. 256 and 257, Table 9.1a). Predominance of male over female serial killers is further reflected in data from the years 1975–2004. In this period, Hickey (2010) identifies

188 male serial killers (ibid., p. 199, Table 7.4). However, only 30 female serial offenders are identified in the slightly longer period 1970–2004 (ibid., p. 257, Table 9.1a).

Gender of Serial Poisoners

With poisoning in general, there is no preponderance of male perpetrators over female offenders (Farrell 2017, passim). A similar picture appears to be found with serial poisoners. Certainly, the high numbers of male sexual predators involved in serial killing generally are not evident among serial poisoners. Also, as Kelleher and Kelleher (1998) point out, female serial killers acting alone tend to choose poison as their weapon.

Female serial poisoners include **Chisako Kakehi** [S63, P22] of Japan, **Christine Malèvre** [S48] of France, **Della Sorenson** [S15] from the US, **Francisca Ballesteros** [S51, P10] of Spain, **Maria Swanenberg** [S6] from the Netherlands, **Madame Popova** [S12] born in Russia, **Marie Alexandrine Becker** [S17] from Belgium, **Christa Lehmann** [S23] of Germany, **Yiya Murano** [S33] from Argentina, Austrian **Elfriede Blauensteiner** [S43, P3], and **Yvonne Fletcher** [S21] of Australia.

Among male serial poisoners are **Graham Young** [S27] of the UK, Indian-Canadian **Sukhwinder Singh Dhillon** [S44, P4], **Lê Thanh Vân** [S47, P7], born in Vietnam, **Mohan Kumar** [S54, P13] of India, **Viacheslav Soloviev** [S56, P15] born in Russia, **Pierre Désiré Moreau** [S5] a French herbalist, and US dentist **Dr. Arthur Waite** [S14].

Regarding healthcare serial poisoners women perpetrators include Swiss nurse **Marie Jeanneret** [S4], US nurse **Jane Toppan** [S10], nursing home manager **Dorothea Waddingham** [S18] of the UK, Canadian nurse **Elizabeth Wettlaufer** [S62, P21], and nurse **Christine Malèvre** [S48] of France.

Among male healthcare serial poisoners are **Dr. Marcel Petiot** [S20] of France, US coronary care nurse **Robert Rubane Diaz** [S29], nurse **Arnfinn Nesset** [S30] of Norway, nurse **Benjamin Geen** [S50, P9] from the UK, nurse **Stephan Letter** [S55, P14] of Germany, and Philippine-born nurse **Victorino Chua** [S60, P19].

Age

Age of Serial Killers

Looking at a sample of 275 US serial killers, Hickey (2010) found that the majority were comparatively young when they first murdered. Some 43.6% were aged 25 years or younger, and 48.4% were aged 26–40 years. Only 8.0% were 40 years or older (ibid., p. 337, Table 11.11). Among the youngest of serial killers is Mary Bell who in 1968 aged 11 strangled two boys aged 3 and 4 years old (Gita 1998). Given that the victims were small children, great physical strength was not required. One of the oldest serial killers is Ray Copeland, convicted aged 75 years in 1991 for (over several years) murdering five drifters at his Missouri farm. Although victims tended to be young men, physical strength was unnecessary for the perpetrator as the victims were shot (Bovsun 2008).

Age of Serial Poisoners

Like the age range of serial killers generally, the age range of serial poisoners is wide, but the 'starting age' higher. Among the youngest serial poisoners is **Graham Young** [S27] in the UK who was committed to Broadmoor maximum-security hospital in 1962 aged 14 for administering poison to family members. His stepmother died during this poisoning period, but her body had been cremated so conclusive evidence of murder was not available. On his release from Broadmoor, Young worked at a photographic supply firm where he killed two co-workers with thallium. He was sentenced in 1972 aged 24. Having a clear intention to poison suggests an understanding that certain substances can do harm, accompanied by a knowledge of how such a substance can be administered undetected by the victim. These factors point to the perpetrator not being very young and having a certain level of cognitive development.

Among older perpetrators is English serial poisoner **Mary Wilson** [S25] aged 64 years in 1957, when she killed for the final time.

Chisako Kakehi [S63, P22] of Kyoto, Japan was 69 years old when she murdered her last victim with cyanide in a supposed health-giving cocktail. Because the administration of poison does not require physical strength to overpower a victim, there is no obvious upper age limit on perpetrators. (The same applies to the use of firearms as we have already seen.)

Ethnicity

Ethnicity of Serial Killers

In a population of US serial killers ($N=249$) where race or ethnicity could be determined, 72% of male offenders were white, 23% African American, 3% Hispanic, 1% Asian, and 1% other racial or ethnic groups (Hickey 2010, p. 192). Between 1995 and 2004 it is reported that 'approximately 44% of identified male serial killers have been African American' (ibid.). Of Hickey's (2010) 64 female serial murderers identified between 1826 and 2004 almost all (93%) were white, while the remainder (7%) were African American (ibid., p. 256). Serial murderers and their victims tend to be of the same ethnic group (ibid., p. 194).

Ethnicity of Serial Poisoners

Among ethnic minority serial poisoners are **Efren Saldivar** [S46, P6] whose parents moved from Mexico to the US where he was born. UK nurse **Victorino Chua** [S60, P19] was born in the Philippines. However, in countries where the predominant ethnic group is white Caucasian such as the US and the UK, there is no evidence that minority ethnic groups are over represented in samples of serial poisoners.

Examples of serial poisoners are found worldwide and again appear to represent the ethnic makeup of the country concerned (and tend to kill victims of the same ethnic origin). In India, the cases of **Mohan Kumar** [S54, P13] and of **K. D. Kempanna** [S58, P17] involved Asian

(Indian) perpetrators and victims. Living in Canada, **Sukhwinder Singh Dhillon** [S44, P4], originally of Punjab, India poisoned Parvesh Kaur Dhillon his wife, and Ranjit Singh Khela his friend and business associate, both of Indian origin. In Japan, **Chisako Kakehi** [S63, P22] poisoned her husband, and two common law partners who were also Japanese, with cyanide. **Lê Thanh Vân** [S47, P7] of Vietnam used cyanide to poison Vietnamese relatives and acquaintances.

Social Background and Occupation

Social Background and Occupation of Serial Killers

Male serial killers in Hickey's (2010) database came from a variety of backgrounds and occupations. Very few possessed college degrees and they mainly held blue collar jobs (ibid., pp. 213 and 217, Table 7.11). Some 64 female serial murderers were identified who had killed between 1826 and 2004. Most of these female poisoners (where occupation was identified) represented a range of occupations, being grouped as unskilled, skilled, or professional (ibid., p. 256, para 2).

Social Background and Occupation of Serial Poisoners

Some serial poisoners were domestic workers. **Hélèna Jégado** [S1] of France administered arsenic to hotel worker colleagues and fellow house servants. Australian **Yvonne Fletcher** [S21], was a domestic help, who used thallium rat poison to kill two husbands. Laundry woman **Maria Swanenberg** [S6] of Leiden, Netherlands killed three people with arsenic for financial gain.

Factory workers include US serial poisoner **Nannie Doss** [S24] who when young worked at the Linen Thread Company. **Mary Ann Britland** [S7] of Manchester, UK, was factory operative who used strychnine exterminator to kill her husband, her daughter, and a neighbour. **Graham Young** [S27] worked at a UK photographic supplier as a store worker and general factotum (whose duties unfortunately for his colleagues included taking round drinks of tea).

Those working in business include **Sukhwinder Singh Dhillon** [S44, P4], originally of the Punjab, India. As a car salesman in Ontario, Canada he killed his wife and later his business partner with strychnine. **Marie Alexandrine Becker** [S17] of Liege, Belgium, was a housewife and sometime dress shop owner, charged with poisoning with digitalis two husbands and an elderly customer of her shop.

State and government workers include **Lynn Turner** [S49, P8] a 911 dispatcher in Cobb County, Georgia, US who killed her husband, and a subsequent common law partner. **Mohan Kumar** [S54, P13], who poisoned women who were hoping for marriage, was a teacher.

In brief we see a range of occupations including domestic helpers, factory workers, business owners or partners, and state and government workers. Sometimes, the perpetrator's occupation allowed the poisoning of associates. **Sukhwinder Singh Dhillon** [S44, P4] poisoned a business partner, while **Marie Alexandrine Becker** [S17] murdered one of her shop customers. Often however, the offender's occupation appears tangential as with domestic help **Yvonne Fletcher** [S21], or 911 dispatcher **Lynn Turner** [S49, P8].

Turning to healthcare professionals, a disproportionally high number are found among poisoners and serial poisoners. Some medical and paramedical professionals kill outside the patient relationship, although helped by their professional knowledge of poisons. **Dr. Edward Pritchard** [S2], the English physician, used antimony and aconite to kill his mother-in-law and his wife. Parisian herbalist **Pierre Désiré Moreau** [S5] killed two wives with copper sulphate. **Lê Thanh Vân** [S47, P7] of Vietnam trained in the army medical corps before using cyanide to poison relatives and others. Hamburg resident **Elisabeth Wiese** [S11] was originally a midwife but was disbarred after conducting illegal abortions. Later she provided care for children whom she poisoned with morphine.

Where healthcare workers kill within the professional–patient relationship, they are aided by professional knowledge, access to patients, and society's basic trust in their vocation. Discussed in a later chapter, they include physicians, nurses, nursing aides, and nursing home managers who poisoned within a professional–patient role.

Personal History of Violent, Criminal, or Abnormal Behaviour

Personal History of Serial Killers

Douglas and Olshaker (1996) state that 'probably the most crucial single factor in the development of a serial rapist or killer is the role of fantasy' for example fantasies relating sex and death in various games as shown by serial killer Ed Kemper (ibid., p. 114). The authors (citing Kemper's background) also refer to a 'triad' of earlier behaviours associated with homicide: enuresis, fire setting, and cruelty to small animals as children (ibid., p. 111). However, Holmes and Holmes (2010) express reservations about overgeneralising such observations. They point out that some serial killers show no such behaviours and that there are people who have shown such conduct including the 'triad' that have not gone on to harm others (ibid., p. 11). Difficulties in defining and identifying such traits and behaviours in childhood, especially retrospectively, limit the credence of such speculations.

Serial killers having previously been incontrovertibly found to have broken laws or norms, provides better evidence that might be associated with later serial homicide. Of Charles Manson, the leader of a group involved in murder it is said that, 'His young adult life was marked by a series of robberies, forgeries, pimpings, assaults, and incarcerations at increasingly tougher institutions' (Douglas and Olshaker 1996, p. 119). Some 211 male serial killers in Hickey's (2010) study (1800–2004), had a history of violent, criminal or 'abnormal' behaviour. Of these, 63% were previously incarcerated in 'prison or mental institution', 45% had previous property crimes, and 38% had committed previous sex-related offences (ibid., p. 220, Table 7.13). However, among female serial killers (1800–2004, $N=64$), 'very few' were known to have criminal records (ibid., p. 276).

Personal History of Serial Poisoners

Just as when considering serial killers generally, in reviewing the personal history of serial poisoners, it is prudent to be sceptical about the predictive and explanatory usefulness of certain supposed traits and behaviours in childhood. Here I concentrate on serial poisoners who prior to their first murder, perpetrated criminal or deviant acts, although such deviance is not of course identified with all serial poisoners.

In the US, **Stella Nickell** [S35] who poisoned her husband and (randomly) a local bank manager had a history of fraud (which led to a jail sentence), forgery, and child beating. Nurse's aide and later care home manager **Dorothea Puente** [S39] of California, US was convicted of three murders using drug overdoses including Tylenol. Much earlier, she served a six-month sentence for forging cheques. Later she was sentenced to three months imprisonment for managing a brothel and soon after was locked up for vagrancy. **Efren Saldivar** [S46, P6] of the US worked as a respiratory therapist and killed six patients by using drugs to induce respiratory arrest or cardiac failure. He had a previous history of petty crime and stealing. UK physician and serial killer **Dr. Harold Shipman** [S41, P1] was convicted for stealing and abusing drugs early in his professional career.

Sometimes the previous offences involve murder or attempted murder by poisoning. **Graham Young** [S27] in the UK had, when only 15 years old, poisoned family members and a school friend. Released from the secure psychiatric hospital where he had been detained, he went on to kill co-workers with thallium. **Dr. Neill Cream** [S9], known for poisoning London prostitutes with strychnine, had previously been imprisoned in Illinois for poisoning Daniel Scott. Relatedly, **Caroline Grills** [S22] of Australia was charged with the attempted murder of three family members, and only then were earlier suspicions confirmed that she had poisoned various relatives six years earlier.

Where such earlier criminal or deviant acts do occur, they might be disinhibiting, making later deviant behaviour including criminal offending more likely. Never the less, in some instances, no such deviant or criminal behaviour is recorded, and poison homicides appear full blown and seemingly without precedent.

Location and Serial Killers

Over half (55%) of male offenders in Hickey's (2010) database of 367 offenders from the years 1800 to 2004 were considered 'local', staying within a general area or county and not carrying on their killings in more than one state. A further 10% of offenders were 'place-specific', their killings occurring in the offender's home or work location. Just above a third of offenders were 'travelling' and killed victims in more than one state (ibid., pp. 194–195 and 199, Table 7.4). In the period 1975–2004, the comparable figure was 'local' 61%, 'place-specific' 11% and 'travelling' 28% ($N=188$) (ibid., p. 199, Table 7.4).

Turning to female serial killers for the years 1821–2004, of 64 offenders, 22% were classified as 'travelling', 44% as 'local' and 34% as 'place-specific' (Hickey 2010, pp. 265 and 266, Table 9.7). Holmes and Holmes (2010) note that, while male serial perpetrators appear to be 'almost equally divided between the stable and the transient types', nearly all female serial offenders fall into 'the geographically stable category' (ibid., p. 175).

Location and Serial Poisoners

Place-Specific and Travelling Poisoners

Where serial poisoners hold medical or related occupations and perpetrate their crimes in a hospital or clinic, these offences are 'place-specific'. Physicians, nurses, and nursing home managers usually come into this category. **Dr. Harold Shipman** [S41, P1] killed in the various homes of his patients and occasionally in his surgery but always within a constrained locality determined by his patient 'pool'.

Similarly, a perpetrator who poisons family members tends to do so in their shared home or when visiting a family member in their (usually) nearby residence. **Chisako Kakehi** [S63, P22] in Japan poisoned her husband and two common law partners at home. Russian **Viacheslav Soloviev** [S56, P15] appears to have poisoned family members at home, although he administered poison to a police officer at the local station where he was being questioned. Equally, serial killers who poisoned work colleagues targeted workers whom they regularly met in their shared locality.

Travelling serial poisoners are rare, reflecting the different nature of poisoning compared with serial homicide generally. For example, a serial sexual predator who rapes and kills strangers may travel to different locations to avoid detection because once a body is discovered it will usually be obvious that a murder has taken place. (Some killers of course hide the bodies of their victims to delay or avoid them being found.) But a serial poisoner may be able to kill without it being apparent to anyone that a crime has taken place because the killing is mistaken for natural death. Therefore, there is no reason to travel to kill or to escape detection. **Dr. Michael Swango** [S42, P2] travelled to commit further crimes and to avoid detection, but once in a new setting Swango's crimes can be considered place-specific. He was not a 'travelling' offender in the sense that he did not go regularly from clinic to clinic looking for victims.

Locations Reducing the Risk of Apprehension

The perpetrator is likely to choose a location for (serial) poisoning that reduces the likelihood of being apprehended. Where the perpetrator poisons short term acquaintances, the setting may be relatively public. **Mohan Kumar** [S54, P13] chose various bus stations in southern Karnataka, India, to persuade his lovers to take seeming contraceptive pills which were in fact cyanide tablets. He further persuaded the women to first lock themselves in the public toilets to avoid premature discovery. This successful modus operandi was repeated because it allowed his escape.

Also, in India, **K. D. Kampana** [S58, P17] poisoned worshipers whom she lured to temples away from their homes, finding a quiet part of the temple complex before administering the poison. Occasionally, the victim is a stranger as when **Stella Nickell** [S35] killed a local bank manager through product tampering to cover the previous murder of her husband. In this case the venue where the poison is inadvertently taken by the victim may be the victims home, workplace or elsewhere.

Workplace and Home

For nurses such as **Niels Hogel** [S61, P20] in Germany, and other hospital serial poisoners, the location is their place of work. This is a setting in which they are familiar with the spaces and the times at which supervision is likely to be reduced. Where homicides take place in nursing homes, the same principles apply. Home manager **Arnfinn Nesset** [S30] in Norway was not only familiar with the setting but arranged the routines himself as the person responsible for the venue. Places of work (other than hospitals or nursing homes) may sometimes be the location for poisoning especially where the poisoner has reason to handle food and drink.

For those who kill their spouse or partner such as **Lynn Turner** [S49, P8] the venue is often their home (or the victim's home). Here, the perpetrator is familiar with the space and the victim's routines and is likely to have the added safeguard of privacy. This allowed Lynn Turner to kill her first husband police officer Glenn Turner without being detected. **Nannie Doss** [S24] too tended to kill in her own home or in the familiar homes of relatives. **Yiya Murano** [S33] visited the familiar homes of relative and friends to poison them.

Different locations are not just defined by the place but also by the sorts of activities and routines associated with them. These, known by the poisoner, can be exploited. The mealtimes and eating habits of a victim in a domestic home is one such set of routines. Another is the procedure of administering medication in a hospital, or a nursing home.

Motives of Serial Killers

Douglas and Olshaker (1996, p. 114) refer to the three 'watchwords' of violent serial offenders, namely, 'manipulation', 'domination', and 'control'.

In Hickey's (2010) study, the motives of *male* serial killers (1800–2004, $N=367$) were predominantly sexual. Sex was the motive with one or more victims in 47% of offences and the sole motive in 8%.

Other common motives were: control ('sometimes' 31%), money ('sometimes' 18% and 'solely' 7%) and enjoyment ('sometimes' 15% and 'solely' 2%) (ibid., p. 219, Table 7.12). Motives of *female* serial killers ($N=64$) were money 'sometimes' for 47% and 'exclusively' for 26%. Sex was only the motive 'sometimes' for 10% and never the sole motive (Hickey 2010, p. 267, Table 9.8).

Regarding child victims, the motive for male offenders ($N=75$) was most commonly 'sexual gratification' (71%) and 'control' (41%). For female perpetrators against children, the main motive was 'monetary gain' (49%) for example family life insurance (Hickey 2010, p. 295).

Motives of Serial Poisoners

Motives of serial poisoners include: financial gain, jealousy and revenge, power and control, sadism, seeking excitement, factitious disorder imposed on another, and (claimed) mercy killing. There are also instances where motive is indirect or cannot be established, or where the perpetrator is judged to be 'insane'. These are each discussed below. (Healthcare Serial Poisoner cases are briefly mentioned and discussed more fully in the next chapter, 'Healthcare Serial Poisoning'.)

Financial Gain

Financial incentives appear to be common motives in serial poisoning. **Nannie Doss** [S24] gained financially from some of her murders as shown by adjusting the amounts to modern values. However, others have attributed the killings to 'enjoyment' and she herself by some accounts purported simply to be bored. In India **K. D. Kempanna** [S58, P17] was driven by robbery. **Lynn Turner** [S49, P8] killed her husband and later her boyfriend for insurance payouts. **Stella Nickell** [S35] murdered her husband for insurance money then tampered with shop medicines, killing a second random victim. In France,

Pierre Désiré Moreau [S5] poisoned two wives with copper sulphate for financial gain. **Maria Swanenberg** [S6] of Leiden, Netherlands, killed three victims with arsenic for money from life insurance and inheritance. UK Factory worker **Mary Ann Britland** [S7] poisoned her husband, her daughter and a neighbour with strychnine pest exterminator for life insurance money. German-born US resident **Sarah Whiteling** [S8] used arsenic rat poison to kill her husband, son, and daughter for life insurance. US dentist **Dr. Arthur Waite** [S14] sought to make money through inheritance by poisoning his mother-in-law and his father-in-law with diphtheria and tuberculosis germs, and arsenic. **Elisabeth Wiese** [S11] of Germany, having set up a service to care for children, poisoned them for financial gain.

Mixed motives including financial gain drove Russian **Madame Popova** [S12] who used arsenic, and other methods to kill the husbands of women clients. As well as the small amounts of money she made from fees, she possibly harboured (to her) altruistic motives in freeing some of her clients from abusive husbands.

Rare examples of healthcare serial poisoners having a financial motive are discussed in the relevant chapter and include nursing home manager **Dorothea Waddingham** [S18] who killed patients for their money.

Jealousy and Revenge

Jealousy was a motive for French domestic servant and hotel worker **Hélèna Jégado** [S1] who poisoned colleagues with arsenic when she considered that they were treated preferentially. Australian **Yvonne Fletcher** [S21] used thallium rat poison to kill her first and her second husbands, and a motive in the second murder may have been revenge for abuse. **Yiya Murano** [S33] of Argentina gave out cyanide in confections killing a neighbour, a friend, and a cousin mainly for financial gain, and possibly resentment at her precarious social position and limited education.

Regarding healthcare serial poisoners, motives of jealousy and revenge are uncommon. Nurse **Vickie Dawn Jackson** [S53, P12] found guilty of poisoning ten patients, may have become vengeful towards patients who had been shown compassion by other nurses.

Power and Control

Feelings of power and control are not often identified among non-healthcare serial poisonings. However, a version of power and control (over life and death) seem to be a motive in some healthcare serial murders. These include UK serial poisoner **Dr. Harold Shipman** [S41, P1], US coronary care nurse **Robert Rubane Diaz** [S29], and **Arnfinn Nesset** [S30] a Norwegian nursing home manager.

Sadism

It is uncommon to see sadism as a motive in non-healthcare serial poisonings. However, **Graham Young** [S27] the UK serial poisoner, sadistically kept records of the effects of the thallium that he was administering to co-workers.

Sadism more often arises with healthcare serial poisoners. Sadistic motives have been suggested in the cases of various nurses: **Marie Jeanneret** [S4], **Jane Toppan** [S10], **Victorino Chua** [S60, P19], **Colin Norris** [S57, P16], **Vickie Dawn Jackson** [S53, P12], and **Brian Rosenfeld** [S38].

Seeking Excitement

With non-healthcare serial poisoners, seeking excitement and thrills seems a rare motive.

Some healthcare serial poisoners however are in a sense motivated by seeking thrills and excitement, perhaps linked to the self-aggrandisement of resuscitating some patients. This may have been part of the motivation of nurses **Niels Högel** [S61, P20] of Germany; **Benjamin Geen** [S50, P9] in the UK; and **Kristen Gilbert** [S45, P5] and **Richard Angelo** [S37] both of the US.

Factitious Disorder Imposed on Another

Factitious disorder imposed on another (American Psychiatric Association 2013, pp. 324–327) has also been called 'factitious disorder by proxy', 'fabricated or induced illness' and 'Munchausen's syndrome by proxy'. The perpetrator (often a parent or carer) causes or invents symptoms of illness in the victim (often a child) to attract admiration or sympathy for themselves. Accurately defined, it is rare among serial poisoners, one example being paediatric nurse **Genene Jones** [S32] who endangered the lives of her child patients then sought admiration by 'saving' them, eventually killing children with drug injections.

Claimed Mercy Killing

For non-healthcare poisoners, euthanasia is rarely a claimed motive. **Maria Velten** [S31] of Germany used E605 from herbicide to kill her father, an aunt (which she claimed were mercy killings) and murdered two husbands and a lover for financial gain.

Healthcare serial poisoners sometimes state that their motive is mercy killing because the patients are suffering or dying, examples being nurse **Stephan Letter** [S55, P14] of Germany, nurse **Charles Cullen** [S52, P11] of the US, French nurse **Christine Malèvre** [S48] and hospital worker **Donald Harvey** [S34].

Indirect or Unestablished Motive

The motives of serial poisoners (non-health or health care) are highly unlikely to be sexual. Indirectly motivated by sex, **Dr. Edward Pritchard** [S2], the English physician, may have decided to kill his wife (and his mother-in-law) so that he could continue an affair with a housemaid. One of the rare cases of a direct sexual motive was that of dentist Dr. Etienne Deschamps, but it was not serial homicide. It involved regularly chloroforming a child over a period of months to sexually abuse her while she was unconscious, which on the final occasion led to her death (Tallant 1853). Whereas a male serial killer might rape and kill a victim by strangulation or some other overtly violent means, a serial poisoner has no such motives.

Caroline Grills [S22] of Sydney, Australia killed relatives with thallium. German **Christa Lehmann** [S23] killed her husband and her father-in-law, and (inadvertently) a friend with E605. **Martha Grinder** [S3] poisoned acquaintances with arsenic and antimony. In these three cases the motives are obscure.

Among healthcare serial poisoners motives are sometimes unclear. Instances include US physician **Dr. Michael Swango** [S42, P2], Los Angeles respiratory therapist **Efren Saldivar** [S46, P6], Canadian nurse **Elizabeth Wettlaufer** [S62, P21] and **Kimberley Clark Saenz** [S59, P18].

Insanity Judgement

I have tended not to describe cases in which the accused was found 'insane' because the implication is that they are not responsible for their actions and therefore not legally guilty. However, to illustrate that such cases sometimes arise, I have included a few.

Bertha Gifford [S16], a farmwife from Missouri tried for the murder of two husbands, was found not guilty 'by reason of insanity' and committed to Missouri State (Mental) Hospital. Although revenge partly motivated **Della Sorenson** [S15] of Nebraska, US who poisoned several relatives and others, she was finally judged insane, and committed to a State Mental Asylum.

Healthcare serial poisoner **Frederick Mors** [S13], working as a hospital porter, confessed to killing patients in New York, and was found criminally insane.

Team Serial Homicide

Team Serial Killers

Team killers that have become well known through wide publicity include in the US, Charles Manson and his 'family'; and in the UK, Fred and Rosemary West. An aspect unavailable to lone serial killers is that team killers can both participate in the killing and observe one or several others doing so. For some killers, this voyeuristic aspect may provide a greater thrill or satisfaction than acting alone. Joint action may also elicit mutual encouragement and shared justification for the activities.

A substantial number of serial killers in general acted with other offenders as 'team killers'. In Hickey's (2010) study (1850–2004) in the US, 114 such offenders were identified representing 26% of all serial murder offenders This comprised 49 cases as each involved several perpetrators (ibid., p. 235, Table 8.2). In most cases the number of offenders was two although there were instances of five perpetrators. The offenders might be, husband and wife, brothers, parent and child, or might be non-relatives, for example lovers (ibid., p. 227, Table 8.1). As for gender, women participated in 17 of the 49 cases. Regarding the ethnicity of offenders, 72% were white, 27% African American and 1% were Asian (ibid., p. 226). The occupation of team killers was mainly blue-collar requiring 'limited training', and offenders were generally 'ill prepared to achieve occupationally successful careers' (ibid., p. 233).

Of the 114 team offenders, most (53%) acted 'locally', 34% were 'travelling', and 13% were 'place-specific'. Similar proportions were shown when the killings were represented as cases (ibid., p. 235, Table 8.2).

Methods of killing ($N=45$ cases) were most commonly firearms (64%), strangulation (36%), and stabbing (32%). Notably, 52% of cases involved more than one method, reflecting the tendency keep the victim alive for pleasure and to torture them (ibid., p. 246, Table 8.8). Various motives ($N=49$ cases) for team killers included sexual (49%), financial (31%), control (33%) and enjoyment (25%) (ibid., p. 246, Table 8.9). Offender history indicated ($N=49$ cases) prior incarceration in prison or mental institution (43%), theft (43%) and sex-related crimes (27%) (ibid., p. 247, Table 8.10).

Team Serial Poisoners

By its nature, poisoning tends to be secretive and therefore solitary and individualistic. The intention is often to present the killing as a natural death, or less often as suicide or accident. This can be accomplished by individual perpetrators without accomplices. For such reasons, even team poisonings of single (i.e. not serial) victims are rare. Roger and David Cooper, in the UK, were sentenced for poisoning Roger Cooper's lover with chloroform (Gibons, 21 October 2015). Mary Creighton and Everett Applegate, in the US, were electrocuted for killing Everett's wife with arsenical rat poison (Farrell 1992). Dan Keisberg and several others used carbon monoxide gas to poison Mike Malloy, a vagrant (Read 2005).

Given the added risks associated with team poisoning, serial team poisoning is almost unheard of. A serial team homicide was perpetrated by Augusta Fullam, and Dr. Henry Clark who in colonial India, in 1911, used arsenic to kill Augusta's husband Edward McKean Fullam. They also procured the murder of Louisa Clarke (Henry Clarke's wife) by sword, in 1912. Strictly speaking, even this rare example is not team serial poisoning because the two perpetrators while they colluded did not act directly together to commit the poisoning, and the second murder was by sword and carried out as a proxy killing (Farrell 1992).

Methods of Serial Killing Including Poisoning

For male serial killers in Hickey's (2010) study (1800–2004, $N=367$), firearms were the commonest method of killing with 38% of offenders using them for one or more victims, and 18% using firearms as their sole weapon. By contrast only 6% used poison for one or more victims and only 5% used poison solely (ibid., p. 219, Table 7.12).

In data relating to female serial killers Hickey (2010) found that of 64 offenders, most (45%) perpetrated 'some' poisoning and 34% used poison only. 'Some' shooting was used by 19% and exclusively shooting by only 8% (ibid., p. 267, Table 9.8). Relatedly, Holmes and Holmes (2010) observe that, 'women who kill sequentially kill in a process-focused manner' (ibid., p. 176).

Conclusion

Serial killers generally and serial poisoners were compared in relation to gender; age; ethnicity; social background and occupation; personal history of violent, criminal or abnormal behaviour; location; methods of killing; and motives. Serial team killers in general were compared with team serial poisoners.

Suggested Activities

Consider the main similarities and differences between serial killers and serial poisoners regarding: gender, age, ethnicity, social background and occupation, and personal history. Discuss which similarities and which difference you find most informative.

Reflect on how a perpetrator's choice of murder location is influenced by serial killing and serial poisoning.

Key Texts

Farrell, M. (2017). *Criminology of Homicidal Poisoning: Offenders, Victims and Detection*. London and New York: Springer.

This book covers topics regarding homicidal poisoning in general: theory, the nature and types of poisons, poisoners, and their characteristics, victims, detection and its avoidance, and poisoners at trial.

Hickey, E. (2010). *Serial Murderers and Their Victims* (5th ed.). Belmont, CA: Wadsworth Cengage Learning.

A comprehensive coverage of the demographics of serial killers.

References

American Psychiatric Association. (2013). *Diagnostic and Statistical Manual of Mental Disorders Fifth Edition (DSM5)*. Washington, DC: APA.

Bovsun, M. (2008, March 25). The Case of the Vanishing Vagrants. *The New York Daily News*.

Douglas, J., & Olshaker, M. (1996). *The Mind Hunter*. New York, NY: Scribner.

Farrell, M. (1992). *Poisons and Poisoners: An Encyclopaedia of Homicidal Poisonings*. London: Robert Hale.

Farrell, M. (2017). *Criminology of Homicidal Poisoning: Offenders, Victims and Detection*. London and New York: Springer.

Gibons, D. (2015, October 21). Coventry Costco Murder: Brothers Jailed for Thirty Years After Killing Sameena Imam. *Coventry Telegraph*. (www.coventrytelegraph.net/news/coventry-news/coventry-costco-murder-brothers-jailed-10307312.

Gita, S. (1998). *Cries Unheard: The Story of Mary Bell*. London: Macmillan.

Hickey, E. (2010). *Serial Murderers and Their Victims* (5th ed.). Belmont, CA: Wadsworth Cengage Learning.

Holmes, R. M., & Holmes, S. T. (2010). *Serial Murder* (3rd ed.). Los Angeles and London: Sage.

Kelleher, M. D., & Kelleher, C. L. (1998). *Murder Most Rare: The Female Serial Killer*. New York, NY: Dell.

Read, S. (2005). *On the House: The Bizarre Killing of Michael Malloy*. New York: Berkley Publishing.

Tallant, R. (1953). *Murder in New Orleans*. London: William Kimber.

Trestrail, J. H. (2007). *Criminal Poisoning: Investigational Guide for Law Enforcement, Toxicologists, Forensic Scientists and Attorneys* (2nd ed.). Totowa, NJ: Humana Press.

5

Healthcare Serial Poisoning

Introduction

Healthcare professionals who have serially killed patients include physicians, nurses of various specialisms, nurses' aides, and nursing home managers and staff. Examples come from jurisdictions including US, Canada, UK, Germany, France, Norway, and Switzerland.

Defining Healthcare Serial Poisoning

A healthcare serial killer has been defined as, 'any type of employee in the healthcare system who use their position to murder at least two patients in two separate incidents, with the psychological capacity for more killing' (Ramsland 2007, pp. xi–xii). Helpfully, the first part of this definition locates the perpetrator in the setting and, like broader definitions of serial killing, refers to at least two killings. However, the reference to a 'psychological capacity for more killing' is problematic. It goes beyond the usually accepted understanding of serial killing, citing a

© The Author(s) 2018
M. Farrell, *Criminology of Serial Poisoners*,
https://doi.org/10.1007/978-3-030-01138-3_5

supposed capacity which in practice would be difficult perhaps impossible to determine.

In further understanding the term, 'health care serial poisoning', one needs to refer to the nature of healthcare settings, and the roles of people working in them. Healthcare employers and settings include hospitals ranging in size from large multi-department venues, to small local 'cottage' hospitals. Other settings and organisations are variously known as medical centres, clinics, community surgeries, nursing homes, long-term care facilities, assisted living provision, and home healthcare agencies.

Personnel working in health care are also diverse. In discussing 'health care killers', Hickey (2010) mentions, '…doctors, nurses, orderlies, nursing assistants, and certified home health workers' (ibid., p. 168). Certainly, doctors and nurses are most often thought of as providing care, but other occupations are also represented. Nursing assistants help patients or clients having healthcare needs under the supervision of a nurse. An orderly provides basic assistance to patients such as help with eating and dressing; transports patients by wheelchair or gurney to different locations such as the operating theatre or dining room; and ensures that the venue is clean. Home healthcare workers may help with eating, bathing, lifting and moving, and self-care, and following training they may supervise clients in taking medication. Employed by an agency, they may work in a client's home.

As well as involving such settings and occupations, serial healthcare killing normally relates to healthcare duties. In the context of the present chapter, it refers to cases where a perpetrator has been convicted of at least two poisonings of patients or clients. The killings also meet the definition of serial homicide concerning a time gap between instances (Holmes and Holmes 2010, pp. 5–6; Hickey 2010, p. 27; Behavioural Analysis Unit 2005, pp. 8–9).

Excluded Cases

Specifying that the circumstances of the healthcare serial poisoning normally relates to healthcare duties, excludes certain cases. I do not look at instances where healthcare professionals have been convicted of serial killing but have used methods other than poisoning, for example suffocation. Also excluded are cases where healthcare workers have poisoned outside the context of their duties. **Dr. Neil Cream** [S9] murdered four women prostitutes by giving them strychnine capsules supposed to improve their complexion. But this was peripheral to his role as a physician and the women were not under his care. Similarly, **Dr. Edward Pritchard** [S2] used aconite (and antimony) to poison Mary Jane Taylor his wife, and Jane Cowan his mother-in-law but not primarily in exercising his healthcare role.

Generally, I leave out wartime state endorsed killings including those carried out by medics under the Nazis during the Second World War. I do however include **Dr. Marcel Petiot** [S20] who in occupied France, over several years, poisoned 24 people. Using his position as a physician, he duped victims wishing to escape the occupation. They would visit his surgery at night thinking that they were getting vaccinations for the country of their supposed escape. In fact, he murdered these victims using cyanide, took the fee that they had paid for his services, and robbed them of the possessions that they had brought with them.

Scale of Healthcare Serial Poisoning

Single Poison Killings by Healthcare Workers

It has long been observed that among single instances of poisoning, a disproportionate number of perpetrators have been healthcare professionals (Farrell 1992, pp. 151–154; Kinnell 2000). Sometimes, where healthcare professionals have committed single acts of murder it has been outside their medical or caring role. Dr. Edme Castaing a French physician, poisoned a fellow conspirator in forging a Will (Parry 1927). English physician Dr. William Palmer killed a racing companion with strychnine pills (Watson [1856] 1952). To be free to pursue another woman with whom he was infatuated, Canadian homeopathic physician Dr. William King killed his wife with arsenic (Dougall 2016). In such instances, the motive tends to be financial gain from a Will or life insurance, or the desire to be rid of a partner to be with a lover.

Fewer instances seem to occur where a carer is convicted of killing once within the healthcare relationship. An example is carer He Tiandi in China who was sentenced to death in 2016 for killing a 70-year-old client using sleeping pills and dichlorvos insecticide administered in soup. Even in this case, the perpetrator admitted to having killed others previously although the sentence applied to the single murder (Li, 5 May 2016).

Healthcare Serial Killings: Physicians, Nursing Home Managers, and Nurses

Turning to healthcare serial killing, it is maintained that medicine has 'thrown up more serial killers than all the other professions put together, with nursing a close second' (Kinnell 2000). It is difficult to give accurate estimates of the scale of healthcare poisoning, but instances can be identified across time and in several countries, that indicate the range of cases.

Healthcare Serial Poisoning in North America and Europe

Healthcare Serial Poisoners in the US and Canada

US healthcare serial killers include **Dr. Michael Swango** [S42, P2] who killed four patients with arsenic and may have murdered many more.

Nurse **Jane Toppan** [S10] poisoned patients as well as killing some of her relatives. **Robert Diaz** [S29], a coronary care nurse, injected lethal doses of lidocaine into patients at two Riverside hospitals. In Texas, **Genene Jones** [S32], a paediatric nurse, used injections of succinylcholine and other drugs to kill children in her care. Nurse **Bobby Sue Dudley-Terrell** [S36] administered insulin overdoses to patients at a healthcare centre in Florida. So that he could intervene and demonstrate 'competence', **Richard Angelo** [S37], a New York nurse, injected Pavulon and Anectine into patients' IV tubes to create respiratory problems. Nurse **Brian Rosenfeld** [S38] pleaded guilty to murdering three patients, with overdoses of the drug Demerol.

Nurse **Kristen Gilbert** [S45, P5] was found guilty of first-degree murder of three patients and second-degree murder of one other patient, through administering epinephrine injections. **Charles Cullen** [S52, P11] a nurse confessed to murdering thirty patients in hospitals in Pennsylvania and New Jersey over a sixteen-year period using injections of the heart drug digoxin. Nurse **Vickie Dawn Jackson** [S53, P12] was found guilty of killing 10 patients with mivacurium chloride (Mivacron). It was suggested that she became vengeful towards patients when other nurses were compassionate to them.

Kimberley Clark Saenz [S59, P18] was tried for murders of 5 patients and sentenced to life imprisonment without the possibility of parole. She injected sodium hypochlorite (bleach) into the dialysis lines of patients. Respiratory therapist **Efren Saldivar** [S46, P6] killed patients using injections of drugs causing respiratory arrest or cardiac failure. The drugs included pancuronium (Pavulon) and possibly morphine and suxamethonium chloride. **Dorothea Puente** [S39], a nurse's aide and later care home manager, killed her patients with drug overdoses including Tylenol. Originally of Vienna, Austria-Hungary, porter **Frederick Mors** [S13] used arsenic and chloroform to kill elderly patients in a nursing home in New York and was found criminally insane. Hospital worker **Donald Harvey** [S34] killed patients at hospitals in Kentucky and Ohio, using cyanide and other poisons and methods.

Found guilty of the murder of patients in Ontario, Canada, with insulin injections, nurse **Elizabeth Wettlaufer** [S62, P21] was sentenced to imprisonment without parole for 25 years.

Healthcare Serial Poisoners in Europe: UK, Germany, France, Norway, Switzerland

UK serial poisoners include physician **Dr. Harold Shipman** [S41, P1] and nursing home manager **Dorothea Waddingham** [S18]. Among other cases is that of nurse **Benjamin Geen** [S50, P9] convicted of murdering two patients and other crimes at a UK hospital using drugs causing respiratory arrest or hypoglycaemic arrest. **Colin Norris** [S57, P16] (now Colin Campbell) was sentenced for murdering several patients with insulin injections at hospital patients in England. Nurse **Victorino Chua** [S60, P19] killed patients in the UK by introducing insulin into saline bags so that it was unwittingly administered by other nurses.

German nurse **Niels Högel** [S61, P20] was convicted of murdering two intensive care patients and attempting to murder three others, and was suspected of killing many more. He used unauthorised drug injection overdoses including ajmaline (Gilurytmal), sotalol (Sotalex), lidocaine/xylocaine, amiodarone (Cordarex), and potassium chloride. In Westphalia, Germany, nurse **Stephan Letter** [S55, P14] was found guilty of 16 counts of murdering patients and other crimes, using drugs including the muscle relaxant lysthenon.

In France, nurse **Christine Malèvre** [S48] administered lethal doses of morphine, potassium and other drugs killing six seriously ill patients in her care at a Paris hospital. **Dr. Marcel Petiot** [S20] killed victims trying to flee occupied France, giving them cyanide injections purporting to be vaccinations for victims' country of destination.

In Norway, **Arnfinn Nesset** [S30] serially killed 21 of his nursing home residents with succinylcholine chloride.

Swiss nurse **Marie Jeanneret** [S4] was convicted of killing seven patients with belladonna (and other poisons) administered as medicines.

Some Themes

Examples from North America and from European countries illustrate the international nature of the phenomena of healthcare serial poisoning. They also show that such poisonings have existed from earlier periods and are not solely contemporary. For example, nurse **Marie Jeanneret** [S4] of Switzerland was sentenced in 1868. US nurse **Jane Toppan** [S10] was arrested in 1901. **Frederick Mors** [S13] was committed to Hudson River State Hospital, New York in 1915. Moving forward in time, Canadian nurse, **Elizabeth Wettlaufer** [S62, P21] was sentenced in 2017. Nurse **Niels Högel** [S61, P20] of Germany was convicted of murder in 2015, as was nurse **Victorino Chua** [S60, P19].

A further feature is the specialisms of some of the poisoners. Nursing duties included looking after patients with heart problems, respiratory difficulties, and diabetes. In each of these areas, there are drug regimens helping to keep the patient's health stable. Interfering with the drug doses that are used is a modus operandi for killing these victims. Doing so tends to create signs and symptoms which can be mistaken for the patient's illness. For example, if the patient has cardiac problems, and a nurse secretly administers a drug overdose that effects the heart, the symptoms may be thought to relate to the patient's original illness.

Demographics and Healthcare Poisoning

A study by Yorker et al. (2006) covers demographics of serial healthcare killing in general which has relevance to serial healthcare poisoning. This research was reported in an article on serial murder perpetrated by healthcare professionals. Carrying out a LexisNexis® search (which involves a legal library database drawing on media and case law) the researchers identified 90 criminal cases meeting inclusion criteria for the serial murders of patients. Additionally, the study used data from epidemiologic studies, toxicology evidence, and court transcripts on healthcare professionals prosecuted between 1970 and 2006.

Prosecutions were reported from 20 countries with the most represented country being the US which accounted for 40% of cases. The next highest number of prosecutions were from Germany and the UK. Nursing personnel comprised 86% of the healthcare providers prosecuted; physicians 12%, and allied health professionals 2%. Victims were mainly the elderly, the very young, or the otherwise vulnerably ill. Some 317 patient deaths resulted in a murder conviction. In all, the number of suspicious patient deaths attributed to the 54 convicted caregivers was 2113. Injection was the main method used followed by suffocation, poisoning, and tampering with equipment.

Of the 90 criminal cases identified by Yorker and her colleagues meeting inclusion criteria for serial murders of patients, 45 were listed as involving convictions for serial murder. (In a few instances, e.g. that of Randy Powers, the conviction was for one murder although the individual may have been suspected of others.)

Where the method of killing was specified, at least 51 of the healthcare providers used injection, and 12 employed suffocation. Other less used methods were drowning, air embolus, oral medications, tampering with equipment, and poisoning. Poisoning was specified as a separate category accounting for a small percentage (1%). However, if one uses the usual legal definition of poisoning, it appears that it was by far the commonest method with administering an injection accounting for 52%, and oral medication for 3% of deaths. As Yorker confirms (Personal communication, September 2017) these percentages refer to the 90 cases originally identified, and it is unclear what the percentages would be for the up to 45 serial poison convictions. Never the less, the Yorker study raises important issues relevant to the discussion of healthcare serial poisoning.

Motive

A serial perpetrator may have several motives which may interact and change over time. The motives that we considered when looking at serial poisoners overall were: financial gain, jealousy/revenge, power/control, sadism, seeking excitement, factitious disorder imposed on another, mercy killing. We also touched on instances when there seemed to be no motive or there was a judgement of insanity. Below we revisit these motives and consider the extent that they typify healthcare serial poisoners.

Financial Gain

Compared with other serial poisoners, healthcare serial poisoners rarely kill for financial gain. French physician **Dr. Marcel Petiot** [S20], murdering victims seeking to escape occupied France in the Second World War, used cyanide injections purporting to be vaccinations for victims' country of destination. Part of his motive was financial gain from payments for arranging the 'escapes', and robbing victims of their valuables. In the UK, nursing home manager **Dorothea Waddingham** [S18] killed residents with overdoses of morphine tablets to gain from inheritance that had been made over in exchange for the patients' care.

Jealousy/Revenge

Regarding healthcare serial poisoners, motives of jealousy and revenge appear uncommon. This is likely because the circumscribed carer–patient relationship limits the opportunity to develop such deep emotions. A rare exception may be licenced vocational nurse **Vickie Dawn Jackson** [S53, P12] who was found guilty of killing ten patients with mivacurium chloride (Mivacron). It has been suggested that she became vengeful towards patients when other nurses showed them compassion.

Power and Control

In Holmes and Holmes (2010) typology, a 'power/control' serial killer, tends to select and stalk specific victims who are otherwise strangers. Method of killing is focused on the process rather than the outcome and is planned and organised, typically using dispersed locations (Holmes and Holmes 2010, p. 159, Table 10.2). US serial killer Ted Bundy's crimes included control through rape, and necrophilia.

For some serial healthcare poisoners, there may be 'issues of power and control as well as a fundamental objectification of people' (Hough and McCorkle 2017, p. 158). However, the power and control in these instances relate to being able to select the moment of death, not as is the case with serial killers in general, control of the person themselves (e.g. eliciting from victims their pleading to live).

Power and control over life and death may have been a driving force for UK serial poisoner **Dr. Harold Shipman** [S41, P1] who, although being uncooperative in police interviews, did not reveal a clear motive. **Robert Rubane Diaz** [S29], a US coronary care nurse, killed elderly patients with injections of lidocaine a drug used to control irregular heartbeat. A motivation for some of these deaths may have related to Diaz' feelings of power and control as he is reported to have predicted the death of some victims. **Arnfinn Nesset** [S30] in Norway, who killed residents of his nursing home with succinylcholine chloride administered as supposed medication, may have been driven by similar feelings.

Sadism

Some caregivers may be motivated by sadistic satisfaction from killing patients or certain perceived types of patients for example ones seemingly difficult or complaining. (There is perhaps also an element of seeking excitement.)

Nurse **Victorino Chua** [S60, P19] may have had sadistic motives in introducing insulin into saline bags to be unwittingly administered by other nurses. Nurse **Colin Norris** [S57, P16], sentenced for the murder of several patients with insulin injections, was said by the legal prosecution to harbour a hatred of caring for elderly people. US licenced vocational nurse **Vickie Dawn Jackson** [WS53, P12] killed patients using mivacurium chloride (Mivacron) and may have become vengeful to patients when other nurses showed them compassion. US nurse **Brian Rosenfeld** [S38] pleaded guilty to murdering three patients, using overdoses of drug pethidine (as Demerol). At his trial, prosecutors stated that he had a voracious appetite for inflicting abuse. US nurse **Jane Toppan** [S10] killed patients (and relatives) which was reported to give her satisfaction. **Marie Jeanneret** [S4], a Swiss nurse, killed patients with belladonna and other poisons administered as medicines from likely sadistic motives. Nurse **Orville Lynn Majors** [S40], who used potassium chloride and epinephrine to kill elderly patients, was said to hate old people.

Seeking Excitement (and Self-Aggrandisement)

In Holmes and Holmes (2010) typology, 'thrill hedonistic' serial killers have strong fantasies and find the act of killing thrilling so that it tends to involve long drawn out death and torture, but not necrophilia.

Victims are stalked and of a specific type but are strangers. Method of killing is process focused and organised, and the murder location tends to be dispersed (ibid., p. 129, Table 8.1). There are similarities and differences to this typology and healthcare serial poisoning. Patients as victims may be observed and chosen for example if they are perceived as complaining or otherwise difficult. They are not stalked in the usual sense, but they are made available by the carer–patient relationship. Circumstances usually dictate that death is not drawn out but is relatively quick, so that torture does not figure in the normal sense.

Hospital or health service authorities may notice a significant increase in the number of cardiopulmonary arrests on a unit, and the number of successful resuscitations may be higher than expected. This could indicate caregiver-induced cardiac arrests. Here a killer may be seeking secondary gain from these incidents, intending to create and deal with a 'code', rather than to kill. (A 'code blue' refers to cardiac arrest.) In such instances, the motive appears to be seeking excitement.

Seeking thrills and the elation of resuscitation may have been part of the motive of nurse **Niels Högel** [S61, P20] of Germany who killed intensive care patients with unauthorised drug injection overdoses. **Benjamin Geen** [S50, P9] convicted of murdering two patients in the UK (using drugs causing respiratory arrest or hypoglycaemic arrest) was conjectured to be seeking the thrill of resuscitating patients. **Kristen Gilbert** [S45, P5] of Massachusetts, US was indicted with killing patients with injections of epinephrine, a heart stimulant. Her motive was thought to be self-aggrandisement in inducing cardiac arrest then displaying supposed nursing skills in trying to save patients. US nurse **Richard Angelo** [S37] was convicted of murdering several patients by injecting pancuronium and succinylcholine chloride into IV tubes. His motive was seemingly to create respiratory problems in his victims, before stepping in to demonstrate apparent competence.

Factitious Disorder Imposed on Another

Sometimes the perpetrator's motive appears to relate to 'factitious disorder imposed on another' (American Psychiatric Association 2013, pp. 324–327) previously known as 'factitious disorder by proxy'. 'Factitious' here means that the disorder is created and artificial rather than being real or 'natural'. In the UK, an alternative term 'fabricated or induced illness' may be used and sometimes the older term, 'Munchausen's syndrome by proxy'.

In factitious disorder imposed on another, the victim is often a child and the perpetrator often a parent (typically the child's biological mother) or a carer. In causing or inventing symptoms of illness in the victim, the perpetrator aims to attract admiration or sympathy for themselves. To sustain the supposed illness, the perpetrator may harm the victim. In a sense, factitious disorder imposed on another has a built-in reward. This comprises the esteem and the attention accruing to the perpetrator, rather like the self-aggrandisement sometimes linked to the motive of seeking excitement.

Genene Jones [S32] a paediatric nurse endangered the lives of the children in her care then sought adulation by 'saving' them, eventually killing children with injections of succinylcholine and other drugs.

Mercy Killings

Sometimes, perpetrators claim that their motive in killing is merciful, because the patients are suffering or dying. This can be contradicted in various ways. Nurse **Stephan Letter** [S55, P14] of Germany killed patients with drugs including the muscle relaxant succinylcholine chloride (as lysthenon) and claimed that he acted to end suffering. However, some of the patients involved were in a stable condition when killed. Nurse **Charles Cullen** [S52, P11] of New Jersey, US confessed murdering thirty patients in hospitals in Pennsylvania and New Jersey using injections of digitoxin a heart drug. He claimed to be easing suffering but contrary to this, some patients were not terminally ill. French nurse **Christine Malèvre** [S48] was found guilty of killing those in her care by administering lethal doses of morphine, potassium and other drugs. Her claim that the deaths were mercy killings was rejected by the patients' families. Hospital worker **Donald Harvey** [S34] killed patients with cyanide and other poisons and methods claiming to be easing their suffering.

Indirect or Unestablished Motive, and Insanity

It is not always possible to establish a motive for healthcare serial poisoning. This is exemplified in the case of **Dr. Harold Shipman** [S41, P1] the UK physician and serial poisoner of patients. A possible motive for Shipman's murders as suggested earlier might be his exercising power over life and death. But a judge-led public enquiry conducted over several years to investigate the killings which produced several volumes of detailed findings was reticent. Psychiatrists asked to try to identify possible motives found it very difficult (Shipman Inquiry, December 2005). (Adding to their difficulties, the psychiatrists were trying to work out possible motive from reports and other sources rather than from direct interviews and assessments involving Shipman.)

The motives of US physician **Dr. Michael Swango** [S42, P2] who killed patients with arsenic are hard to ascertain. So are those of **Efren Saldivar** [S46, P6], a Los Angeles respiratory therapist, charged with six counts of murder. **Kimberley Clark Saenz** [S59, P18] killed patients with sodium hypochlorite (bleach) injected into dialysis lines from unclear motives. Similarly obscure, are the motives of Canadian nurse, **Elizabeth Wettlaufer** [S62, P21] who murdered those in her care by using insulin injections.

A legal judgement of insanity is an indication that the individual was unaware of the consequences of his or her actions at the time of the offence. An example is **Frederick Mors** [S13] who, working as a hospital porter in New York, US, killed patients with arsenic and later chloroform and was judged criminally insane.

Opportunity: Perpetrator–Patient Role, Location, and Routines

Healthcare roles as well as being vehicles for care and compassion offer opportunities to perpetrate murder. By the nature of their work, healthcare workers have access to clients including for their physical care. Again, by the nature of the relationships these patients are often vulnerable. Where care involves individuals who are very ill, death is sometimes expected, which can disguise killing. If death is expected and there are no apparent unusual circumstances, autopsies may not be performed, it being assumed that they would reveal nothing new.

Medical professionals have opportunity to acquire drugs. Physicians prescribe as well as administer medications. Nurses and other healthcare staff administer drugs under certain circumstances, although where they have been found in possession of medication outside circumscribed situations, this has raised concerns. Never the less, where drugs are routinely used, it is possible to find ways of administering them nefariously and disposing of any evidence without arousing suspicion.

As well as having access to both medication and patients, physicians and others have knowledge of how drugs work and the symptoms that overdoses are likely to cause. Such knowledge can be used to administer drugs whose effects will appear like symptoms of the underlying illness or simply look like natural death. Other professionals may then misconstrue the real cause of death. Where the physician who has killed is also instrumental in assessing the cause of death this can allow abuse to go undetected for long periods.

Healthcare professionals generally enjoy the trust and respect of the local community. It does not routinely cross the minds of patients or relatives and friends of the patient that this respected role might be being abused. In hospitals, medical centres and similar settings, administrators, and other staff may be slow to recognise or respond to suspicious behaviour by a staff member. Managers may worry about the implications for the medical setting of any scandal and so they may deliberately, or subconsciously, minimise what is reported or suspected.

Holmes and Holmes (2010, pp. 205–206) point out that healthcare professionals who kill are often able to do so in their 'comfort zones'. These are physical areas with which they are very familiar, such as a hospital ward, surgery, or nursing home. Not only are they comfortable with the physical surroundings, but these staff are conversant with the routines and expectations associated with the setting. Such familiarity enables healthcare serial killers to sometimes choose or arrange night shift working where supervision may be less apparent than during busy day shifts. Knowing the supervisory routines that are in place at any given time can also assist a staff member intending to harm patients.

Yorker et al. (2006) point out several factors that may be relevant where hospitals are implicated in healthcare murder prosecutions. Injectable medications may be easily accessible, and several patients may have intravenous lines. Oversight during evening and night shifts might be slight, and 'float' nursing personnel might often be used. General quality assurance activities may be weak. In the Yorker et al. (2006) study, while very few killers had a known criminal record, many had histories of falsifying aspects of their background. These were often not picked up during recruitment, and where they were, it did not seem to hinder hiring.

It is important that a poisoner (including a serial poisoner) knows the routines of victims. Where the perpetrator–victim relationship is that of a spouse or partner, the mealtime routines and food and drink preferences will be familiar, information which is useful if the poison is administered orally. In the case of healthcare serial poisoners, where the patient is in hospital, routines are often proscribed by that setting. Administration of specified drugs at agreed times is largely determined by the hospital. A perpetrator will also know the times and places when supervision may be lighter than is typical. Such knowledge of routines and control of routines is used by a serial healthcare killer in a similar way to other serial poisoners, to provide opportunity to administer the poison and to decrease the chances of being caught.

Identifying Concerns in the Behaviour and Personality of Healthcare Workers

Ramsland's 'Red Flags' and Later Refinements

Can staff in healthcare venues (and those advising their managers) identify possible causes for concern where patients might be being harmed by staff? Attempts have been made to shed light on this question by looking at the apparent personality and behaviour of healthcare killers.

Ramsland (2007) examined characteristics of healthcare serial killers, their motives and methods. In doing so she suggested preventative reforms to the health care and criminal justice systems. Drawing together some of the issues, Ramsland proposed a 'red flag' checklist, providing items which were found in cases of healthcare serial killing. Twenty-two items were listed. Some of these describe specific behaviour, such as, 'Moves from one hospital to another' (Item 1) and 'Predicts when someone will die' (Item 4). Other items concern broader personality issues such as, 'Appears to have a personality disorder' (Item 21) and 'History of mental instability/depression' (Item 3).

Yardley and Wilson (2016) suggest refinements to Ramsland's (2007) 'red flag' checklist. They identify 16 cases where nurses have been convicted of the serial killing of patients. For each item, the percentage of cases where the item was noted is given. The highest scoring three items were number 7, 'Higher incidences of death on his/her shift' evident in 94% of cases; item 3 'History of mental stability/depression' (63% of cases) and item 13, 'Make colleagues anxious/suspicious' (56% of cases).

Strengths and Limitations of Behavioural and Personality Checklists

Among potential strengths of checklists such as the ones discussed is that they can raise awareness of some of the behaviours and traits among healthcare workers that might compromise patient safety. Being expressed briefly, the items can crystallise concerns about a worker that otherwise might be felt only nebulously by staff colleagues and others. This might lead to investigation raising further questions that need to be addressed.

Reservations arise however. The brevity of items which makes checklists appealing and manageable can conceal potential misunderstanding and confusions. 'Lied about personal information' (Item 18) could mean that an individual lied on an application form or at interview about a previous hospital job from which they were dismissed. Or it could mean that the person evaded enquiries by colleagues about a painful divorce. 'Predicts when someone will die' (Item 4) could refer to a single occasion when a worker mentioned to a colleague that a patient was near death so that relatives could be informed. Alternatively, it could convey that a nurse or physician had persistently predicted the death of patients where it was unexpected. Once one begins to make such matters clearer, the checklist becomes a lengthy and unwieldy. At the same time, it likely becomes a more accurate depiction of issues that might or might not raise concerns.

There is no systematic and widely accepted guidance about how behavioural and personality observations (as reflected in checklist items) might interact and how different combinations or clusters of items might be more pertinent than others. For example, 'Has a substance abuse problem' (Item 22) and 'In possession of drugs etc. at home/in locker' (Item 17) might or might not relate to each other depending on what exactly they convey. Do the items occurring together refer to a worker who is addicted to harmful drugs which have been found to be missing from hospital supplies and have been subsequently found in the person's locker? Or does the concurrence refer to a nurse who has accidentally left a medicine in their uniform pockets, and has a supply of legitimate medicines at home which they happen to use?

Is there a potentially more useful response to such attempts to identify behavioural or personality traits in workers that might raise alarms? One possible reaction to the issues that the brief items reflect is to treat them more broadly and more subtly. 'Prefers night shifts – fewer colleagues about' (Item 10) could be further analysed to raise questions about night shift work. Do certain staff expressed preferences for certain shifts including night shift? If so what are the reasons? How does staff supervision operate and how effective is it in different shifts? Such questions could lead to a general review of night shift supervision and of the quality of care and the capability of staff on night shift.

Furthermore, item 7, 'Higher incidences of death on his/her shifts' is fraught with difficulties. A cluster of cardiopulmonary arrests and/or deaths may occur in a patient group. Patients may suffer multiple cardiopulmonary arrests. Resuscitation rates may be unusually high. Deaths may cluster on the evening or night shift. Epidemiologic studies may appear to link the presence of a specific staff member to an increased likelihood of death. With such observations, the context is important as well as the statistical assumptions being made. Which shifts are being compared? In what circumstances? Over what periods of time? What exactly does 'higher incidences' mean and who is defining it? What are the statistical probabilities of apparent differences in deaths arising by chance? (Ascertaining this can require specialist statistical interpretation and evaluation.) What other explanations are there for the deaths other than that a staff member is responsible? Questions about incidence of deaths have arisen in several cases of healthcare poisoning or suspected killing and need to be examined rigorously and with care.

Improving Background Checks, Monitoring, and Communicating Concerns

As well as looking at possible personality and behavioural indications of risk to patients from healthcare workers, other steps have been suggested. Some convicted healthcare providers in a study by Yorker et al. (2006) had falsified their credentials and/or had fabricated critical events (such as sexual assault) before being suspected of murdering patients. The study authors suggest that healthcare employers should consider fraud or misrepresentation a serious risk factor for the safety of patients. They propose a better balance between the employment rights of caregivers, and the need for healthcare facilities to know employee's backgrounds.

Holmes and Holmes (2010) refer to good practice in the Coroner's office in Louisville, Kentucky, where the doctor's name is tabulated against every death. If a physician's name appears more often than might be expected, the situation may be investigated. Naturally specific circumstances are noted, as when a doctor has a practice or speciality such as oncology where the likelihood of deaths is increased (ibid., p. 204).

The Yorker and colleagues (2006) study argues that healthcare employers need to say if a worker was fired, or if their presence was associated with adverse patient outcomes. Hospital administrators and physicians may fear negative publicity, civil suits for negligence, and civil suits by nurses who are being investigated. But if they do not fully cooperate with police enquiries and other investigations they risk harm to patients (ibid., paraphrased).

Illustrations of the importance of information about past employment include the case of nurse **Bobby Sue Dudley-Terrell** [S36] who killed four elderly patients with insulin overdoses in a centre in Florida. Her employment had previously been terminated elsewhere after the suspicious deaths of those in her care. She had had treatment for various mental disorders thought to include schizophrenia, depression, and (as it was then called) Munchausen's syndrome, including self-harm. Serial poisoner **Dr. Michael Swango** [S42, P2] of the US had a long history of crimes and deviance, some of which likely preceded his first murder. As a medical student, he faked check-ups during his obstetrics and gynaecology clinical clerkship ('rotation') and was held back for a year. Working as an ambulance corps emergency medical technician, he was convicted of aggravated battery for poisoning co-workers and sentenced to imprisonment. Swango subsequently forged documents allowing him to work, despite his criminal record.

Notes of Caution

Clearly, the work of researchers, administrators, healthcare staff, and others in recognising the risks to patients of aberrant staff is likely to help patient safety. At the same time, some notes of caution have been sounded. These imply developing the best strategies for preventing harm to patients by healthcare workers, while at the same time avoiding unjustly suspecting staff members.

Indeed, cases have arisen in which staff have been unjustly accused and convicted. Lucia de Berk a nurse from the Netherlands was convicted of serial murder but later exonerated. In Italy, a 42-year-old nurse Daniela Poggiali was accused of killing 'up to 38 patients because she found them annoying' (Day, 14 October 2014). In fact, Daniella Poggiali was acquitted.

In other instances, support groups are convinced that an individual has been incorrectly convicted. An example is nurse **Colin Norris** [S57, P16] sentenced in 2008 for the murder of several patients in hospital in Leeds, England. Another instance of suspected miscarriage of justice is the case of **Ben Geen** [S50, P9] convicted of murdering two patients at Horton General Hospital, Oxfordshire, UK and in 2004, given 17 life sentences.

Conclusion

Defining healthcare serial poisoning relates to the nature of healthcare settings and the roles of their workers. While the suspected scale of healthcare serial poisoning causes concern, it remains difficult to establish. Yorker et al. (2006) outline demographics of serial healthcare killing generally, which includes poisoning. Financial gain and jealousy/revenge tend to be rare motives for healthcare serial poisoning. Other motives are: power and control, sadism, seeking excitement, and factitious disorder imposed on another. Opportunity to kill patients implicates healthcare venues and related professional roles. Attempts have been made to identify concerns in the behaviour and personality of healthcare workers. Proposals have been made for improving staff background checks, monitoring, and communicating concerns. In some instances, healthcare workers have been unjustly accused. Other possible miscarriages of justice have been publicised.

Suggested Activities

Review the potential causes of concern that may relate to a risk of healthcare serial killing.

Examine the extent might these could be useful preventative guides and look also at the degree to which they could lead to injustices towards professionals.

Consider what changes might be made that prioritise patient safety while taking account of the just and fair treatment of healthcare staff.

Key Texts

Ramsland, C. (2007). *Inside the Minds of Healthcare Serial Killers: Why They Kill.* Westport, CT: Praeger.

The book makes useful distinctions between healthcare killers and serial healthcare killers, and those who kill inside and outside the profession. Suggestions for reform are also made.

References

American Psychiatric Association. (2013). *Diagnostic and Statistical Manual of Mental Disorders Fifth Edition (DSM5).* Washington, DC: APA.

Behavioural Analysis Unit. (2005). *Serial Murders: Multi-disciplinary Perspectives for Investigators.* Washington, DC: National Center for the Analysis of Violent Crime, US Department of Justice.

Day, M. (2014, October 14). Italian Nurse Daniela Poggiali Is Accused of Killing 'Up to 38 Patients Because She Found Them Annoying'. *The Independent.* http://www.independent.co.uk/news/world/europe/italian-nurse-under-investigation-for-killing-up-to-38-patients-because-she-found-them-annoying-9793181.html.

Dougall, C. (2016). *King, William Henry. Dictionary of Canadian Biography Vol. 8 (1851–1860).* Toronto: University of Toronto.

Farrell, M. (1992). *Poisons and Poisoners: An Encyclopaedia of Homicidal Poisonings.* London: Robert Hale.

Hickey, E. (2010). *Serial Murderers and Their Victims* (5th ed.). Belmont, CA: Wadsworth.

Holmes, R. M., & Holmes, S. T. (2010). *Serial Murder* (3rd ed.). London: Sage.

Hough, R. M., & McCorkle, K. D. (2017). *American Homicide.* Thousand Oaks, CA and London: Sage.

Kinnell, H. G. (2000). Serial Homicide by Doctors: Shipman in Perspective. *British Medical Journal, 321,* 1594–1597.

Li, L. (2016, May 5). Death Sentence for Carer. *Shanghai Daily.* www.shanghaidaily.com/nation/Death-sentence-for-carer-who.../shdaily.shtml.

Parry, L. (1927). *Some Famous Medical Trials.* London: Churchill.

Ramsland, K. (2007). *Inside the Minds of Healthcare Serial Killers: Why They Kill.* Westport, CT: Praeger.

Shipman Inquiry. (2005, December). Fifth Report. *Safeguarding Patients: Lessons from the Part—Proposals for the Future.* http://webarchive.national-archives.gov.uk/20090808154959/http://www.the-shipman-inquiry.org.uk/fr_page.asp.

Watson, E. R. (Ed.). ([1856] 1952). *Trial of William Palmer* (Notable British Trials Series) (3rd ed.). London: William Hodge.

Yardley, E., & Wilson, D. (2016). In Search of the 'Angels of Death': Conceptualising the Contemporary Nurse Healthcare Serial Killer. *Journal of Investigative Psychology and Offender Profiling, 13*(1), 39–55.

Yorker, B. C., Kizer, K. W., Lampe, P., Forest, A. R. W., Lannan, J. M., & Russell, D. A. (2006, November). Serial Murder by Healthcare Professionals. *Journal of Forensic Science, 51*(6), 1–10.

6

Victims of Serial Poisoners

Introduction

Studying the victims of crimes, or 'victimology' (Doerner and Lab 2012, passim), can apply to different types of crime including serial poison homicide. Victimology can be informative and useful for several reasons. Examining the perpetrator's apparent choice of victim can illuminate the offender's characteristics and motives. Information about the nature of early serial homicide victims of a sequence can suggest to investigators the type of likely future victims. Interactions between perpetrator and victim, the 'social dynamics' of the crime, can also be informative.

Data Sources for Serial Homicide Victims

Federal Bureau of Investigation US Data

The FBI's Uniform Crime Reporting Program publishes annual statistics of criminal offences known to law enforcement and on arrest, including homicide. For example, Table 10 concerns 'Murder circumstances by relationship' and deals with the relationships between offender and victim

(FBI 2014a). While this does not show serial homicide, there is a category of 'unknown' relationship which has attracted interest. In the year 2014, the total number of murder victims was 11,961 while the number where the relationship between perpetrator and victim was 'unknown' was 4506 (ibid.). Holmes and Holmes (2010) suggest (concerning earlier figures) that, '…it may be that a significant percent of "unknown" are works of serial killers' (ibid., p. 220).

Hickey's US Data

Hickey (2010) collated US data based on the 'biographical case study analysis of serial murderers and their victims' from 1800 to 2008 (ibid., p. 34). Sources included 'newspapers, journals, bibliographies, biographies, computer searches and social science abstracts' and a few interviews with serial killers. Cases cited by Hickey involved reported convictions of two or more victims over an extended period (ibid.).

Reliability and Validity of Data on Serial Killer Victims

As pointed out when discussing data on serial killers, there are difficulties in establishing the reliability and validity of the information. Trying to estimate the number of serial killer victims from FBI data is speculative. As Hickey's (2010) sample also demonstrates, estimates of victim numbers vary widely from 3000 to 4600 homicides because 'a few serial murderers killed so many people that only close approximations of the actual numbers can be ascertained' (ibid., pp. 35–36).

Data on Serial Poisoner Victims

Trestrail's Database

Wider sources of data on serial homicide generally do not tend to analyse serial poisonings separately, so databases that are specific to poison murders are helpful. Trestrail (2007) collated a database of 1026 cases of offenders convicted of homicidal poisoning. Most cases were from either the US (404) or the UK (255) (ibid., pp. 56–57). Although mainly from the twentieth century, the dates of cases ranged from 339 B.C.E. to 2007 (Trestrail, personal communication, November 2016). This database includes information on serial poisoners and their victims but has not, so far as I am aware, been analysed solely according to these cases. One can however examine poison cases and groups of cases, making tentative generalisations.

Reliability and Validity of Data on Serial Poisoning Victims

Given that serial poisoning may have gone unsuspected for long periods, establishing information about victims is challenging. There are arguments for considering perpetrator confessions, suspicions harboured by police and others, and the number of killings for which the offender has been convicted. Each source has its own strengths and difficulties, and it is not possible to say that in every instance one source is better than another.

Perpetrator confessions cannot be taken at face value. On the one hand, it may be in the offender's interests to deny everything. On the other hand, perpetrators who consider that they have nothing to lose can vaingloriously exaggerate the numbers of their victims. Furthermore, the numbers of victims that the perpetrator claims to have killed may change from time to time. They may claim to have killed many, then perhaps having reflected on lawyers' advice, state that they have killed none. Where many victims have been poisoned, the perpetrator may pretend not to know the number or may genuinely be unable to recall.

Police and others may suspect that there are more poison victims than is at first apparent, trusting years of experience and a developed 'instinct' for such matters. But such suspicions can of course be incorrect. There may be a snowball effect where, if it seems clear that several poisonings have been committed, other suspected deaths can be attributed to the offender. This might occur where a staff member is suspected of killing in a hospital setting.

Yet even if one restricts oneself to only the poisonings for which an offender has been placed on trial and found guilty, there is no guarantee that this is the 'real' number. Police may have evidence of several other poisonings but may decide to bring charges for only a few where there is the highest possibility of conviction. This can, from a prosecution point of view, avoid potentially muddying the waters with cases that are more difficult to present to a court convincingly. Also if the presented crimes that are selected are likely to attract very lengthy sentences, it may seem less fruitful to pursue convictions on others where the evidence might not be quite as compelling.

Some commentators tend to accept possible killings as likely ones and attribute more victims to a perpetrator than is justifiable. Others are perhaps over cautious. Where conviction, perpetrator confession, and police and other suspicions all settle on the same number of victims, then the ground is more secure. Sometimes, it is especially difficult to determine the number of victims. Those killed by **Dr. Harold Shipman** [S41, P1] is estimated to be around 250 patients over decades. But even a rigorous judge-led enquiry over several years could not categorically state the number of victims and had to include informed judgements about whether deaths were natural or unlawful.

Numbers of Victims

Numbers of Victims of Serial Murder

In his study of serial killers in the US during 1850–2004 Hickey (2010) refers to 431 serial killers representing 367 cases of serial murder (ibid., p. 278). The 367 cases accounted for an estimated 2760–4340 victims (ibid., p. 279, Table 10.2). Most cases fell in the period 1950–1974 (107 cases) and 1975–2004 (183 cases) (ibid.).

Numbers of Victims of Serial Poisoning

Given that serial homicide is defined in the present context as involving a minimum of two victims, there are examples such as **Lynn Turner**

[S49, P8] who was convicted of poisoning both her husband and later a common law husband. At his home in Glasgow, Scotland, **Dr. Edward Pritchard** [S2] used antimony and aconite to poison Jane Tailor (his mother in law) and his wife Mary Jane Cowan.

There are also convictions of serial poisoners, often in medical or related occupations, involving many victims. Many examples could be given. US nurse **Charles Cullen** [S52, P11] confessed to murdering thirty patients in hospitals in Pennsylvania and New Jersey over a sixteen-year period using injections of the heart drug digitoxin. **Elisabeth Wiese** [S11] of Germany using morphine, poisoned five children left in her care then destroyed the bodies by burning them in her apartment stove.

Gender

Gender of Victims of Serial Killers

From a sample of 418 offenders between 1800 and 2004. Hickey (2010) looked at the percentage of perpetrators who murdered according to the victim's gender (ibid., p. 288, Table 10.8). Most offenders (40%) murdered both males and females. A further 39% murdered females only while only 21% killed males only. Represented among victims were adults, teens, and children.

Gender of Victims of Serial Poisoners

Male-on-female serial poisonings include those of **Mohan Kumar** [S54, P13] in India who poisoned women to whom he had promised marriage, and then stole their belongings. In France, **Pierre Désiré Moreau** [S5] poisoned his wife, Félicye-hortense Aubry and later his second wife, Adelaide-Louise for financial gain.

Female-on-male cases include that of **Lyn Turner** [S49, P8] in the US who poisoned both her husband and her common law husband. In England, **Mary Wilson** [S25] poisoned her second and third husbands. Where a woman poisons a succession of partners, the popular press might refer to 'black widow' murders. In a variation on this theme,

Madame Popova [S12] in Russia killed the husbands of women clients, including by administering arsenic. She received only small financial gain, and part of her motive may have been a sense of freeing women from abusive husbands.

An instance of female on female serial poisoning was that of **K. D. Kempanna** [S58, P17] who killed and robbed women temple worshipers having convinced them that she could help with their problems. Kempanna may have considered that female victims would be more likely to trust another woman whom previously they did not know. Nursing home managers **Dorothea Waddingham** [S18] in England gave overdoses of morphine tablets to two female residents but there is no indication that they were chosen because of their gender, more because of the enticing financial gain that their deaths offered. **Yiya Murano** [S33] of Argentina poisoned women friends and neighbours with cyanide in confections. These victims likely came into Murano's orbit because she could gain their confidence to get them to lend her money (which she could not repay).

Male on male serial poisoning appears uncommon. **Graham Young** [S27] killed two male work colleagues. However, he had poisoned several members of his family when he was a boy of 14-years-old. Although his stepmother died at that time, he was not convicted of her murder but sent to a secure hospital. If Young's victims were exclusively male, it does not seem as though this was planned. Similarly, UK nurse **Benjamin Geen** [S50, P9] was convicted of murdering two male patients with drugs causing respiratory arrest or hypoglycaemic arrest but their gender appears not to be relevant.

In other instances, both male and female victims were killed. In Germany, **Christa Lehmann** [S23] administered E605 to her husband and to her father-in-law but also poisoned (inadvertently) her friend Annie Hamann. **Dr. Arthur Waite** [S14], a US dentist, poisoned both his mother-in-law and father-in-law for financial gain. Members of medical and related occupations who poison serially tend not to have any gender preferences for victims. Nurses **Niels Högel** [S61, P20], **Victorino Chua** [S60, P19] and **Charles Cullen** [S52, P11] killed both male and female patients. Victim choice here centred not on gender but on the availability and vulnerability of patients.

Age

Age of Victims of Serial Killers

In Hickey's (2010) database of cases of serial murder covering the dates 1800–2004 and with a sample of 431 offenders, the age groupings of victims were categorised as: children, teens, adults, and the elderly, and different combinations of these. The most frequent age group killed by serial murders was 'adults only' (36%) and 'at least one adult' (78%) (ibid., p. 287, Table 10.7). Hickey (2010) also notes that by 2004, serial offenders 'were increasingly targeting the elderly' (ibid., p. 287).

Age of Victims of Serial Poisoners

Victims of serial poisoners cover all ages. In the US, as a paediatric nurse, **Genene Jones** [S32] injected succinylcholine and other drugs killing infants including 15-month-old Chelsea McClellan. **Viacheslav Soloviev** [S56, P15] of Russia poisoned several adults with thallium but also Nastya his 14-year-old daughter, and (inadvertently) his sister Oksana's one-year-old child. To gain financially from their deaths, **Elisabeth Wiese** [S11] in Germany poisoned children in her care with morphine. **Della Sorenson** [S15] of Nebraska, US killed several members of her family including her first husband's nephew aged 4 months, two of her daughters aged 8 years and 1 year, and the one-year-old daughter of a relative.

Norwegian **Arnfinn Nesset** [S30] killed elderly residents of the nursing home that he managed. **Elfriede Blauensteiner** [S43, P3] murdered a husband and a companion (both elderly) for financial gain. In Japan, **Chisako Kakehi** [S63, P22] poisoned a husband and two common law partners for their money using cyanide, all three victims being in their 70s. US nurse **Bobby Sue Dudley-Terrell** [S36] killed four patients at a centre in Florida using insulin overdoses. The oldest victim was Aggie Marsh aged 97 years, and two others were in their mid-80s. Nurse **Orville Lynn Majors** [S40], who was said to hate elderly people, killed patients with potassium chloride and epinephrine at Vermillion County Hospital, the oldest being Luella Hopkins, age 89 years.

Where victims are poisoned between the two age extremes the perpetrator may wish to gain sexual freedom. **Francisca Ballesteros** [S51, P10] killed her husband for this reason (although she also killed her daughter). **Mohan Kumar** [S54, P13] killed his victims for robbery.

Ethnicity

Ethnicity of Victims of Serial Killers

With homicides generally, in the USA, in 2014 more than half the victims (6095 of a total of 11,961) were 'Black or African American' (FBI 2014b). By contrast for serial homicide most victims (and perpetrators) are Caucasian (Hickey 2010, p. 286). Racial killings are perpetrated by serial killers, but victims who are *sought out* because of race (while of course they do occur) appear to be uncommon compared with other groups. For example, where serial killers seek out strangers, the most common are 'young women alone' while 'racial killings' were listed as the least frequent (Hickey 2010, p. 286, Table 10.6).

Ethnicity of Victims of Serial Poisoners

Where serial poisoning is perpetrated by offenders in medical and related occupations, the victims tend to be those available in the setting (hospital, clinic. elderly home, or community served by home healthcare visits). **Dr. Harold Shipman** [S41, P1], himself Caucasian, killed patients because they were available in his community, not because they were of any specific racial group. The generally Caucasian ethnicity of victims simply reflected the communities in which he lived. US Respiratory therapist **Efren Saldivar** [S46, P6] was born of Mexican parents and killed victims with different ethnic backgrounds that reflected the geographical areas where he worked. Racial or ethnic aspects did not influence his choice of victim, they were simply available. In healthcare serial poisoning then, there may be cross-ethnic or intra-ethnic killing, but this is guided by availability, not by the ethnic origin of perpetrator or victim.

In other instances, serial poisoning tends to be intra-racial, again guided by the potential victims available to the perpetrator rather than any kind of preference. **Nannie Doss** [S24] poisoned spouses and was suspected of killing her children and relatives all of whom were from the same ethnic group. Indian **Mohan Kumar** [S54, P13] killed Indian women whom he met and robbed. **K. D. Kempanna** [S58, P17] poisoned Indian women like herself. But in these intra-ethnic killings too, victims were not actively selected according to ethnicity, but more guided by convenience and availability.

Social Background and Occupation

Social Background and Occupation of Victims of Serial Killers

Hickey (2010) listed (in order) the types of victims selected by serial murderers from most to least sought out. Three lists were made: of 'strangers', 'acquaintances' (which could give an indication of social background and occupation) and 'family' (ibid., p. 286, Table 10.6).

The *'strangers'* list included several occupations. Among 'young women alone' (the most sought out group) were included, 'female college students' and 'prostitutes'. 'Business people including store owners and landlords' were listed sixth of thirteen groups. 'Police officers' came ninth. The general category of 'employees' was tenth. The *'acquaintances'* list comprised seven groups. Third was 'young women working alone including waitresses, prostitutes'. Fifth was 'people in authority, including landlords, employers, guards' (Hickey 2010, p. 286, Table 10.6).

This list is difficult to interpret because it does not specify an exhaustive set of categories according to occupation (where this was known). Some of the categories are likely to overlap for example 'young women alone' and 'hitchhikers'. It is based on reported victims as sought out by offenders, not on the occupations of victims as recorded in crime figures. Yet it does point to categories of occupations that are likely to be more vulnerable to being selected by some serial killers, such as 'prostitute', and 'police officer'.

Concerning broader social issues, Fox and Levin (2001) found that victims tended to come from areas with high rates of divorce, one-person households, and areas with high rates of unemployment.

Social Background and Occupation of Victims of Serial Poisoners

With healthcare serial murders, it is the role of the victim (that of 'patient') rather than their social background or occupation that is pertinent. Being a patient makes them available. Being in everyday life an engineer, a shop assistant, or a computer analyst does not add to the victim's accessibility in this sense.

In other circumstances, where serial poisoners kill a spouse or family member, the social background of perpetrator and victim is likely to be similar. With non-familial serial poisonings, where the motive is financial gain such as robbery the victims may enjoy better social circumstances than the perpetrator, as was so with **K. D. Kempanna** [S58, P17] and her victims, whom she robbed.

Among the varied occupations of victims of serial murderers are a police officer and a firefighter the husband victims of **Lynn Turner** [S49, P8]. Their occupations are not relevant to their being victims except as occupations with which Lynn Turner came into regular contact in her job as a 911 dispatcher and from which pool her husbands were chosen. However, the occupation of Lynn's first husband likely contributed to her being apprehended. His police colleagues had suspicions about his death which re-emerged when Lynn's second husband died and was investigated leading to her apprehension.

The occupations of two of the victims of **Graham Young** [S27] in England were simply fellow workers in the photographic supply factory where Young worked. They were killed because of Young's fascination with poisoning, and because the killer had the opportunity in his duties of giving out refreshments to colleagues.

Christa Lehmann [S23] in Germany, administered E605 killing her husband Karl as well as her father-in-law and (inadvertently) a friend. Work was relevant only in the sense that her husband was uninterested in working which added to the strains of their marriage.

Mary Wilson [S25] married several times and poisoned her second husband (a retired estate agent/realtor) and her third husband (a retired engineer). The relevance of their occupations lies not in what they were exactly. Rather, they had provided property and a comfortable living for the two men, which offered Mary her motive of financial gain when she poisoned them.

The husband victim of **Stella Nickell** [S35] in the US was a heavy equipment operator, but it was for insurance that she poisoned him with cyanide. Her second victim, a local bank manager was random, and that death resulted from Stella Nickell tampering with over the counter medication to cover her earlier murder.

Victim–Perpetrator Relationship and Serial Killers

In his study, Hickey (2010) distinguished the perpetrator-victim relationship as 'stranger', 'acquaintance' or 'family'. These categories were further subdivided according to whether the perpetrator killed a member of the category exclusively (e.g. 'stranger only' or 'family only') or whether the offender killed a member of the category 'at least once'.

Identifying 420 offenders (356 males and 64 females) for the period 1800–2004 in the US, Hickey (2010) considered the preferences of offenders to killing family, acquaintances, or strangers as victims. For male and female perpetrators combined, 'stranger only' represented a full 61% of killings and 'family only' represented a relatively small 8% (ibid., p. 284, Table 10.5). Among reasons for the tendency for serial killers to prefer murdering strangers is that offenders seem to perceive that it offers safety from detection. Also, offenders can more easily view strangers as objects, making it easier to dehumanise these victims (ibid., p. 185). For serial homicides 'the most salient factor' among the groupings of strangers, acquaintances, and family members is that most of the victims are women and children (ibid.). This contrasts with homicides in general where the great majority of victims are male.

Gender differences relating to serial perpetrators are complex but there are some broad differences. For the period 1800–2004, the percentage of 346 US male offenders murdering 'strangers only' (71%) is vastly greater than for 'family members only' (3%) (Hickey 2010, p. 207, Table 7.7). On the other hand, with 64 US female serial killers from the period 1826–2004, the difference between killings of 'family only' (35%) and 'strangers only' (25%) was less marked (see also Hickey 2010, pp. 261–262, Table 9.3).

Victim–Perpetrator Relationship and Serial Poisoners

General Points

For serial poisoning, statistics are lacking in perpetrator–victim relationships, such as those of 'stranger', 'acquaintance', and 'family' and their possible relationship to gender. This precludes comparisons with such information regarding serial killers in general. However, serial poisoners and the perpetrator–victim relationships can still be informative, for example relating to the perpetrator's motives. Relationships include: family or de facto family members and others; friends, acquaintances, neighbours, and work colleagues; and strangers. (Healthcare serial poisoners discussed in an earlier chapter are not considered below.)

Family or de facto Family Members

Where family members or de facto family members are serially poisoned, male perpetrators seldom come to light. Where men are perpetrators, the motive is either financial gain or a desire for sexual freedom from a partner. **Dr. Arthur Waite** [S14], a US dentist, used diphtheria and tuberculosis germs and arsenic to murder his mother-in-law and his father-in-law to gain inheritance. Parisian herbalist **Pierre Désiré Moreau** [S5] killed two wives with copper sulphate for financial gain. **Dr. Edward Pritchard** [S2] used antimony and aconite to kill his wife and his mother in law, likely wanting to continue an affair with a housemaid.

Cases of women serially poisoning family members are more common. Where a woman serially poisons husbands and common law husbands typically for financial gain, popular media may adopt the sobriquet 'black widow'. **Mary Wilson** [S25] in England used phosphorus beetle poison, to kill her second and third husbands to acquire money and property. **Lynn Turner** [S49, P8] of Texas, US poisoned food with ethylene glycol anti-freeze, killing her former husband, and her common law husband, for financial gain. **Chisako Kakehi** [S63, P22] in Kyoto, Japan poisoned a husband and two common law partners with cyanide to gain inheritance money to pay off debts. Financial gain did not appear to drive Australian **Yvonne Fletcher** [S21] a domestic help who used thallium to kill two husbands. Her motive for killing her first husband is unclear and her second husband was said to be abusive.

Sometimes, husbands and children are serially poisoned. **Francisca Ballesteros** [S51, P10] in Melilla, Spain used calcium cyanamide to kill her daughter Florinda, aged 6 months, and many years later poisoned her husband Antonio, and her daughter Sandra, aged 14 years. The motive for killing her baby daughter is unclear, but it appears Francisca killed her husband and older daughter to be free to join a man she had met online. **Sarah Whiteling** [S8] in Philadelphia, US used arsenic rat poison to kill her husband, her daughter, and her son for life insurance money.

A wider circle of family members has been the victims of serial poisoning. Sometimes, the motive is financial. **Anjette Lylles** [S26] of Georgia, US employed arsenic to poison her first and second husbands and her first husband's mother for insurance money. **Janie Lou Gibbs** [S28] of Georgia, US used arsenic rat poison to kill her husband; her sons Marvin, Melvin, and Roger; and her grandson (Roger's son) aged 1 month. Gibbs donated a tithe of the resulting insurance money to her church. **Nannie Doss** [S24] of Alabama, US was convicted of murdering her fifth husband Samuel Doss, and confessed to killing her second, third, and fourth husbands, and by some reports admitted murdering other family members. These are reported to include: her mother, her two daughters aged 1½ and 2½ years, her newly born granddaughter, a two-year-old grandson, a mother-in-law, and Nannie's sister. Nannie

Doss' motives are debated, but financial gain played a part. In Germany, **Maria Velten** [S31] killed with E605 from herbicide administered in food. Her victims were her two husbands, and a lover who were killed for money. Velten also poisoned her father, and an aunt, claiming that these deaths were mercy killings. **Della Sorenson** [S15] of Nebraska, US killed members of her family with an unnamed (seemingly unidentified) poison, apparently out of long-standing revenge. Victims were John Weldman (her first husband), her first husband's niece and nephew, two daughters, her mother-in-law, the daughter of a relative, and another infant. Sorenson was deemed insane. Australian **Caroline Grills** [S22] used thallium to murder her step-mother, her sister-in-law, and two other relatives by marriage. Here the motive was unclear.

In these cases where family members have been serially poisoned, they have often formed a 'pool' of accessible victims whose deaths provided financial gain. Less often, the motives may be released from a partnership to allow sexual freedom to be with a lover; or very occasionally claimed mercy killing.

Mixed Family Members and Others

Family members have sometimes been poisoned in a sequence with non-family members. A commonly arising motive for these 'mixed' murders is financial gain. **Martha Marek** [S19] of Vienna, Austria, killed mainly her family using thallium. She killed her husband, daughter, and a relative, but also murdered a lodger. From all these deaths, she gained life insurance or inheritance. UK factory worker **Mary Ann Britland** [S7] killed her husband and her daughter, as well as a neighbour with strychnine to acquire life insurance money. **Marie Alexandrine Becker** [S17] of Liege, Belgium, a housewife and sometime dress shop owner, used digitalis to poison her victims. She was charged with murders of two husbands from whose deaths she gained life insurance, and an elderly customer of her dress shop whom she robbed. Austrian **Elfriede Blauensteiner** [S43, P3] used the drugs anafrinil and glyburide to kill for money. Her victims were Alois Pichler a companion, Friedrick Doecker her third husband, and Franziska

Koeberl a former neighbour. **Sukhwinder Singh Dhillon** [S44, P4] born in the Punjab, India but living in Ontario, Canada murdered Parvesh Kaur Dhillon, his wife and Ranjit Singh Khela, his friend and business associate. Her poisoned them with strychnine, for insurance money.

In an unusual variation, **Stella Nickell** [S35] conspired to increase the already expected income from murdering her husband. She poisoned her husband with cyanide, then added cyanide to shop stores of Excedrin capsules to support her claim that these were responsible, and therefore increase the insurance payout. In doing this, she randomly killed a local bank manager. Financial gain can drive some killings in a series while different motives lay behind the other murders. **Lê Thanh Vân** [S47, P7] of Vietnam used cyanide administered in food and drinks to kill 13 people. She poisoned her foster mother, lovers, and acquaintances for money from forged wills and other means. However, she appears to have murdered her mother in law, and her brother in law, owing to family conflicts.

Christa Lehmann [S23] in Germany administered E605 to her husband Karl, and Valentin Lehman her father-in-law, although the motive was unclear. She also inadvertently poisoned her friend Annie Hamann. **Viacheslav Soloviev** [S56, P15] in Russia poisoned mainly family members with thallium. They were wife Olga, daughter Nastya, a common law wife, and his sister Oksana's one-year-old child (in attempting to poison his sister and brother-in-law). He also poisoned a friend's grandmother Taisiya, and a police investigator of a brawl involving Soloviev. An obsessive fascination with poisons seems to have partly driven this.

Where victims are a mixture of family and non-family members, financial gain as a motive still looms large. Less often the motive is obscure, or is related to family conflicts, or concerns an obsession with poisons.

Friends, Acquaintances, Neighbours, and Work Colleagues

Clearly, friends, acquaintances, neighbours, and work colleagues are known with varying degrees of closeness. A certain level of intimacy is necessary for the victim to have the confidence in the perpetrator or at least lack suspicion of their intentions. As we have seen, non-family members can be victims of serial poisoners along with family members. In other instances, the victims are exclusively non-family members.

Yiya Murano [S33] of Argentina poisoned with cyanide, a friend, a neighbour, and a cousin for financial gain (to avoiding paying promissory notes). **Martha Grinder** [S3] killed two acquaintances with arsenic and antimony. **Dr. Neill Cream** [S9] killed successively four prostitutes in London, with strychnine including in drinks and as pills. His motive may have been sadistic although it is suggested that he planned to make money by accusing and blackmailing others of the killings. **Maria Swanenberg** [S6] of Leiden, Netherlands used arsenic to kill neighbours whom she purported to help and from whom she received life insurance money or inheritance.

A loose client relationship somewhere between friendship and acquaintanceship enables some killings. **Elisabeth Wiese** [S11] set up as a child carer in Hamburg, Germany killed five children with morphine, gaining financially from being paid in advance for the children's care. **Madame Popova** [S12] in Russia poisoned the husbands of clients for a small payment, using arsenic.

Hélèna Jégado [S1], driven by jealousy, poisoned fellow work colleagues and domestic servants with arsenic. UK serial poisoner **Graham Young** [S27] killed two work colleagues with thallium out of an obsession with poisons and their effects.

Financial motives are predominant, although there are examples of perpetrators being obsessed with poison, being uncontrollably jealous, or having an unknown motive.

Strangers

Where a perpetrator serially poisons strangers, it may involve product tampering as with the Tylenol killings in Chicago in 1982. Also, in Japan in 1985, a series of poisonings occurred leaving 12 people dead when the herbicide Paraquat was added to drinks left in or near vending machines. In both instances, the perpetrator or perpetrators were never caught.

Also, such killings do not strictly meet the criteria for serial murder. The victims die one after the other, but this is largely outside the perpetrator's control. There is no 'cooling off' period between killings because the perpetrator is not involved directly in the murders in the same way as a sexually predatory killer.

'Sets' of Victims

Victims of poisoners can be from an identifiable set. With a 'successful' modus operandi, **Mohan Kumar** [S54, P13] focused on vulnerable women whom he poisoned and robbed. He chose victims who were unlikely to be recognised as missing or reported as missing, so reducing the chances of being apprehended. These women were desperate to marry and were prepared to leave their homes to do so. Choosing victims in this way tends to relate to poisoners' roles and victims' habits. The London poisonings of **Dr. Neil Cream** [S9] were prostitutes. **Dr. Michael Swango** [S42, P2] and many other medical killers murdered patients. Such common features often have to do with motivation and availability. If the motive is financial gain, then family members who have life insurance become possible victims as with **Nannie Doss** [S24] who killed husbands and possibly other family members.

Location

Location and Victims of Serial Killers

In Hickey's (2010) study, offenders were categorised as 'local' (staying within a general area or county and not carrying on their killings in more than one state), 'place specific' (killing in the offender's home or place of work), or 'travelling' (killing victims in more than one state) (ibid., p. 282, Table 10.4). Looking at 431 offenders from the years 1800–2004, showed that 'local' killing accounted for most cases (52%). Notably, only 14% were 'place specific' but these accounted for the highest number of victims per offender (9–17 victims). Turning to the mobility of offenders against child victims, male offenders were more likely to travel to hunt for child victims than were female offenders (ibid., p. 294).

Location and Victims of Serial Poisoners

Serial poisoners may administer poison to family members at their shared home in meals that they (partly) share. This tends to be so where a spouse kills their partner or a parent murders their children. **Pierre Désiré Moreau** [S5], the Parisian herbalist, poisoned his first and second wives at their homes using copper sulphate. **Mary Wilson** [S25] poisoned her second and third husbands at their home in Tyne-and-Wear, England. **Francisca Ballesteros** [S51, P10] in Melilla, Spain killed members of her family at home. In a slight variation, US dentist **Dr. Arthur Waite** [S14] poisoned Hannah Peck his mother in law, and later John Peck his father-in-law at Waite's New York apartment where the relatives had been invited.

Where relationships are more tenuous, as with acquaintances or even friends, and with neighbours, the administration of the poison may be at the perpetrator's or the victim's homes. The perpetrator may take the victim gifts as did **Yiya Murano** [S33], the Argentinian poisoner, who mixed cyanide with confections which she gave as presents to some of her victims. Co-workers will tend to administer poison in the setting where they have greatest contact with the victims, that of the place of work, as did **Hélèna Jégado** [S1] in France, and **Graham Young** [S27] in the UK, each of whom poisoned fellow workers.

Elisabeth Wiese [S11] in Germany; poisoned the children in her care and disposed of their bodies in her apartment. **Mohan Kumar** [S54, P13] in India arranged that his victims would die taking cyanide tablets in the toilets of public bus stations. **K. D. Kempanna** [S58, P17] in India poisoned her victims in the remote temples to which she had lured them.

Generally, where the perpetrator is intimately related to the victims, the poisoning is likely to take place in their shared home. Work colleagues tend to be poisoned at their shared place of work. The more tenuous the relationship, the more likely the poisoning is to be administered in a neutral or even a public place. All this relates to opportunity and practical considerations about where the offender can administer poison while avoiding suspicion.

As we saw in the chapter concerning healthcare serial poisoners, these perpetrators kill relative strangers in a professional health care–patient relationship where the location is determined by the hospital, care home setting, or local community that is served.

Interaction of Characteristics, Relationships and Location and Serial Poisoning

Demographics, perpetrator–victim relationship and location all interreact. In the case of **Nannie Doss**, [S24] her social situation, the relationship with her spouses, and the setting of the family home formed part of the milieu of the killings. Similarly, with healthcare professionals the demographics of their work, the relationship between professional and patient, and the location (care home, hospital or local community surgery) forms part of the pattern in which killing takes place.

Gathering Detailed Information on the Victims

Recent Contacts

We can better understand the interaction between perpetrator and victim by examining the victim's contacts prior to the killing. These may have been the intimate relationships of spouse or family member. Or it may have been the brief contact of the subject of a confidence scam such as that of **K. D. Kempanna** [S58, P17] and women temple worshipers.

Routines and Preferences

Victims' routines and preferences may suggest an opening for the poisoner. A spouses' eating habits will be well known to a killer. The vulnerabilities of a lonely seeker of a husband can be exploited by a murderer such as **Mohan Kumar** [S54, P13] in India.

Why Victimised?

All the above considerations suggest that certain individuals might be victimised. They may be temple worshipers seeking solace in grief or ways of resolving problems. They may be unwanted lovers or partners, or prostitutes. They may be defenceless patients in a hospital or nursing home. Such considerations suggest why some individuals are more likely to become victims than others.

Team Murder Victims

Victims of Team Serial Killers

In Hickey's study (2010) team offenders were considered for the period 1850–2004. Regarding victim selection, team killers equally selected male or female victims, especially if the victims were adults. Half the team offenders killed both male and female victims. Strangers were the most common type of victim, and adult strangers were more predominant than child strangers (Hickey 2010, p. 241).

Victims of Team Serial Poisoners

In a rare serial team homicide perpetrated in colonial India, Augusta Fullam and Dr. Henry Clark used arsenic to kill Augusta's husband Edward McKean Fullam. They also procured the murder of Louisa Clarke (Henry Clarke's wife) by sword, in 1912. Although the perpetrators colluded, they did not act directly together to achieve the poisoning, and the second murder was by proxy and did not implicate poison (Farrell 1992).

Conclusion

Data sources and statistics relating to the victims of serial killing are various and their accuracy cannot always be relied upon. Regarding serial poisoning, observations can be made about cases, and guarded generalisations can be made. Demographic features of victims of serial killing and serial poisoning were compared. Perpetrator–victim relationship and crime location were discussed and their interaction with demographic factors considered. Information about the victim's contacts, routines, and preferences can be informative. All these considerations can suggest why the individual became a victim. The rare instances of team serial poisoning, and victims were briefly considered.

Suggested Activities

Select an example from the case studies of serial poisoning at the end of this book. Research further information about several of the victims involved, including the apparent first and last victims in the series.

What are the similarities and differences in the victims including demographics, relationship with perpetrator and location?

What does this information add to your understanding of the case?

Key Texts

Doerner, W. G., & Lab, S. P. (2012). *Victimology* (6th ed.). New York and London: Elsevier.

While this volume does not specifically consider poisoning, it does give a general orientation to thinking about crime by examining victims. Early chapters on 'The Scope of Victimology' and 'Measuring Criminal Victimisation' offer an overview. Chapter 4 looks at 'Personal Victimisation' including homicide.

Fox, J. A., Levin, J., & Fridel, E. E. (2015). *Extreme Killing: Understanding Serial and Mass Murder* (4th ed.). Thousand Oaks, CA: Sage.

The sections on serial murder include a chapter on victims which includes discussion on the vulnerability of some victims and how this can inform police approaches to investigation.

References

Doerner, W. G., & Lab, S. P. (2012). *Victimology* (6th ed.). New York and London: Elsevier.

Farrell, M. (1992). *Poisons and Poisoners: An Encyclopaedia of Homicidal Poisoning*. London: Robert Hale.

Federal Bureau of Investigation. (2014a). *United States, 2014 Uniform Crime Reports Homicide Data 'Expanded Homicide Data, Table 10, 'Murder Circumstances by Relationship, 2014'*. Washington, DC: Federal Bureau of Investigation. https://ucr.fbi.gov/crime-in-the-u.s/2014/crime-in-the-u.s.-2014/tables/expanded-homicide-data/expandedhomicidedatatable10_murder_circumstancesby_relationship_2014.xls.

Federal Bureau of Investigation. (2014b). *United States, 2014 Uniform Crime Reports Homicide Data 'Expanded Homicide Data, Table 3, Murder Offenders by Age, Sex, Race and Ethnicity, 2014'*. Washington, DC: Federal Bureau of Investigation. https://ucr.fbi.gov/crime-in-the-u.s/2014/crime-in-the-u.s.-2014/offenses-known-to-law-enforcement/expanded-homicide.

Fox, J., & Levin, J. (2001). *The Will to Kill: Making Sense of Senseless Murder*. Boston, MA: Allyn & Bacon.

Fox, J. A., Levin, J., & Fridel, E. E. (2015). *Extreme Killing: Understanding Serial and Mass Murder* (4th ed.). Thousand Oaks, CA: Sage.

Hickey, E. W. (2010). *Serial Murderers and Their Victims* (5th ed.). Belmont, CA: Wadsworth Cengage Learning.

Holmes, R. M., & Holmes, S. T. (2010). *Serial Murder* (3rd ed.). Los Angeles and London: Sage.

Trestrail, J. H. (2007). *Criminal Poisoning: Investigational Guide for Law Enforcement, Toxicologists, Forensic Scientists and Attorneys* (2nd ed.). Totowa, NJ: Humana Press.

7

Investigating Serial Poisoning

Introduction

The point of entry for investigating serial poisoning can be distinctive and requires consideration. Aspects of theory can help keep open lines of enquiry in investigations. 'Case logic', and profiling have their role. Demographic information can also suggest lines of enquiry.

Point of Entry of Investigation

Consider a situation in which there is evidence that several non-poison homicides have taken place, and that investigators believe that the crimes are a series committed by the same perpetrator. In this scenario, the several recognisable crime scenes over time provide information that can be examined and analysed. Even if the perpetrator has disposed of the bodies and they are not found for some time, there are often reports of a missing person to alert police and others of a possible crime. Except for serially murdered vagrants or run-aways, generally someone is reported missing and/or a body is found. Given this, the point of entry of an investigation can be quite early in a series even though several more killings might occur before the offender is caught.

With serial poison homicides, the situation can be different. Several murders may have taken place without anyone being aware of even one of them. Previous deaths may have been attributed to natural causes, accidental ingestion of a harmful substance, or suicide. Then the poisoner makes a mistake, or commits one murder too many, arousing suspicion, or in some other way attracts attention leading to investigation, and perhaps to criminal charges.

Investigators may begin their task looking at one suspicious death but then become aware that there are likely others committed by the same suspect. Their task is then to examine earlier deaths in an apparent series to see if a case can be brought concerning each of them. This task may take place months or even years after the suspected murders have occurred.

Where a victim's body has not been cremated, investigators can turn to evidence from exhumation and autopsy. Witnesses can still be interviewed although their recollection of events may be vague if they were unaware of murder taking place at the time. Patterns suggesting malign motives can be sought such as the deaths of suspected victims all having financially benefited the suspect. Never the less, the investigation is made more challenging by the delayed point of entry because of the remoteness of the events, the possible contamination of evidence, and the potential unreliability of delayed witness statements.

Using Theories of Serial Poisoning in Investigation

Do any aspects of theories relating to serial poisoning help to inform investigation? Although some theories appear to be isolated psychological explanations, each has a social and cultural context. In each of the theories shedding light on poisoning, there are potential environmental and cultural influences. Accordingly, examining information in the physical environment, and looking at what the suspect or witnesses say and do can raise investigative questions.

Moral reasoning theory (Kohlberg 1978) proposed that such reasoning develops sequentially with maturity. Serial poisoning often involves a type of calculated planning and reasoning, yet the perpetrator may lack sufficient moral reasoning to resist the temptation towards criminal conduct. A prospect of money or a desire to escape an unwanted relationship may eclipse all else, leading to an act of criminal poisoning, which if successful once, may be repeated. In short, the serial poisoner persistently lacks moral constraint. So, is there anything in the suspect's environment or social contacts that might have fed the hypothesised 'temptation'? How does the suspect respond to temptations of making money or the opportunity to end unwanted relationships? Do any past behaviours including any legal transgressions have a bearing on this?

Merton (1938) argued that crime emerges from tension between society's cultural goals and structural social limitations. Unfulfilled goals of wealth can lead some individuals to respond by adopting deviant means. These implications of anomie contributed to 'strain theory' (Farrell 1991) later adapted to include crimes precipitated through frustrations in not achieving status and self-reliance (Agnew 2001). This allows strain theory to be applied to understanding homicide (Brookman 2005, pp. 103–104). In part, this may explain some serial poisonings. So, in investigation, are there any aspects of the environment in which the suspect moves that could build up frustrations and act as obstacles? Does the suspect seem frustrated in pursuing legitimate ways of achieving goals? How would this inform the possible offence? Does this line of exploration provide a social or personal context for jealousy, revenge, and other powerful emotions that could sustain several poison homicides?

Differential association theory (Sutherland 1947) takes account of social factors defining crime, and the environment in which deviance most frequently occurs. It proposes that criminal behaviour is learned in a social context. Taking up the implications of learned behaviour, Jeffrey (1965) developed differential reinforcement theory. This highlighted the role of 'operant conditioning' concerning the effects of reward, punishment and the avoidance of unpleasant circumstances on how often certain behaviour occurs (Skinner 1938). This theory could apply to serial poisoning, where the behaviour of a perpetrator is 'reinforced' if he escapes punishment yet gains financially or otherwise from a victim's death. Second attempts at poisoning where an earlier one has (in the perpetrator's terms) 'succeeded' constitute further reinforcement. This leads to investigative questions such as, 'What "gains" have been open to the suspect in the environment in which they move?' and 'What avoidance of potential losses have operated?'

Rational choice theory concerns opportunities for crime according to environmental variables, but also views individuals as able to reason and work out risks. Clarke (1992) identifies factors that can influence crime by making it harder or riskier to commit, or by reducing its associated rewards (ibid., p. 13, paraphrased). Among factors making crime harder to carry out are 'controlling facilitators'. Examples relevant to criminal poisoning are limiting the sale and purchase of poisons; and tightening rules for death certification to deter poisoning or collusion in poisoning by physicians. One can therefore ask in the investigation, whether any controlling facilitators expected to deter serial poisoning have been evaded. For example, if the suspect is a medical professional, have death certification procedures been scrupulously followed, or have they rather been side-lined?

Control theory implies that many people would commit crimes if inducements to comply with social rules were eliminated. Hirschi (1969) suggested inducements to rule compliance such as 'attachment' and 'commitment'. In an application of control theory, Laub and Sampson (2003) focused on the life course of men over many years, and how they resisted or accepted delinquency. The researchers studied how social bonds (e.g. friends, family, employment) create informal controls, filtering influences from the wider social structure. Control theory informs understanding of a 'career' of serial poisoning involving little or no adherence to social rules. Over time, refinements are made to the modus operandi, making the perpetrator better at avoiding detection. Where serial poisoning remains undetected the offender may feel no social pressure because others are ignorant of the wrong doing. Controls would be diminished. Another control diminishing factor could be self-justifications as when health care serial poisoners claim to be mercy killers.

In labelling theory (Becker 1963) and the process of developing a 'career' of deviance, language is important. Labelling within the criminal justice system is associated with power and authority. An individual commits an initial delinquent act ('primary deviance'), experiences the reactions of others identifying them as deviant, and responds in a deviant role perhaps as a means of defence or attack. Therefore, the deviance becomes, 'secondary', incorporating the knowledge, stereotypes, and experience of others in shaping identity and future behaviour (ibid.). An adaptation of labelling theory might involve a serial poisoner witnessing accounts of their crimes in the mass media (or from unwitting conversations of others) and gradually shaping their offending according to these depictions. The person is not directly confronted by others' views and reactions. Instead they experience these responses secretly through the media and through what others around them say unknowingly. This suggests several points of enquiry. In the suspect's environment, what exposure do they have to mass media and social media? What part does it play in their lives? Have they been exposed to discussions of the crimes (of which they are suspected) among friends and acquaintances?

In brief, investigators can use the range of explanations of crime and homicide (and in the present context, serial poisoning) to ensure an open mind to various possibilities and lines of enquiry. These apply to the milieu in which the suspect moves as well as to the behaviour and views of the suspect themselves.

What Is Case Logic?

By 'case logic' I mean an assessment of the apparent facts of a case to see how convincing they are and where they might be questioned. In serial killings including serial poisonings, this involves examining the series of murders or supposed murders. I illustrate case logic with reference to **Nancy 'Nannie' Doss** [S24] convicted in June 1955 of murdering her fifth husband Samuel Doss.

Case Logic and the Nannie Doss Killings

How Many Did Nannie Doss Murder?

Media reports on the case of Nannie Doss are sometimes sketchy and contradictory. Although convicted 'only' of the murder of her fifth husband Samuel Doss, Nannie Doss was suspected of other deaths. Harvey (2014) states that regarding her husbands, Nannie '…confessed to murdering four and maintained that she never harmed her "blood kin"'. He adds that law enforcement officials 'speculate that she is likely to have murdered as many as 12 people'. Jackson and Pittman (2015) concur that Nannie 'admitted to killing four husbands with rat poison' and that she 'denied poisoning any of her blood relatives' (ibid.).

Cole (2016) affirms that, 'in the end, Nannie Doss confessed to killing four of her husbands, her mother, her sister Dovie, her grandson Robert, and her mother-in-law (Lanning)' (ibid.). Hickey (2010) asserts, 'She murdered four husbands, her mother, two sisters, two children, one grandson, and one nephew' (ibid.). Trestrail (2007, p. 18) citing Nash (1990) states that Nannie Doss, '…poisoned 11 victims: 5 husbands, 2 children, her mother, 2 sisters, and a nephew'. Clearly not all these contradictory reports can be correct, and an evaluation of them is clouded where commentators do not cite their own sources.

What Were the Possible Motives for Murder?

Nannie is said to have collected life insurance for some of the deaths possibly providing a motive of financial gain for the deaths occurring at various dates.

- In 1927 her two 'middle' daughters one aged 1½ and the other 2½ years old (Jackson and Pittman [2015] state that 'Nannie collected $500 each on their life insurance policies').

- In July 1945, Nannie's two-year-old grandson Robert Lee Haynes (Both Cole [2016] and Harvey [2014] say that Nannie collected $500 in life insurance).
- In September 1945, her second husband Frank Harrelson (Cole [2016] states that Harrelson was killed apparently after forcing Nannie to have sex with him; Jackson and Pittman [2015] maintain that 'insurance policies paid Nannie $2,000').
- 1950 Arlie Lanning, her third husband (Cole [2016] mentions 'insurance money'; Jackson and Pittman [2015] say that 'Nannie collected $1,500 on his insurance policy').
- 1953 Richard Morton, Nannie's fourth husband (Cole [2016] asserts, 'Nannie had promptly poisoned him to death', Jackson and Pittman [2015] state 'his life was insured for $1,500').
- 1954 Samuel Doss, Nannie's fifth husband (Jackson and Pittman [2015] say that, 'his life was insured for $1,400').

If the lives that are said to have been insured were in fact insured, and for the amounts specified, the total payments would have been as follows with estimated 2018 values in brackets:

$1,000 in 1927 ($13,600)
$2,500 in 1945 ($34,000)
$1,500 in 1950 ($15,400)
$1,500 in 1953 ($13,600)
$1,400 in 1954 ($12,600).

The total income would have been equivalent to more than $89,000. Hickey (2010) rejects a financial motive, asserting, 'the truth was that Nannie liked to kill' (ibid., p. 264). Jackson and Pitman (2015) report that 'investigators believed that Doss committed the murders for convenience and money' (ibid.).

How Convincing Are the Views of the Perpetrator?

It seems at first glance that when we are considering motive, the views of a perpetrator or suspect might carry weight, for surely, the motive for crimes would be best known by the person involved. In fact, the perpetrator may not always have the clearest insight into what drove them. Evidence that Nannie Doss took out life insurance policies might point to possible motives of financial gain, yet her explanations of her behaviour are different.

Canter (1994, p. 228) refers to 'narratives' that we live by. An example might be the account that Nannie Doss gave of a head injury when she was a child that led to headaches and supposedly accounted for her crimes. Harvey (2014) writes that 'Nannie claimed to have suffered a head injury when a train in which she was riding slowed' and she 'later cited this injury as the source of her destructive future behaviour' (ibid.). Furthermore, Nannie 'had confessed to killing her husbands and blamed it all on the head injury she had sustained as a child, which she claimed had given her headaches all her life' (ibid.). Jackson and Pittman (2015) apparently quoting a statement given to a police stenographer say that, 'in her confession, Doss said she killed Samuel (Doss) "because he got on my nerves". She said he wouldn't let her read *True Detective* magazines, have a radio or visit neighbours to watch television' (ibid.).

According to Hickey (2010) Nannie told police that Harrelson, her second husband, 'was an "awful drunkard"' and that she, 'decided to teach him a lesson' (ibid., p. 264). She poisoned her third husband Arlie Lanning it is reported 'because "he was running around with other women" and killed husband number four, Richard Morton because "he was fixing to run around with another woman"' (ibid.). Overall, it seems she "was searching for the perfect mate, the real romance of life" (ibid.).

Hickey (2010) rightly treats these 'explanations' with caution. He suggests instead that Nannie killed because she 'liked to kill'. However, this view does not explain (if she really did kill her two infant daughters) why there was such a long gap between the 1927 killings and later murders that took place from 1945. Serial killers do sometimes kill in what appear to be single instances before later embarking on serial killing, but if their motive is that they enjoy killing, one must explain the reason for wide gaps in murder sequences.

Internal Logic of the Deaths

There are clear differences in what commentators considered to be the number of murders committed by Nannie Doss. Given that evidence was tested at her trial, the most certain murder is that of Samuel Doss. The next highest probabilities are that she poisoned husbands two, three and four to which by all accounts not just some, she confessed. Reasonable doubts can be raised about some other deaths. If she killed her two young daughters in 1927, why was there a gap of 18 years before the suspected murder of her grandson? If the motive was financial gain or that Nannie simply liked killing, such a gap is hard to explain. At the very least, the deaths other than the poisoning of her second, third, fourth, and fifth husbands, attract differing likelihoods of her (or anyone) being the perpetrator.

In the killing of Samuel Doss and the likely killing of the spouses two, three and four Nannie knew their routines and prepared the food and drink that they consumed. This would make poisoning these victims (with arsenic) relatively easy. Repeating the similar modus operandi seems to have worked from Nannie's point of view as she was not suspected until the fourth murder. Also repetitive was the method of meeting future spouses, through lonely hearts columns.

Nannie married her second husband Frank Harrelson in 1929 and likely killed him in 1945. She wed her third husband Arlie Lanning in 1947, probably murdering him in 1950. Richard Morton became Nannie's fourth husband in October 1952 and was likely murdered in May 1953. Marrying her fifth husband Samuel Doss in June 1953, Nannie killed him in October 1954. This death was deemed suspicious and an autopsy showed it to be caused by poisoning. With each marriage, the duration of the liaison grew shorter—Harrelson 16 years, Lanning three years and Morton and Doss even less.

Importance of the Sequence of Murders

In suspected serial murder cases, it is important to establish after several killings have taken place, the order in which they occurred. If one can pin down the date and details of the first murder, it may be possible to trace precursors to it such as less serious and less violent breaches of the law. The situation is different if one is looking at second and subsequent killings because the perpetrator has already killed and therefore committed the most serious transgression. It is also important to establish the first murder in the series because subsequent killings are likely to be informed by this as the killer learns from mistakes and near mistakes and perhaps modifies later actions and killings accordingly.

In the example of Nannie Doss, the lack of agreement on what was her first murder hinders developing a fuller understanding of what she did, the possible motives, and the trajectory of adaptations that might have taken place as she repeatedly killed.

Fact Checking

To aid accuracy in summarising accounts of serial murder, researchers, and others need to check basic facts as far as possible. This involves journalistic, historical and biographical skills. Sources may include court transcripts, documents, and physical evidence. In the example of Nannie Doss, given the range of conflicting reports, it would be relevant to try to establish information such as the following:

- The number of murders to which Nannie Doss at various times confessed and when and to whom the confessions were made.
- If she made and then retracted any confessions and to who any retractions were made.
- The companies with which she took out insurance policies and whether they expressed contemporary suspicions about claims.
- Cause of death entered on the death certificates of all those whom Nannie Doss is said (by at least some sources) to have killed.

In brief, in serial killings (including serial poisonings) the number of murders, the various possible motives, perpetrators views and confessions, the internal logic of the series of deaths, their sequence, and the checking of key assumed facts, can help in reviewing and learning from cases.

Crime Investigation and Profiling

What, Why, and Who

FBI agents and others who were taught elements of criminal-personality profiling and crime scene analysis at the National Academy at Quantico Virginia, were encouraged to think about, 'the entire story of the crime' (Douglas and Olshaker 1996, p. 36). Roy Hazelwood, in teaching the basic profiling course, structured the analysis around three questions: What? Why? Who?

- What took place? (everything that might be 'behaviourally significant about the crime'),
- Why did it happen in the way that it did? (the reasons for every behaviourally significant factor in the crime),
- Who would have committed this crime for these reasons?

It is a challenge to determine what represents 'behaviourally significant' aspects of what took place in connection with the crime. In asking why events happened in the way that they did, getting an answer also depends on identifying behaviourally significant factors. In part, being alert to what such factors are will be informed by the agent's previous experience and by reports of earlier cases.

Signature and Modus Operandi

Reviewing serial killings mainly involving explicit violence and sexual abuse, Douglas discusses a criminal's 'signature'. A signature is 'something inherent, deep within the criminal's mind and psyche that compelled him to do things in a certain way' (Douglas and Olshaker 1996, p. 69). In looking at the mentality and motivations of serial killers and in examining crime scenes for behavioural clues, the signature is the element(s) 'that made the crime and the criminal stand out, *that represented what he was*' (ibid., italics in original). It is distinguishable from the modus operandi of the crime. Modus operandi is learned behaviour, potentially dynamic and changeable over time as the perpetrator progressively learns. A signature expresses the perpetrator's personality and is something that he 'needs' to do. It does not help in the perpetrating of the homicide, indeed it might over time attract attention and arouse suspicion (ibid., pp. 251–252).

Consider a *modus operandi* associated with (serial) poisoning. A hospital nurse may plan to kill a patient through directly poisoning the victim, intending the poison to take effect after a few minutes when the offender can be away from the patient's bedside. However, the dose may be misjudged so that attention is drawn to the patient's distress too quickly while the perpetrator is still present. Next time, the killer is likely to learn from the close shave. They might be more accurate in their judgement of the dosage, its timing, and the current health of the victim. They might contaminate medication supplies so that another nurse inadvertently administers the fatal poison (perhaps even calculating the time when this is likely to occur so that they can be in the vicinity). Modus operandi is therefore modified towards successfully achieving the crime. In this context, a *signature* might be that the nurse needs to make an apparent attempt to save the patient perhaps to gain admiration. This is a need in the perpetrator that the killing serves and is more static.

Understanding the Offender

FBI agent and profiler John Douglas emphasised the importance of the crime scene in the slogan, 'if you want to understand the artist, look at his work' (Douglas and Olshaker 1996, p. 116). In other words, examining the crime scene and other aspects of the crime can inform the investigator about the perpetrator. When investigating a case, Douglas took account of evidence, such as case reports, crime scene photographs and descriptions, victim statements, or autopsy protocols. Using all this, he attempted to put himself, 'mentally and emotionally in the head of the offender' (ibid., p. 151).

Profiling can contribute to the apprehension of a serial offender where investigators and others can identify patterns or other features that indicate a series of homicides suggesting the same perpetrator. With serial poisoning, it is unlikely that anyone is aware that the crimes have taken place. (Exceptions include poisonings such as those by **Dr. Neil Cream** [S9] of prostitutes with cyanide.) This lack of awareness that crimes have taken place is one factor contributing to the relatively high proportion of victims in healthcare serial poisoning.

A possibility of detecting a series arose with the homicides of **K. D. Kempanna** [S58, P17] in India. The first few murders showed the features of the series. They were of women, involved the same poison (cyanide), and usually took place in temples which were not closest to the victim's home. Police missed several lines of enquiry. Had the victims been persuaded to visit the temples where their bodies were discovered? Who could have persuaded them? Was it more likely that the offender was a man or a woman? Would the perpetrator have an interest in temples or regularly frequent temples?

Profiling may be useful when an individual is suspected or has been charged and it is apparent that several poisonings have taken place, and there is debate about the number and their sequence. Along with other information, profiling can help in estimating these issues. It could then enable investigators to understand what may have led to the first homicide, and how the sequence of homicides then developed. In a sense, this is what Douglas describes in relation to his work on the case of Robert Hansen a serial killer in Alaska. Police had strong suspicions but no physical evidence to bring a charge. When Douglas was asked to contribute, he recognised that 'this was the opposite of what we normally do in that we were working from a known subject, trying to determine whether his background, personality and behaviour fit a series of crimes' (Douglas and Olshaker 1996, p. 242).

Investigative Implications of Demographics and Related Matters

To what extent can general demographic information inform cases being investigated? This can be considered in relation to serial poisoners in general, health care serial poisoners particularly, and victims.

Serial Poisoners

Some serial poisoners were caught almost fortuitously and may have otherwise committed further murders. Given this, and the linked possibility that there may be other serial poisoners that have not been apprehended, current estimates of the scale of the crime may be too low. This suggests investigators remaining alert to the possibility of serial poisoning.

Regarding the gender of serial poisoners, as with poisoning in general (Farrell 2017, passim), there appears to be no preponderance of male perpetrators over female offenders. This suggests keeping an open mind about the gender of a poisoner where the perpetrator is unknown and certainly not assuming a female offender without supportive indications or evidence.

The age range of serial poisoners is wide, as it is with serial killers generally, but the 'starting age' is generally higher because of the knowledge and planning required for poisoning.

Turning to ethnicity, serial poisoners appear to represent the ethnic makeup of the country concerned (and tend to kill victims of the same ethnic origin). In countries where the predominant ethnic group is white Caucasian, minority ethnic groups do not appear to be overrepresented among serial poisoners. This suggests that the perpetrator is likely to be of the same ethnic origin as the victim, except for health care serial poisoners who tend to draw from the available patient 'pool' irrespective of ethnicity.

Serial poisoners come from a range of occupations, but a disproportionally high number of health care professionals, are represented.

In the personal history of serial poisoners, the predictive and explanatory usefulness of certain childhood traits and behaviours is limited. However, where serial poisoners prior to their first murder, perpetrated criminal or deviant acts, these are likely to be more easily verifiable. While they may point to an erosion of boundaries and restraints that has led to subsequent deviance including poisoning, sometimes, no such deviant or criminal behaviour is recorded, and poison homicides appear seemingly without precedents.

Investigators need to remember that the motives of serial poisoners include: financial gain, jealousy and revenge, power and control, sadism, seeking excitement, factitious disorder imposed on another, and (claimed) mercy killing. There are also instances where motive is indirect or cannot be established, or where the perpetrator is judged 'insane'.

Regarding location, where serial poisoners hold medical or related occupations and perpetrate their crimes in a hospital or clinic, these offences are 'place specific'. Similarly, a perpetrator who poisons family members tends to do so in their shared home or when visiting a family member in their nearby home. Likewise, serial killers who poisoned work colleagues targeted workers whom they regularly met in their shared locality. 'Travelling' serial poisoners are rare. Unlike other serial killers, a serial poisoner may be able to kill without it being apparent to anyone that a crime has taken place, making it unnecessary to travel to kill or to escape detection. A serial perpetrator tends to choose a location that reduces the likelihood of being apprehended. Where the perpetrator poisons short-term acquaintances, the setting may be relatively public. For those who kill their spouse or partner the venue is often their home (or the victim's home). Here, the perpetrator is familiar with the space and the victim's routines and finds protective privacy. Locations have their associated activities and routines, such as the mealtimes and eating habits of a victim in a domestic home, which the serial poisoner can exploit.

Healthcare Serial Poisoners

Healthcare serial poisoners work in a healthcare setting and, through their privileged role, serially poison at least two patients or clients, with a 'cooling off' time gap between killings. Yorker and colleagues (2006 and personal communication, September 2017) suggest that for health care serial killers, poisoning was the commonest method of killing especially using injection. Some healthcare serial poisoners with specialist duties involving patients with heart problems, respiratory difficulties, and diabetes interfere with the drug regimens to kill their victims.

A serial perpetrator may have several interacting motives. Healthcare serial poisoners rarely kill for financial gain. Jealousy and revenge, probably constrained because the circumscribed carer-patient relationship, appear uncommon motives. While some serial healthcare poisoners, are driven by 'power and control' (Hough and McCorkle 2017, p. 158) this concerns selecting the moment of death, not as with other serial killers, control of the person themselves. Some caregivers may have sadistic motives.

In relation to the 'thrill hedonistic' broader serial killer typology (Holmes and Holmes 2010, p. 129) healthcare serial poisoners may observe and choose complaining or 'difficult' patients as victims, but do not conventionally stalk them. Circumstances usually dictate relatively quick death precluding torture. With caregiver-induced cardiac arrests the perpetrator may want to create and deal with a 'code' rather than to kill; and may be motivated by excitement. A poisoner with 'factitious disorder imposed on another' (American Psychiatric Association 2013, pp. 324–327) may seek esteem and attention. Perpetrators may claim mercy killing because the patients are suffering or dying, despite victims not being terminally ill.

Healthcare professionals have opportunity for serial killing through access to patients including through physical care, access to drugs, and knowledge of their use and effects. As Holmes and Holmes (2010, pp. 205–206) indicate, such killings take place where perpetrators are familiar with the venues and its routines.

Yorker et al. (2006) identify possible factors when hospitals are implicated in healthcare murder prosecutions. Injectable medications may be easily accessible, and several patients may have intravenous lines. Oversight during evening and night shifts may be slight, and 'float' nursing personnel may be used. General quality assurance activities may be weak. Perpetrators may have falsified aspects of their background unnoticed or unchallenged.

Ramsland (2007) developed a 'red flag' checklist of potential concerns relating to healthcare workers. Yardley and Wilson (2016) suggest refinements to the approach. Checklists can raise awareness of some of potentially harmful behaviours and traits among health care workers. However, the brevity of items can conceal potential misunderstanding and confusion. Data interpretation of hospital in-house statistics can be complex in investigations into suspected serial poisoning. Any apparent relationship between patients dying under possible suspicious circumstances and the presence of a suspected nurse can mislead. Managers should therefore consider getting professional statistical help to interpret data.

Some convicted health care providers in the Yorker et al. (2006) study had previously falsified their credentials and/or had fabricated critical events. Clearly, employers should consider fraud or misrepresentation a serious risk factor for patient safety. Also, healthcare employers should say if a worker was fired, or was associated with adverse patient outcomes. Hospital administrators and physicians may fear negative publicity, civil suits for negligence or wrongful accusation, but if lax in co-operating with external investigations they risk harm to patients (ibid). Recognising the risks of aberrant staff is likely to help patient safety but managers need to ensure that their strategies avoid pointing suspicion unjustly at staff members.

Victims of Serial Poisoning

Victims numbers in serial poisonings range from two (fitting the definition of serial killing) to sometimes hundreds.

Exclusively male on female (and female on male) serial poisonings are often of spouses or casual partners. Solely male on male (and female on female) serial poisonings seem less common perhaps reflecting fewer equivalent homosexual relationships. Poisoners of both male and female victims include healthcare serial killers where the patient role rather than gender is paramount.

The age of victims of serial poisoning ranges from babies to the very elderly, reflecting vulnerability. Where victims are of other ages the perpetrator may kill for sexual freedom or money.

In general, serial poisoning tends to be intra-racial, guided by the victim availability rather than perpetrator preference. In health care serial poisoning, there may be both cross ethnic or intra-ethnic killing also steered by availability.

Where serial poisoners kill a spouse or family member, perpetrator and victim social background is likely to be similar. With non-familial serial poisonings, where the motive is financial gain such as robbery, victims may be socially above the perpetrator. Health care serial murderers prioritise the victim as patient rather than their social background or occupation.

When men (rarely) poison family or de facto family members, the motive tends to be financial gain or desiring sexual freedom from a partner. Women more commonly serially poison family members, as when a media labelled 'black widow' poisons spouses for financial gain. Sometimes, husbands *and* children are serially poisoned, and the motive may be financial. A wider circle of family members can be victims, perhaps for financial gain or revenge. Less often, the motive may be a wish for sexual freedom from a partner; or very occasionally claimed mercy killing.

Where victims include family and non-family members, financial gain may be the motive; or less often family conflicts, or obsession with poisons. Clearly, friends, acquaintances, neighbours, and work colleagues are familiar in varying degrees, making the victim less likely to suspect the perpetrator. Where victims are exclusively non-family members, financial motives tend to predominate. A perpetrator may serially poison strangers through product tampering, although this is not strictly serial murder, because there is no 'cooling off' period between killings.

If the perpetrator is intimately related to the victims, poisoning is likely to be in their shared home. Work colleagues tend to be poisoned at their common place of work. The more tenuous the relationship, the more likely the poisoning is to be administered in a neutral or even a public place. Healthcare serial poisoners kill relative strangers in a professional health care-patient relationship where the location is the hospital, care home setting, or local community. All this relates to opportunity and practicalities about where the offender can administer poison undetected.

The perpetrator-victim interaction before the killing may be the intimate relationships of spouse or family member, or brief interaction of a victim of a confidence scam. Victims' routines and preferences for example a spouses' eating habits may suggest an opportunity, while the vulnerabilities of a lonely seeker of a spouse can also be exploited. Such considerations suggest that certain individuals might be become victimised whether unwanted lovers or partners, or defenceless hospital patients.

Effective Police Investigation

Effective police investigation led to the conviction of **Lynn Turner** [S49, P8] a Texas 911 dispatcher. Using ethylene glycol anti-freeze, she poisoned her former husband, police officer Glenn Turner in 1995. Years later, she used the same modus operandi to kill her boyfriend Randy Thompson. This alerted authorities to similarities with Glenn Turner's death, leading to Lynn's arrest. **Sukhwinder Singh Dhillon** [S44, P4], a car salesman in Canada, used strychnine to kill Parvesh his wife, and Ranjit Singh Khela, his business associate. Investigating the Canadian murders, police visited Dhillon's native Punjab, where indications that he had committed murders while there, reinforced tenacious police efforts to examine his crimes in Canada.

Less effective was the police investigation of **Dr. Harold Shipman** [S41, P1] the UK physician who poisoned 250 of his patients. Officers who investigated the concerns of a local physician about excessive deaths at Shipman's practice lacked expertise to analyse the relevant data. A doctor recruited to help the investigation appeared to assume there was nothing amiss. Attempts to give **Graham Young** [S27] a fresh start hampered investigators. In 1962, aged 15, Young had been admitted to a secure psychiatric hospital, confessing to administering poison to his father, and others, and was released in 1970. Support workers did not inform his new employers of his previous convictions. A year later, Young killed two co-workers with thallium.

Other Aspects of Investigation

Several further aspects of investigation into poisonings and related implications have been examined elsewhere (Farrell 2017, pp. 131–146). These are: establishing a suspicious death; investigating motives;

interpreting physical evidence; understanding exhumation and autopsy findings; using modern toxicology; examining a suspect's knowledge of poison; and establishing how a suspect gained access to poisons.

Conclusion

Finding a starting point for investigation can be complex for serial poison murder. Aspects of theory and explanation of serial poisoning can act as a prompt to keep open a range of possibilities in reviewing strategies for investigation. Case logic scrutinises cases of serial poisoning to test various interpretations of contentious or conflicting accounts. Profiling has possible if limited usefulness in cases of serial poison homicide. Demographics can also inform investigation. Examples of effective and unsuccessful police investigation were mentioned.

Suggested Activities

Select an example from the summary case list where there is debate about the number and sequence of victims. Research it further to see if you can apply case logic and profiling to clarify accounts of the events involved.

Key Texts

Daniszewska, A. (2017). *Serial Homicide: Profiling of Victims and Offenders for Policing.* New York: Springer.
 A thoughtful overview.

Trestrail, J. H. (2007). *Criminal Poisoning: Investigational Guide for Law Enforcement, Toxicologists, Forensic Scientists and Attorneys* (2nd ed.). Totowa, NJ: Humana Press.
 A broad ranging book, engagingly written.

References

Agnew, R. (2001). Strain Theory. In E. McLaughlin & J. Muncie (Eds.), *The Sage Dictionary of Criminology*. London: Sage.

American Psychiatric Association. (2013). *Diagnostic and Statistical Manual of Mental Disorders Fifth Edition (DSM5)*. Washington, DC: APA.

Becker, H. ([1963] 2008). *Outsiders: Studies in the Sociology of Deviance*. New York: Free Press.

Brookman, F. (2005). *Understanding Homicide*. London and Los Angeles: Sage.

Canter, D. (1994). *Criminal Shadows: Inside the Mind of the Serial Killer*. London: HarperCollins.

Clarke, R. V. (Ed.). (1992). *Situational Crime Prevention: Successful Case Studies*. New York: Harrow and Heston.

Cole, C. (2016, September 26). *Nannie Doss: The Femme Fatale Next Door*. www.americas-most-haunted.com/2016/09/26/nannie-doss-the-femme-fatale-next-door/.

Daniszewska, A. (2017). *Serial Homicide: Profiling of Victims and Offenders for Policing*. New York: Springer.

Douglas, J., & Olshaker, M. (1996). *Mindhunter: Inside the FBI Elite Serial Crime Unit*. London: William Heinemann.

Farrell, M. (1991). Strain Theory. *The Criminologist, 15*(2), 107–108.

Farrell, M. (2017). *Criminology of Homicidal Poisoning: Offenders, Victims and Detection*. London and New York: Springer.

Harvey, G. (2014, August 19). Nannie Doss. *Encyclopaedia of Alabama*. www.encyclopediaofalabama.org/article/h-3619.

Hickey, E. (2010). *Serial Murderers and Their Victims* (5th ed.). Belmont, CA: Wadsworth Cengage Learning.

Hirschi, T. (1969). *The Causes of Delinquency*. Berkeley: University of California Press.

Holmes, R. M., & Holmes, S. T. (2010). *Serial Murder* (3rd ed.). London: Sage.

Hough, R. M., & McCorkle, K. D. (2017). *American Homicide*. Thousand Oaks, CA and London: Sage.

Jackson, D., & Pittman, H. (2015, August 27). Throwback Tulsa: Charming, Friendly Nannie Doss Poisoned Four Husbands. *Tulsa World*. www.tulsaworld.com/blogs/news/throwbacktulsa/throwback-tulsa-charming-friendly-nannie-doss-poisoned-four-husbands/article_c43b83ff-f12e-5952-a64b-21a1c0fbdcd4.html.

Jeffrey, C. R. (1965). Criminal Behaviour and Learning Theory. *Journal of Criminal Law, Criminology and Police Science, 56,* 294–300.

Kohlberg, L. (1978). Revisions in the Theory and Practice of Mental Development. In W. Damon (Ed.), *New Directions in Child Development: Moral Development.* San Francisco, CA: Jessey-Bass.

Laub, J., & Sampson, R. (2003). *Shared Beginnings Divergent Lives: Delinquent Boys to Age 70.* Cambridge, MA: Harvard University Press.

Merton, R. K. (1938). Social Structure and Anomie. *American Sociological Review, 3,* 672–682.

Nash, J. R. (1990). *Encyclopaedia of World Crime* (6 vols.). Wilmette, IL: Crime Books.

Ramsland, K. (2007). *Inside the Minds of Healthcare Serial Killers: Why They Kill.* Westport, CT: Praeger.

Skinner, B. F. (1938). *The Behaviour of Organisms: An Experimental Analysis.* New York: Appleton-Century-Crofts.

Sutherland, E. H. (1947). *Principles of Criminology* (2nd ed.). Philadelphia, PA: Lippincott.

Trestrail, J. H. (2007). *Criminal Poisoning: Investigational Guide for Law Enforcement, Toxicologists, Forensic Scientists and Attorneys* (2nd ed.). Totowa, NJ: Humana Press.

Yardley, E., & Wilson, D. (2016). In Search of the 'Angels of Death': Conceptualising the Contemporary Nurse Healthcare Serial Killer. *Journal of Investigative Psychology and Offender Profiling, 13*(1), 39–55.

Yorker, B. C., Kizer, K. W., Lampe, P., Forest, A. R. W., Lannan, J. M., & Russell, D. A. (2006, November). Serial Murder by Healthcare Professionals. *Journal of Forensic Science, 51*(6), 1–10.

8

Summary Note of Serial Poisonings

The list is in chronological order usually of date of sentencing (set in bold). Entries are further grouped in fifty-year sections from 1850–1899 through to 1950–1999, then from 2000 to 2017. References are flagged in the entry then cited fully at the end of the listings. Entries typically include:

P Poisoner, year of birth, their country/nationality, occupation/role, sentence and date, and whether a healthcare serial poisoner as indicated by 'HSP' in bold lettering
PA Poison used, and how it was administered
V Victim, their relationship to the poisoner, year of their death, location of the murder
M Motive where this can be judged
R References for further reading
N Notable other information.

1850–1899

[S1]
P: Hélèna Jégado, born 1803, Brittany, France, domestic servant, guillotined **1852**
PA: Arsenic administered in food and drink
V: Perotte Mace, fellow worker at Bout-du-Monde Hotel, Rennes, 1850 (at the hotel); Rose Tessier, 1850; Rosalie Sarrazin, 1851, both fellow servants for Theophile Bidard a law professor in Rennes (at their workplace Bidard's home)
M: Jealousy where she considered other workers were preferred over her
R: Heppenstall (1970)
N: At trial HJ was accused of three murders, three attempted murders and various thefts, and was highly suspected of many other murders.

[S2]
P: Dr. Edward Pritchard, born 1825, Hampshire, England, physician, hanged **1865**
PA: Antimony (and aconite) at his home in Glasgow, Scotland. For Jane Tailor (mother-in-law) in the opiate medicine Battley's Solution. For Mary Jane Cowan (wife) in food
V: Jane Tailor (70) who was nursing her ill daughter, February 1865; and Mary Jane Cowan, March 1865, both murders were revealed following an anonymous letter to authorities
M: Possibly to allow continuation of an affair with a housemaid
R: Roughhead (1906)
N: Dr. James Patterson declined signing the death certificates, so Pritchard signed them (wife, gastric fever). Wife recovered on staying with her mother Christmas 1864, but relapsed on returning to husband.

[S3]
P: Martha Grinder, born 1815 (or 1833), in Allegheny, Pennsylvania, US; arrested August 1865, convicted of the first-degree murder of acquaintance Mary Caruthers (and confessed to killing another acquaintance Jane Buchanan) November 1865, hanged January **1866**

PA: Arsenic and antimony administered in coffee and food
V: Jane Buchanan, February 1864; Mary Caruthers, August 1865 Alleghany City, Pennsylvania, US
M: Unclear
R: Reporter (1866) *NYT*.

[S4]
P: Marie Jeanneret, born 1836, Switzerland, nurse, sentenced to 20 years imprisonment **1868**, died 1884 **HSP**
PA: Belladonna (and other poisons) administered as medicines
V: Charged with killing: Douise Junod, Jeanne Gray, Jenny Juvet, Louise Henriette, Mme. Bourcart, Jaques Gros, Julie Bonvier, Mme. Legeret, Demoiselle Fritzges. Convicted of killing seven patients
M: Probably sadistic.
R: Reporter (1884) *NYT*.

[S5]
P: Pierre Désiré Moreau, born 1842, Paris, herbalist, guillotined 1874
PA: Copper sulphate (found in both exhumed bodies) unclear how administered
V: Wife Félicye-hortense Aubry, 1869; Second wife, Adelaide-Louise (Lagneau) 1874, both at home
M: Financial gain
R: *Quotidien Le Gaulois*, 11 September 1874.

[S6]
P: Maria Swanenberg, born September 1839, Leiden, Netherlands, laundrywoman, caught attempting to kill members of the Frankhuizen family in December 1883; April **1885** found guilty of three killings, sentenced to life imprisonment, died in prison in Gorinchem 1915
PA: Arsenic administered in food and drink
V: Charged with killing three people. Suspected of killing many more victims including family and other relatives in her neighbourhood while purporting to help them
M: Financial gain from life insurance or inheritance

R: Moerman, I. ([1985] 2013)
N: In 1868 married Johannes van der Linden and subsequently had seven children.

[S7]
P: Mary Ann Britland (née Haigh), born 1847, Ashton-Under-Lyne, Manchester, UK, factory operative, arrested May 1886 and charged with murder; July 1886 trail at Manchester Assizes; August **1886** hanged at Strangeways Prison, Manchester
PA: Strychnine in pest exterminator administered in food
V: Elizabeth Hannah (19) her daughter, died March 1886; Thomas Britland (44), her husband 3 May 1886; Mary Dixon (29), neighbour 14 May 1886; all at Ashton-Under-Lyne
M: Financial gain from life insurance
R: Reporter (1886) *TE*
N: Following the death of her husband, MAB moved in with neighbours Mr. and Mrs. Dixon. After the deaths, the bodies were exhumed, and strychnine was found in Mary Dixon's stomach.

[S8]
P: Sarah Whiteling, born 1848, possibly in Germany, lived in Philadelphia, US; found guilty of murder November 1888, hanged June **1889** Philadelphia, PA
PA: Arsenic as rat poison
V: John Whiteling (38) her husband on 20 March, Bertha (9) her daughter on 25 April, Willie (2) her son on 26 May 1888 at their home in Philadelphia
M: Financial gain from life insurance
R: Reporter (1888) *StPDG*
N: Coroner was suspicious and ordered exhumations and autopsies which found arsenic after which SW confessed. Defence of insanity rejected.

[S9]
P: Dr. Neill Cream, born 1850, Glasgow (Lived Canada, US, and London), physician, hanged **1892**
PA: Strychnine including in drinks

V: Four prostitutes: Helen Donworth (Oct 1891), Matilda Clover (later in October 1891), Emma Showell, and Alice Marsh jointly murdered (April 1892) at various venues

M: Probably sadistic although he did not remain to witness the deaths of his victims, possibly hoped for monetary gain from extortion.

R: Farrell (1993a, b)

N: In 1881 Cream imprisoned in Illinois for poisoning Daniel Scott with strychnine. Released 1891. In London murders, NC attracted attention by sending accusatory letters fictitiously implicating others and demanding money.

1900–1949

[S10]

P: Jane Toppan (née Honora Kelley) born 1857, Massachusetts, US, nurse, arrested **1901**, died 1938 **HSP** also killed relatives

PA: Included strychnine administered to Elizabeth Brigham

V: Israel Dunham (87) patient, died 26 May 1895; Lovely Dunham (87) patient, 19 September 1897; Elizabeth Brigham (69) foster sister, 29 August 1899; Mary McNear (70) patient, 28 December 1899, Florence Calkins (45) Elizabeth's housekeeper, 15 January 1900; William Ingraham (70) patient, 27 January 1900; Sarah Connors (48) patient, 11 February 1900; Mattie Davis (62) Alden's wife, 4 July 1901; Genevieve Gordon, Alden and Mattie's daughter, 31 July 1901; Alden Davis (64) 8 August 1901; Mary Gibbs (40) Alden and Mattie's daughter, 13 August 1901; Edna Bannister (77) EB's sister-in-law, 26 August 1901.

M: It is reported that JT gained satisfaction from killing patients

R: Reporter (1902).

[S11]

P: Elisabeth Wiese, born 1853, St Pauli, Hamburg, Germany; originally a midwife but prevented after conducting illegal abortions, later provided care for children, convicted of murder and other offences 1904, guillotined **1905**

PA: Morphine then destroyed the bodies by burning them in a stove in her apartment
V: Five children left in her care. Berta Blanck, Peter Schultheiss, Franz Sommer, Wilhelm Klotsche and the unnamed aborted child of her daughter Paula which she drowned
M: Financial gain
R: Bahnsen (2005)
N: Husband was tradesman Heinrich Wiese. EW imprisoned for various crimes before her killings. For some children AW took a single adoption fee, but poisoned them. Police grew suspicious and searched her apartment finding morphine and other drugs.

[S12]
P: Madame Popova, born in Samara, Russia, date unknown, arrested 1909, executed by firing squad in St Petersburg, March **1909**
PA: Arsenic administered in food and drink, and other methods
V: Husbands of women clients. Number reported to be numerous between 1879 and 1909
M: Small financial gain and possibly sense of freeing women from abusive husbands
R: Reporter (1909a, b)
N: Arrested after a remorseful client reported her to police and MP confessed.

[S13]
P: Frederick Mors, born Carl Menarik October 1889, Vienna, Austria-Hungary; emigrated to US, 1914; worked as a porter, confessed killing patients in New York, found criminally insane. In **1915**, committed to Hudson River State Hospital. Escaped May 1916. Fate unknown. **HSP**
PA: Initially used arsenic and later chloroform
V: Eight elderly patients in a nursing home in New York between September 1914 and January 1915.
M: Insanity
R: Ephemeral New York (2015)

N: Employed as porter for German Odd Fellows Home in Unionport (The Bronx), New York.

[S14]
P: Dr. Arthur Waite, born 1889, US, dentist, electrocuted **1917**
PA: Diphtheria and tuberculosis germs (and arsenic)
V: Hannah Peck mother-in-law (January 1916) and John Peck (March 1916) father-in-law (at Waite's Grand Rapids, NY apartment)
M: Financial gain from inheritance
R: Buhk (2014).

[S15]
P: Della Sorenson, born in Dannebrog, Howard County, Nebraska, US; February 1897; arrested April **1925**, judged insane, committed to State Mental Asylum, died June 1941
PA: Nature of poison unclear but administered in food such as candy and cookies
V: Killed at DS home in Dannebrog: John Weldman, first husband, 1920; Viola Cooper (John Weldman's niece) July 1918; Clifford Cooper, 4 months (John Weldman's nephew) 1922; Wilhelmina Weldman (mother-in-law) 1920; Minnie Weldman, 8 (daughter) 1921, Delores Sorenson, 1-year-old (daughter of DS second marriage) 1924; Ruth Brock, under a year old (daughter of a relative) 1923; another infant, 1924
M: Supposed revenge on family members, deemed insane
R: Reporter (1925).

[S16]
P: Bertha Gifford (née Williams), born October 1872, Morse Hill, Missouri, US; a farmwife in Catawissa, Missouri. First husband Henry Graham died. Second husband Eugene Gifford. In 1928, arrested Eureka, Missouri. Tried for three murders. Found not guilty 'by reason of insanity'. Committed to Missouri State (Mental) Hospital, where she died 1951
PA: Arsenic assumed to be administered in food and drink

V: Edward Brinley aged 49 (May 1927), farmhand; Elmer Schamel age 6 years 10 months (September 1925), Lloyd Schamel aged 7 years 11 months (August 1925)

M: Insanity

R: Popper, J. (n.d.)

N: Noted in her local community for her cooking skills and for caring for others. Autopsy revealed arsenic in bodies of victims. Suspected of killing 17 people in total.

[S17]

P: Marie Alexandrine Becker, born 1877, Liege, Belgium, housewife, dress shop owner and sometime nurse. Arrested following an anonymous tip-off to police, and sentenced to imprisonment **1936**, died in prison 1938

PA: Digitalis administered in food or drink. Found in police search of MAB home

V: Victims included first husband Charles Becker a cabinetmaker in 1932, and second husband, Lambert Beyer (age untraced) November 1934; Marie Castadot an elderly customer of her dress shop, July 1935. Suspected of killing other victims for money

M: Murdered husband Charles Becker to be with her then lover Lambert Bayer and for insurance money; financial gain from killing Lambert Bayer (will), and Marie Castadot (robbery)

R: Gibson (2010) and Lange (2015)

N: The time frame of killings and the number of murders is disputed.

[S18]

P: Dorothea Waddingham, born 1899, Hucknall, Nottinghamshire, England, nursing home manager, found guilty **1936** hanged, **HSP**

PA: Overdose of morphine tablets

V: Louisa Baguley (aged 89) May 1935, and her daughter Ada Baguley (aged 50) September 1935 (both at DW's nursing home, Nottingham, England)

M: Financial gain from inheritance made over in exchange for the patients' care

R: Glaister (1954)

N: DW claimed untruthfully that Dr. Mansfield had given her surplus morphine tablets for Ada Baguley.

[S19]
P: Martha Marek (née Lowenstein) born 1904, Vienna, Austria; guillotined **1938**
PA: Thallium bought from a pharmacist in Vienna probably administered in food
V: Her husband Emil Marek (July 1932), her daughter Ingeborg (August 1932), a relative Susanne Lowenstein (July 1934), and a lodger Frau Kittenberger (1937)
M: Financial gain from life insurance and inheritance
R: Emsley (2005, pp. 332–333)
N: Frau Kittenberger's son suspecting MM persuaded authorities to exhume his mother's body in which thallium was found. Previous victims' bodies were then exhumed, and thallium was detected.

[S20]
P: Dr. Marcel Petiot, born 1897, Auxerre, France, physician, in **1946** guillotined **HSP**
PA: Cyanide injections purporting to be vaccinations for victims' country of destination
V: 24 men and women 1942–1944 during Nazi occupation of France (at his Paris home)
M: Financial gain from payment for 'escape' and robbery of victims' valuables
R: Maeder (1980).

1950–1999

[S21]
P: Yvonne Fletcher, born 1922, Australia, domestic help, arrested May 1952, sentenced to death **1952**, commuted to life imprisonment, released 1964
PA: Thallium as rat poison

V: Desmond Butler (30) her first husband, July 1948; Bertrand Fletcher (29) her second husband, March 1952 (Newtown, New South Wales, Australia)
M: Motive for killing first husband unclear. Second husband possibly revenge as he was said to be abusive
R: Reporter (1952)
N: In rat infestation in Sydney in the 1940s and 1950s thallium sulphate used as a rat poison 'Thall-rat' was available 'over the counter'. Other murderers used thallium at that time.

[S22]
P: Caroline Grills (née Mickelson), born 1888 in Balmain, Sydney, New South Wales, Australia. In 1953, charged with murders and attempted murders. Death sentence October **1953**. Commuted to life imprisonment in Long Bay Prison, Sydney. Died October 1960
PA: Thallium (used as rat poison) possibly administered in food
V: Murder in 1947 of Christine Mickelson (87) CG's stepmother, Angelina Thomas and John Lundberg both relatives by marriage, and Mary Anne Mickelson her sister-in-law. Attempted murder of three other family members in 1953 with thallium led to her arrest
M: Unclear
R: Garton (1996)
N: Married Richard Grills 1908. First suspected of murder in 1947 following the deaths of her family members. Following her father's death in 1953 Grills lived in Gladesville.

[S23]
P: Christa Lehmann (née Ambrose), born 1922, Worms, Germany, life imprisonment **1954**
PA: E605 administered to her husband Karl in milk, to Valentin Lehman in yoghurt, to Annie Hamann in candies/sweets
V: Her husband Karl (often unemployed), 1942, and Valentin Lehman her father-in-law 1952, her friend Annie Hamann 1954
M: Poisoning of Annie Hamann was inadvertent; motive for other murders unclear
R: Farrell (1992).

[S24]
P: Nannie Doss, born 1905, Aniston, Alabama; for murdering her fifth husband Samuel Doss sentenced to life imprisonment **1955**, died 1965
PA: Arsenic administered in food and drink
V: Her mother, sister Dovie, grandson Robert, the mother of one of her five husbands Arlie Lanning, and four husbands 1920–1954 (Alabama, Oklahoma, Kansas, North Carolina)
M: Financial gain from insurance, although ND claimed boredom
R: Cole (2016), Harvey (2014), Jackson and Pitman (2015)
N: Suspected of killing: her two 'middle' daughters aged 1½ and 2½ died apparently of food poisoning, 1927; newly born granddaughter died apparently of birth complications, 1945; two-year-old grandson Robert Lee Haynes died seemingly of asphyxia, July 1945; Frank Harrelson, second husband, September 1945, Arlie Lanning, third husband seemingly from heart failure, 1950; Arlie Lanning's mother (Nannie's mother-in-law), 1950; Nannie's sister Dovie, 1950; Nannie's mother Sue Hazel, 1952; Richard Morton, fourth husband, died 1953.

[S25]
P: Mary Wilson, born 1893, South Tyneside, England, sentenced to death **1958**, commuted to life imprisonment, died in prison 1962
PA: Phosphorus beetle poison, possibly administered with medication
V: Oliver Leonard retired estate agent/realtor, aged 75 (second husband) killed 1956, Ernest Wilson, retired engineer, aged 76 (third husband) killed 1957 (at her home in Gateshead, Tyne-and-Wear, England)
M: Financial gain from money and property
R: Farrell (1994)
N: Suspected of murdering John Knowles (first husband) and John Russell (her lover).

[S26]
P: Anjette Lylles, born August 1925, Macon, Georgia, US; arrested May 1958, sentenced to death **1958**, commuted, AL sent to State Hospital for the Insane, Milledgeville. Died December 1977

PA: Arsenic administered in food and drink over prolonged periods
V: Ben Lylles Jr. (husband), Joe Gabbert (second husband), Julia Lylles (mother-in-law), Marcia Lylles (daughter aged 9 years) at Macon, Bibb County, Georgia, US
M: Financial gain from insurance
R: White (2007).

[S27]
P: Graham Young, born 1947, London, England, store worker at a photographic supplier, sentenced to life imprisonment **1972**, died in prison 1990
PA: Thallium, administered in tea which he made for co-workers. GY kept a diary of the doses and effects of his poisonings.
V: Work colleagues Bob Egle 1971 and Fred Biggs, 1971 (both ill at work, died in hospital)
M: Sadism, obsession with poisons
R: Emsley (2005)
N: In 1962, aged 15, GY admitted to Broadmoor secure psychiatric hospital, confessing to administering poison to his father a sister and a school friend. He was released in 1970.

[S28]
P: Janie Lou Gibbs (née Hickox), born 1932, Georgia, US; lived in Cordelle, Crisp County, Georgia; arrested December 1967; 1968 considered mentally ill; sent to a state mental hospital; **1976** found guilty of murder and sentenced to five terms of life imprisonment; 1999 released owing to Parkinson's disease; died 2010
PA: Arsenic in the form of rat poison administered in food
V: Charles Gibbs (39) her husband died January 1966; her son Marvin (13) died August 1966; her son Melvin (16) died January 1967; her grandson (Roger's son) Ronnie Gibbs (1 month) died October 1967; her son Roger (19) died Christmas Eve 1967. Each was poisoned at their home.
M: Life insurance money a tithe of which she donated to her church
R: Kellerher and Kellerher (1998).

[S29]
P: Robert Rubane Diaz, born 1938, raised in the mid-west US, coronary care nurse, arrested November 1981, sentenced to death April **1984**. Died still in custody in 2010 aged 72. **HSP**
PA: Lidocaine a drug used to control irregular heartbeat, by injection
V: Patients. Formally charged with the deaths of 12 elderly patients at two Riverside hospitals in 1981. Eleven deaths at Community Hospital of the Valleys in Perris, March and April 1981. One death at San Gorgonio Pass Memorial Hospital in Banning
M: Unclear but possibly feelings of power as he is reported to have predicted the death of some victims
R: Reporter (1984) *NYT*
N: Autopsy revealed the bodies contained many times the legal dose of Lidocaine. Diaz worked as a temporary nurse on night shifts in both hospitals.

[S30]
P: Arnfinn Nesset, born in Trøndelag, Norway, 1936, nurse, sentenced to imprisonment **1983**, released 2004 **HSP**
PA: Succinylcholine chloride administered as supposed medication
V: 21 residents of his nursing home in Orkdallo, Norway, 1977–1980
M: Possibly feelings of power and control over life and death
R: Wilson and Seaman (1983).

[S31]
P: Maria Velten, born Germany, arrested 1980, confessed to killings, sentenced to three terms of life imprisonment **1983**, released early into a nursing home owing to dementia
PA: E605 (including thiophosphoric) from herbicide in food
V: Her father, 1963; an aunt, 1970; a husband, 1976; another husband, 1978; a lover, 1980
M: MV claimed a mercy motive for killing father and aunt; financial gain for other victims
R: Dupke (2009)
N: MV daughter-in-law became suspicious leading to MV arrest.

[S32]
P: Genene Jones, born 1950, Texas, US, paediatric nurse, in **1984** sentenced to extensive prison sentences **HSP**
PA: Succinylcholine and other drugs by injection
V: 15-month-old Chelsea McClellan, another child Rolando Santos, suspected of killing more children (at various medical clinics, San Antonio, Texas) 1977–1982
M: Endangered children's lives then sought adulation by 'saving' them
R: Hickey (2010).

[S33]
P: Yiya Murano, born May 1930 in Corrientes, Argentina; sentenced to 16 years imprisonment **1985**; released 1995; then lived in La Boca, Buenos Aires
PA: Cyanide in confections
V: Nilda Gamba, neighbour, died 11 February 1979; Lelia Formisano de Ayala, a friend died 19 February 1979; Carmen Zulema del Giorgio de Venturini, a cousin, died 24 March 1979
M: Financial gain by avoiding the payment of promissory notes, possibly resentment at her position and education
R: Reporter, 23 June 2007; Reporter, 28 June 2005.

[S34]
P: Donald Harvey, born 1952, Ohio, hospital worker, sentenced to life imprisonment **1987**, March 2017 found in his cell severely beaten and died two days later (attacker not identified)
PA: Cyanide and other poisons and methods **HSP**
V: DH pleaded guilty to 24 killings, mainly patients at hospitals in Kentucky and Ohio, between 1970 and 1987
M: Compulsive serial killer, claimed to be easing patients' suffering
R: Trestrail (2007, p. 23).

[S35]
P: Stella Nickell, née Stephenson, born 1943, Oregon, US, sentenced to 90 years imprisonment **1988**
PA: Cyanide, added to Excedrin capsules

V: Husband Bruce Nickell (52), a heavy equipment operator; Susan Snow (40) a bank manager, 1986 (Auburn, Washington)
M: Financial gain from insurance
R: Trestrail (2007, pp. 22–23)
N: Poisoned husband then replaced shop stock with poisoned capsules ('product tampering') killing Susan Snow randomly.

[S36]
P: Bobby Sue Dudley-Terrell, born October 1952, Woodlawn, Illinois, US, nurse, March 1985 charged with four counts of murder. Legal and psychiatric issues delayed the trial. February **1988**, a plea bargained guilty plea to second-degree murder, sentenced to imprisonment. Died in prison 2007. **HSP**
PA: Insulin overdoses administered as injections
V: Murders all in 1984 of: Aggie Marsh (97) on 13 November; Leathy McNight (85) on 23 November; Stella Bradham (85) and Mary Cartright (79) both on 25 November. All at the North Horizon Healthcare Centre, St Petersburg, Florida
M: Possibly related to Dudley's schizophrenia, depression, and the then designated Munchausen's syndrome (including self-harm). She had previously had hospital treatment
R: United Press International (1986) *OS*
N: October 1984 worked in Centre in St Petersburg, Florida, where after suspicious deaths of patients, her employment was terminated.

[S37]
P: Richard Angelo, born 29 August 1962, Long Island, New York, US, nurse, convicted of murdering several patients, in **1990** sentenced to life imprisonment **HSP**
PA: Injecting pancuroneum and succinylcholine chloride into patients' IV tubes
V: Convicted on two counts of second-degree murder and associated crimes. Patients at Good Samaritan Hospital, West Islip, New York 1987. First murder John Fisher (75) in April. Other victims Milton Pultney (74) 16 September; Joseph O'Niel (79) 21 September;

Frederick LaGois 9 October; Anthony Greene (57) 16 October and possibly others
M: To create patient respiratory problem so he could intervene and demonstrate competence, broadly related to self-aggrandisement and seeking thrills and excitement
R: Associated Press (1990) *TD*
N: Apprehended 11 October 1989 attempting to poison patient Gerolamo Kucich (73). RA's locker searched, revealing drugs used to poison.

[S38]
P: Brian Rosenfeld, born 1958, US, nurse, arrested **1990**, pleaded guilty to murdering three patients, sentenced to imprisonment with no possibility of parole for 25 years **HSP**
PA: Overdoses of drug pethidine (as Demerol)
V: Three patients at nursing homes in St Petersburg, Florida. Suspected of killing more
M: Prosecutors referred to BR having a voracious appetite for inflicting abuse
R: Reporter (1992)
N: Pleaded guilty under a plea agreement. From 1985 to 1990 BR said to have been dismissed from 14 nursing homes.

[S39]
P: Dorothea Puente (née Gray), born 1929, Redlands, California, US; worked as a nurse's aide and later managed a care home in Sacramento; arrested 1988; in 1990 charged with 9 murders, in **1993** convicted of three murders and sentenced to life imprisonment; in 2011 died in prison **HSP**
PA: Overdoses of drugs including Tylenol
V: Convicted of killing three victims: Ben Fink, Dorothy Miller, Leona Carpenter
  Jury could not reach a verdict on another six murder counts
M: Financial gain such as from cashing the security checks of victims
R: Connell (2011)

N: Around 1948, DP served a six-month sentence for forging cheques. In 1960 sentenced to three months imprisonment for managing a brothel; soon after imprisoned for vagrancy.

[S40]
P: Orville Lynn Majors, born 1961, Indiana, US, nurse, in **1999** sentenced to 360 years imprisonment **HSP**
PA: Potassium chloride and epinephrine
V: Patients at Vermillion County Hospital 1993–1994: Mary Anderson 69, Dorothea Hixon, 80, Cecil Smith, 74, Luella Hopkins, 89, Margaret Hornick, 79, Freddie Wilson, 56, Derek Maxwell, 64
M: Hated elderly people
R: Hanna (1999).

2000–2018

[S41]
P: Dr. Harold Shipman, born 1946, Nottingham, England, physician, sentenced to life imprisonment **2000**, committed suicide in prison 2004 **HSP**
PA: Mainly morphine-based drugs
V: 250 of his patients 1970–1990s (Yorkshire and Manchester, England often in their own homes)
M: Difficult to establish, but possibly feelings of power over life and death
R: Peters (2005)
N: Convicted of 15 murders, a subsequent public enquiry established that he was responsible for about 250.

[S42]
P: Dr. Michael Swango, born 1954, Tacoma, Washington, US, physician, arrested 1997, in **2000** sentenced to life imprisonment **HSP**
PA: Arsenic added to food and drink
V: 4 patients (may have been many more between 1981 and 1997)

M: Unclear
R: Stewart (1999).

[S43]
P: Elfriede Blauensteiner, born 1931, Vienna, Austria; sentenced in 1997 and **2001**, died in custody 2003
PA: Anafrinil (an anti-depressant) and glyburide (as euglucon) a drug used to lower blood sugar levels in diabetes
V: Alois Pichler (77) a companion died 1995; Franziska Koeberl (84) a former neighbour, died 1992; Friedrick Doecker () EB's third husband, died 1995
M: Financial gain
R: Bridge (1996), Leidig (2001).

[S44]
P: Sukhwinder Singh Dhillon, born 1959, Punjab, India; car salesman in Stoney Creek, Ontario, Canada; sentenced **2001** to twenty-year imprisonment in Warkworth Institution, Ontario; died serving sentence in May 2013
PA: Strychnine
V: Parvesh Kaur Dhillon his wife (36) on 3 February 1995, in Hamilton; Ranjit Singh Khela (25), his friend and business associate in Riverdale, 23 June 1996
M: Financial gain from insurance money
R: Metroland News Service (2013), Wells (2009)
N: Investigating Canadian murders, police visited SSD's native Punjab and suspected he had committed murders there.

[S45]
P: Kristen Gilbert, born 1967 in Fall River, Massachusetts, US. 1998 indicted with killing patients at VA hospital; **2001** found guilty of first-degree murder of three patients and second-degree murder of one other patient, sentenced to life imprisonment. **HSP**
PA: Epinephrine injections (heart stimulant)
V: Killing of four patients between 1995 and 1996: Stanley Jagodowski (65), Henry Hudon (35), Kenneth Cutting (41), Edward Skwira (69)

M: Self-aggrandisement in inducing cardiac arrest then demonstrating supposed nursing skills trying to save patients. Possibly broadly related to seeking thrills and excitement
R: Reporter (1999), Farragher (2000).

[S46]
P: Efren Saldivar, born 1969, in Brownsville, Texas, US; family later moved to Los Angeles; trained as respiratory therapist; charged with six counts of murder 2001; March 2002, Salvidar pleaded guilty; **2002** sentenced to six consecutive life sentences without parole **HSP**
PA: Injection of drugs causing respiratory arrest or cardiac failure including Panuronium and possibly morphine and suxamethonium chloride
V: Patients: Salbi Asatryan (75) died December 1996; Eleanora Schlegel, (77), Jose Alfaro, (82) and Luina Schidlowski, (87) all in January 1997; Balbino Castro, (87) and Myrtle Brower, (84) both in August 1997
M: Unclear
R: Lieberman (2002)
N: Previous history of petty crime, stealing.

[S47]
P: Lê Thanh Vân, born 1956, Vietnam; trained in army medical corps; August 2001, arrested and charged with murder; sentenced to death **2003**
PA: Cyanide administered in food and drinks
V: LTV confessed to 13 killings between January 1998 and August 2001; mother-in-law, brother-in-law, foster mother, lovers, and acquaintances
M: Financial gain from forged wills and other means; killed her mother-in-law and brother-in-law owing to family conflicts
R: BBC News (2004), ABC News (2004)
N: In 1993, jailed for fraud.

[S48]
P: Christine Malèvre, born January 1970, France, nurse, arrested 1998, found guilty of killing patients **2003**, sentenced to 10 years imprisonment. **HSP**
PA: Administering lethal doses of morphine, potassium and other drugs

V: Six seriously ill patients in her care between 1997 and 1998 at François Quesnay Hospital, Mantes-la-Jolie, Paris
M: Malèvre claimed that the deaths were mercy killings. Families of deceased rejected this
R: Bryant (2003)
N: France does not accept a 'right to die'.

[S49]
P: Lynn Turner (born Julia Lynn Womack), born 1968, Texas, US, 911 dispatcher, sentenced to imprisonment **2004** (and 2007), committed suicide in prison 2010
PA: Ethylene glycol anti-freeze in food
V: Former husband police officer Glenn Turner 1995 (for which sentenced in 2004) and boyfriend fire officer Randy Thompson 2002 (for which sentenced 2007)
M: Financial gain
R: Martinez (2010)
N: Death of Randy Thompson alerted authorities to similarities between his death and the death of Glenn Turner leading to her arrest and conviction.

[S50]
P: Benjamin Geen, born 1979, UK, nurse; **2004**, convicted of murdering two patients at Horton General Hospital, Banbury, Oxfordshire, UK. Sentenced to 17 life sentences **HSP**
PA: Geen was said to have used several drugs including vecuronium (and midazolam) possibly by injection or through drips
V: Anthony Bateman (66) of Banbury died 6 January 2004, David Onley (77) of Deddington, died 21 January 2004
M: Conjectured to be the thrill and excitement of resuscitating patients
R: BBC News (2006), Vinter (2006), Payne (2006)
N: Criminal Case Review Commission investigated.

[S51]
P: Francisca Ballesteros, born 1969, Valencia; Lived in Melilla, Spain/North Africa; confessed to murder of family members, sentenced to 84 years imprisonment in **2005**

PA: Calcium cyanamide administered usually over an extended period in food and drink
V: Her daughter Florinda (6 months) died 1990, husband Antonio (43) died 2004; daughter Sandra (14) died 2004
M: Motive for killing daughter Florinda unclear, motive for killing husband and daughter Sandra appears to be free to join a man she had met online
R: 'Adegüello' Reporter (2006); Ramos, 24 September 2005; 20 minutes, 21 September 2005.

[S52]
P: Charles Cullen, born 1960 in West Orange, New Jersey, US; graduated nursing school 1987, arrested 2003; confessed murdering thirty patients in hospitals in Pennsylvania and New Jersey over a sixteen-year period; sentenced **2006** to multiple life sentences **HSP**
PA: Digitoxin a heart drug by injection
V: Patients at hospitals in New Jersey and Pennsylvania
M: Cullen claimed easing suffering but contrary to this, some patients were not terminally ill
R: Daily Mail Reporter (2013)
N: Suspected of killing many more patients than those for whom he was convicted.

[S53]
P: Vickie Dawn Jackson, born 1966, in Indiana, US; family moved to Nocona, Texas; qualified as licenced vocational nurse, 2002 arrested and charged with murder, found guilty of 10 killings, **2006** VDJ made a no contest plea and sentenced to life imprisonment **HSP**
PA: Mivacurium chloride (Mivacron)
V: Between 2000 and 2001 patients at Nocona General Hospital all of whom died of respiratory arrest: Donnie Jennings (100) died 11 December; Elgie Hutson (87) died 20 December; Sanford Mitchell (62) died 20 December; Barbara Atteberry (50) died 24 December; Boyd Burnett (87) died 24 December
M: Possibly VDJ became vengeful towards patients when other nurses showed them compassion
R: Associated Press, 3 October 2006; Henderson (2002)
N: VDJ worked nightshift.

[S54]
P: Mohan Kumar, born 1963, India; worked as a teacher from 1980 to 2003, sentenced **2006**
PA: cyanide tablets given as supposed birth control pills
V: Anitha Barimar (22) from Barimaru in Bantwaltaluk; Lilavati Mistry (age not reported), Leela (second name not reported) (32) from Kodambettu in Belthangady Taluk; and Sunanda Pujari (32) of Peruvaje in Bellare village of Sullia Taluk
M: Financial gain and sexual gratification
R: Siddiqui (2016).

[S55]
P: Stephan Letter, born 1978, Herdecke, Westphalia, Germany; nurse, arrested 2004; found guilty of 16 counts of murdering patients and other crimes, **2006** sentenced to life imprisonment **HSP.**
PA: Drugs including the muscle relaxant succinylcholine chloride (as lysthenon)
V: Patients at a hospital in Sonthofen, Bavaria. Ages ranged from 40 to 94 but mainly in 70s
M: Although SL claimed he acted to end suffering, but some patients were in a stable condition when killed
R: Cleaver (2006).

[S56]
P: Viacheslav Soloviev, born 1971, Russia; lived in Yaroslavl, Central Russia; found guilty
And sentenced to life imprisonment **2008;** later that year found dead in his cell apparently from the long-term effects of experimenting on himself with poisons
PA: Thallium as a constituent of rat poison, administered in food
V: Six victims: wife Olga; Nastya (14) his daughter; Valery Shcherbakov a police investigator of a brawl involving VS; his common law wife Irina Astakhov died May 2005; a friend's grandmother Taisiya in late 2006; his sister Oksana's one-year-old child (in attempting to poison his sister and brother-in-law)

M: Partly an obsessive fascination with poisons which he administered over extended periods
R: Reuters/Sydney Morning Herald (2008), RIA Novosti (2008)
N: While awaiting trial VS attempted suicide.

[S57]
P: Colin Norris (Colin Campbell), born 1976, Glasgow, Scotland; nurse, sentenced **2008** for the murder of several patients **HSP**
PA: Insulin injections
V: Hospital patients in Leeds, England: Doris Ludlam (80), Bridget Bourke (86), Irene Crookes (79), and Ethel Hall (86) in 2002
M: Prosecution argued that Norris had a hatred of caring for elderly people
R Burns (2008), Campbell (2011)
N: In May 2013, the Criminal Cases Review Commission confirmed that they were re-examining the case in the context of new evidence.

[S58]
P: K. D. Kempanna (also known as Mallika), murdered victims 1999–2007, sentenced various dates in 2010, 2012 and **2013**
PA: Cyanide administered to women worshipers at various temples
V: Mamatha Rajan (30) at her home outside Bangalore, 19 October 1999. Then between 10 October and 18 December 2007; Muniyama (60), of Chikka Bommasandra murdered at Yediyur Siddalingshwara temple, Kunigal; Elizabeth, (52 or 61), of Banaswadi; Yashodamma (60) of Yelahanka; Pillamma (50 or 60), of Hebbal 17 December 2007; and Nagaveni, (30) a housewife from Allalasandra
M: Financial gain through robbery
R: Abraham (2017).

[S59]
P: Kimberley Clark Saenz, born 1973, tried 2012 for murders of 5 patients perpetrated in 2008; sentenced **2012** to life imprisonment without the possibility of parole **HSP**
PA: Sodium hypochlorite (bleach) injected into the dialysis lines of patients

V: Patients: Clara Strange, Thelma Metcalf, Garlin Kelley, Cora Bryant, and Opal Few
M: Unclear
R: Daily Mail Reporter, 31 March 2012; Fox News, 31 March 2012; Graczyk, M. / Associated Press (2015).

[S60]
P: Victorino Chua, born 1956, Philippines, nurse Stockport, UK; 2014 charged with murder; **2015** sentenced **HSP**
PA: Insulin introduced into saline bags by Chua and unwittingly administered by other nurses
V Patients Tracey Arden (44), and Derek Weaver (83)
M: Probably sadistic
R: Scheerhout (2015).

[S61]
P: Niels Högel, born 1975, Germany; nurse, 2008 convicted of attempted murder and sentenced to seven and a half years imprisonment; **2015**, convicted of murder of two intensive care patients and attempted murder of three others; life jail sentence. **HSP**
PA: Unauthorised drug injections overdoses of which can be fatal; included ajmaline, sotalol (Sotalex), lidocaine, amiodarone, and potassium chloride
V: Convicted of murdering two patients but highly suspected of killing many more
M: Possibly compulsively seeking thrills and excitement and the elation when resuscitating a patient
R: Oltermann (2017).

[S62]
P: Elizabeth Wettlaufer, born 1967, Ontario, Canada; nurse, 2016 charged with murder of eight patients, **2017** sentenced to imprisonment without parole for 25 years. **HSP**
PA: Insulin injections
V: Victims were at Caressant Care long-term care home in Woodstock, James Silcox (84) in 2007; and Maurice Granat (84), Gladys Millard

(87), Helen Matheson (95), Mary Zurawinski (96), Helen Young (90), and Maureen Pickering (79) in 2014. At Meadow Park facility, London, Ontario a further victim was Arpad Horvath (75)
M: Unclear
R: Associated Press, Woodstock, Ontario (2017), McQuigge (2017).

[S63]
P: Chisako Kakehi, born 1947, in Kyoto, Japan; December 2014, charged with death of her husband; Later charged with the murder of two common law partners; November **2017** sentenced to death
PA: Cyanide administered in a supposed health cocktail drink
V: Husband Isao Kakehi (75); Masanori Honda (71) common law partner; Minoru Hioki (75) between 2007 and 2013, also attempted murder of Toshiaki Suehiro (79)
M: Financial gain from inheritances to pay off CK debts
R: Reporter (7 November 2017)
N: Defence of incompetence owing to dementia failed.

References

ABC News. (2004, August 23). Vietnam to Try Alleged Serial Killer. http://www.abc.net.au/news/2004-08-23/vietnam-to-try-alleged-woman-serial-killer/2031066.
Abraham, B. (2017, February 18). Meet Cyanide Mallika India's First Woman Serial Killer…. *Times of India*. www.indiatimes.com/news/india/meet-cyanide-mallika-india-s-first-woman-serial-killer.
'Adegüello' Reporter. (2006). La envenadora de Melilla confiesa tres asesinatos. *Adegüello Crítica de Crímenes*. www.adeguello.net/ade04julio6.htm#veneno.
Associated Press. (1990, January 25). Nurse Gets 50 Years to Life. *Times Daily*.
Associated Press. (2006, October 3). Life Term for Ex-nurse in Patient Killings. *NBC News*. http://www.nbcnews.com/id/15119953/ns/us_news-crime_and_courts/t/life-term-ex-nurse-patient-killings/#.WgwGcWi0OM8.
Associated Press, Woodstock, Ontario. (2017, June 26). Former Nurse Who Killed Eight Elderly People in Her Care Gets Life in Prison. *The Guardian*. www.theguardian.com/world/2017/jun/26/canada-nurse-deaths-elizabeth-wettlaufer-prison-life.

Bahnsen, U. (2005, January 23). *Tod unterm Fallbeil – die Engelmacherin von St Pauli Die Welt*. www.welt.de/print-wams/article120605/Tod-unterm-Fallbeil-die-Engelmacherin-von-St-Pauli.

BBC News. (2004, August). Vietnamese Serial Killer on Trial. http://news.bbc.co.uk/1/hi/world/asia-pacific/3597358.stm.

BBC News. (2006, April 18). Nurse Guilty of Killing Patients (Updated).

Bridge, A. (1996, January 21). Fatal Games of the 'Black Widow'. *Independent*. www.independent.co.uk/news/world/fatal-games-of-the-black-widow-1325010.

Bryant, E. (2003, January 31). Nurse Sentenced for Killing Patients. *United Press International*. www.upi.com/Business_News/Security-Industry/2003/01/31/Nurse-sentenced-for-killing-patients/UPI-96721044036550/.

Buhk, T. T. (2014). *Poisoning the Peck of Grand Rapids: The Scandalous 1916 Murder Plot*. Charleston, SC: The History Press.

Burns, J. (2008, March 4). Death Spree of Serial Killer Nurse Colin Norris. *Daily Record*.

Campbell, D. (2011, October 4). 'Angel of Death' Colin Norris Could Be Cleared of Insulin Murders. *The Guardian*.

Cleaver, H. (2006, February 8). Angel of Death 'Driven by Kindness'. *The Telegraph*.

Cole, C. (2016, September 26). *Nannie Doss: The Femme Fatale Next Door*. http://www.americas-most-haunted.com/2016/09/26/nannie-doss-the-femme-fatale-next-door/.

Connell, R. (2011, March 28). Dorothea Puente Dies at 82: Boarding House Operator Who Killed Tenants. *Los Angeles Times*.

Dupke, D. (2009, January 23). Stadt Kempen Giftmörderin im Fernsehen. *RP Online* (in German).

Daily Mail Reporter. (2012, March 31). Nurse Faces Death Penalty After Being Found Guilty of Killing Five Patients by Injecting IV Lines with Bleach. *Mail Online*. http://www.dailymail.co.uk/news/article-2123252/Nurse-Kimberly-Saenz-faces-death-penalty-murdering-patients-bleach.html.

Daily Mail Reporter. (2013, April 29). 'Angel of Death' Nurse Who Murdered at Least 40 Patients to Become One of America's Worst Serial Killers Speaks from Prison for the First Time to Chillingly Claim: 'I Thought I Was Helping'. *Mail Online*.

Emsley, J. (2005). *The Elements of Murder: A History of Poison*. Oxford: Oxford University Press.

Ephemeral New York. (2015). *Serial Killer Frederick Mors*. https://ephemeralnewyork.wordpress.com/tag/serial-killer-frederick-mors/.

Farragher, T. (2000, October 8). Death on Ward C: Caregiver or Killer. *The Boston Globe Online*. http://cache.boston.com/globe/metro/packages/nurse/part1.htm.

Farrell, M. (1992). *Poisons and Poisoners: An Encyclopaedia of Homicidal Poisonings*. London: Robert Hale.

Farrell, M. (1993a, March 19). What's Your Poison? *Solicitors Journal*.

Farrell, M. (1993b). Death Certification and Neil Cream's Murder of Matilda Clover. *The Criminologist, 17*(4), 237–241.

Farrell, M. (1994). The Murders of Mary Wilson. *Justice of the Peace, 158*(32), 523–525.

Fox News. (2012, March 31). *Texas Nurse Convicted in Bleach Deaths Case*. http://www.foxnews.com/us/2012/03/31/texas-nurse-convicted-in-bleach-deaths-case.html.

Garton, S. (1996). Grills, Caroline. In *Australian Dictionary of Biography* (Vol. 14). Carlton, VIC: Melbourne University Publishing.

Gibson, D. C. (2010). *Serial Killing for Profit: Multiple Murder for Money* (pp. 68–79). Santa Barbara, CA: Praeger.

Glaister, J. (1954). *The Power of Poison*. London: C. Johnson.

Graczyk, M. / Associated Press. (2015, Novewmber 14). Nurse's Bleach Injection Deaths Trial Begins. *KIMATV*. http://kimatv.com/news/nation-world/nurses-bleach-injection-deaths-trial-begins-11-14-2015-230029540.

Hanna, J. (1999, November 16). Ex-nurse Gets Maximum Term in Hospital Killings. *Chicago Tribune*. http://articles.chicagotribune.com/1999-11-16/news/9911160161_1_vermillion-county-hospital-orville-lynn-majors-hospital-killings and www.law.justia.com/cases/indiana/supreme-court/2002/08140201-rts.

Harvey, G. (2014, August 19). Nannie Doss. *Encyclopaedia of Alabama*. www.encyclopediaofalabama.org/article/h-3619.

Henderson, J. (2002, July 18). Nocona Seeks Pattern Linking Nurse to Deaths. *Houston Chronicle*.

Heppenstall, R. (1970). *French Crime in the Romantic Age*. London: Hamish Hamilton.

Hickey, E. (2010). *Serial Murderers and Their Victims* (5th ed.). Belmont, CA: Wadsworth.

Jackson, D., & Pittman, H. (2015, August 27). Throwback Tulsa: Charming, Friendly Nannie Doss Poisoned Four Husbands. *Tulsa World*. www.tulsaworld.com/blogs/news/throwbacktulsa/throwback-tulsa-charming-friendly-nannie-doss-poisoned-four-husbands/article.

Kellerher, M. D., & Kellerher, C. L. (1998). *Murder Most Rare: The Female Serial Killer*. Westport, CT: Praeger.

Lange, E. (2015). *Veuve Becker – La Grande Serial Killer de Tous les Temps*. La Boîte à Pandore.

Leidig, M. (2001, April 21). The Black Widow Is Guilty of Two More Murders. *The Telegraph*. www.telegraph.co.uk/news/worldnews/europe/austria/1316893/The-Black-Widow-is-guilty-of-two-more-murders.

Lieberman, P. (2002, April 18). Hospital 'Angle of Death' Gets Life Without Parole. *Los Angeles Times*. http://articles.latimes.com/2002/apr/18/news/mn-38536.

Maeder, T. (1980). *The Unspeakable Crimes of Dr Petiot*. Boston, MA: Little, Brown.

Martinez, E. (2010, August 31). Antifreeze Killer Lynn Turner Dies in Prison. *CBS News*. www.cbsnews.com/news/antifreeze-killer-lynn-turner-dies-in-prison.

McQuigge, M. (2017, June 2). If You Ever Do This Again, We'll Turn You in Pastor Tells Killer Nurse. *The Canadian Press*. www.thestar.com/news/canada/2017/06/02/if-you-ever-do-this-again-well-turn-you-in-pastor-told-killer-nurse.html.

Metroland News Service. (2013, November 22). Hamilton Serial Killer Sukhwinder Dies in Prison. *Toronto Metro*.

20 Minutes. (2005, September 21). La 'envenadora' se contradice sobre la muerte de su marido y dice que no quiso matar a sus hijas. http://www.20minutos.es/noticia/49407/0/envenenadora/juicio/melilla/.

Moerman, I. ([1985] 2013). Swanenburg, Maria Catherina 1839–1915. In *Biographical Dictionary of the Netherlands*. Huygens: The Hague. resources.huygens.knaw.nl/bwn1880-2000/lemmata/bwn2/swanenburg.

Oltermann, P. (2017, August 28). German Nurse Suspected of Murdering at Least 90 Patients. *The Guardian*. www.theguardian.com/world/2017/aug/28/german-nurse-niels-hoegel-suspected-murdering-90-patients.

Payne, S. (2006, April 19). Guilty of Murder: The Nurse Who Got His Kicks from Life-or-Death Drama. *The Telegraph*.

Peters, C. (2005/2006). *Harold Shipman: Mind Set on Murder—Why Shipman Killed and Killed Again—The True Story*. London: André Deutsch.

Popper, J. (n.d.). A Darkness 'Round the Bend'. www.berthagifford.com.

Quotidien Le Gaulois. (1874, September 11). Moreau – L'Herboriste de Saint-Denis (Source: gallica.bnf.fr).

Ramos, T. (2005, September 24). La fiscal eleva la pena para la 'envenenadora de Melilla' a 84 años. *El País*. https://elpais.com/diario/2005/09/24/espana/1127512820_850215.html.

Reporter. (1866, January 20). The American Borgia. *New York Times*. http://query.nytimes.com/gst/abstract.html?res=980DEFD71F3EEF34B-C4851DFB766838D679FDE&legacy=true.

Reporter. (1884, May 11). Marie Jeanneret's Death-Grim Facts in the Career of this Famous Poisoner. *New York Times*, p. 5 (Reprinted from *The London Daily News*).

Reporter. (1886, August 9). Execution of a Woman Today. *The Echo*.

Reporter. (1888, November 29). Philadelphia's Borgia. *St Paul Daily Globe*. www.philadelphiaspeaks.com/threads/philadelphia-stories.40236/.

Reporter. (1902, July 27). Poison Her Passion. *The Clinton Morning Age*. www.news.google.com/newspapers?nid=2267&dat=19020727&id=6nc-mAAAAIBAJ&sjid=CgEGAAAAIBAJ&pg=4194,996821&hl=en.

Reporter. (1909a, June 24). Woman Kills 300 at Wives' Behest. *The Stanstead Journal* (Canada).

Reporter. (1909b, March 25). Woman Murdered 300. *The Coffeyville Daily Journal* (Kansas).

Reporter. (1925, April 28). Woman Remorseless After Taking Eight Relatives' Lives by Poison. *The Sioux City Journal*.

Reporter. (1952, May 20). Woman Charged with Murder of Two Husbands. *Sydney Morning Herald*.

Reporter. (1984, April 12). Nurse Sentenced to Die in Slayings. *New York Times*.

Reporter. (1992, April 10 Friday). Nurse Pleads Guilty to Killing Three Patients. *New York Times*. www.nytimes.com/1992/04/10/us/nurse-pleads-guilty-to-killing-three-patients.html.

Reporter. (1999, May 16). Death Penalty Sought in Patients' Deaths. *Los Angeles Times*.

Reporter. (2005, June 28). Hace veinte años condenaban a la 'envenenadora de Monserrat'. *Clarín (Noticias)*. www.clarin.com/ediciones-anteriores/hace-veinte-anos-condenaban-envenenadora-monserrat_0_Hk7GWtd10Yl.html.

Reporter. (2007, June 23). Mujer Envenenadora: Yiya Murano. *eMujer.com* (in Spanish). https://www.emujer.com/mujer-envenenadora-yiya-murano/.

Reporter. (2017, November 7). Japan's 'Black Widow' Serial Killer Gets Death Sentence. *The Japan Times*.

Reuters/Sydney Morning Herald. (2008, April 10). Poisoner Killed Family for Fun. *Sydney Morning Herald*. http://www.smh.com.au/news/world/poisoner-killed-family-for-fun/2008/04/10/1207420526584.html.

RIA Novosti. (2008, April 9). Trial of Rat Poison Killer Suspended in Central Russia. *Sputnik International*. https://sputniknews.com/russia/20080409104192288/.

Roughhead, W. (Ed.). (1906). *Trial of Dr Pritchard*. Edinburgh: William Hodge.

Scheerhout, J. (2015, May 18). Did Killer Nurse Victorina Chua Pay Someone to Pass His Nursing Exam? *Manchester Evening News* (Updated).

Siddiqui, I. (2016, October 9). Prof Mohan Kumar, the Man Who Killed 20 Women with 'Anti-pregnancy Pills'. *Bangalore Mirror*. www.bangaloremirror.indiatimes.com/bangalore/cover-story//articleshow/54758093.cms.

Stewart, J. B. (1999). *Blind Eye: How the Medical Establishment Let a Doctor Get Away with Murder*. New York: Simon & Schuster.

Trestrail, J. H. (2007). *Criminal Poisoning: Investigational Guide for Law Enforcement, Toxicologists, Forensic Scientists and Attorneys* (2nd ed.). Totowa, NJ: Humana Press.

United Press International. (1986, March 31). Suspected Nurse Had History of Mental Illness. *Orlando Sentinel*.

Vinter, P. (2006, November 24). Killer Nurse—The Full Story. *Oxford Mail*.

Wells, J. (2009). *Poison: From Steeltown to the Punjab—The True Story of a Serial Killer*. Ontario, Canada: Wiley.

White, J. W. (2007, October). Lyles, Anjette Donovan. *American National Biography Online* (Update). http://www.anb.org/articles/20/20-01888.html.

Wilson, C., & Seaman, D. (1983). *Encyclopaedia of Modern Murder: 1962–1982*. London: Barker.

9

Profiles of Selected Serial Poisoning Cases

[P1] Dr. Harold Shipman, UK

Sentenced 2000

Physician Dr. Harold Shipman (born 1946) in England was the UKs most prolific serial killer. A public enquiry deemed him responsible for about 250 murders of his patients from 1970 to the 1990s mainly using morphine-based drugs. He committed suicide in prison in 2004.

He married at age 19 and the union lasted throughout Shipman's life. Graduating medical school aged 25, Shipman worked in hospitals for several years. Entering general practice in 1974, he worked in Todmorden until 1979 when colleagues discovered that he had been dishonestly obtaining controlled drugs (pethidine) for his own use. He pleaded guilty in court to drugs charges. The following year, he became a General Practitioner at the Donnybrook practice in Hyde, near Manchester. Having left this practice in January 1992, Shipman worked as a sole practitioner in the same building. In October, he moved to a surgery nearby, again as a sole practitioner. For many he was a well-liked and respected physician.

From a practice in Hyde, in March 1998, Dr. Linda Reynolds raised concerns with the South Manchester Coroner about the number of Shipman's patients who were dying and the circumstances. Greater Manchester Police conducted a confidential investigation, concluding that there was no substance in Dr. Reynolds' concerns, After the investigation ended on 17 April 1998, Shipman killed three more patients before being arrested.

Shipman patient Kathleen Grundy (81) died at home in 1998. Her daughter, solicitor Angela Woodruff, was suspicious to find that her mother's will which she knew had left her estate to near relatives had been changed to favour Shipman shortly before Kathleen's death. Woodruff reported this to the police. Greater Manchester Police searched Shipman's surgery and home. Kathleen's body was exhumed, revealing unexpectedly high levels of morphine. Police examined 19 deaths implicated in the investigation in March and further bodies were exhumed showing the presence of morphine. Examination of Shipman's computerised medical records showed evidence of tampering to hide the real cause of death by morphine. Shipman was arrested and charged with murder.

In 1999, Shipman pleaded 'not guilty' to 15 counts of murder. Found guilty on all counts, he was given a prison term of 15 life sentences. No further criminal proceedings were proposed, it being considered impossible for Shipman to have a fair trial.

Between August 2000 and April 2001, inquests into 27 deaths of Shipman's patients, recorded verdicts of unlawful killing in 25 and open verdicts in 2. In May 2001, inquests into a further 232 deaths were opened, then immediately adjourned, pending the findings of a public inquiry. This inquiry was established in 2001 ultimately judging that Shipman murdered about 250 patients between 1971 and 1998, of whom it was able positively to identify 218. The typical method of killing was by a lethal dose of an opiate (usually diamorphine).

Reference

Peters, C. (2006). *Harold Shipman: Mind Set on Murder—Why Shipman Killed and Killed Again—The True Story*. London: André Deutsch.

Points of Special Interest

Regarding location, Shipman's victims were all from the area of his practices. All were his patients and they were usually killed in their residence where Shipman was making a 'home visit'. Typically, the patient would be alone, and would not resist being injected, assuming this was part of their treatment.

The age range of victims—the youngest 41-year-old Peter Lewis and the oldest 93-year-old Ann Cooper, conceals that they were mostly in their 70s, 80s and 90s. As such, often relative might be expecting their deaths. Most victims were women—about four times as many as men among killings positively identified—perhaps reflecting the greater preponderance of women among elderly populations. There appeared to be no selection of victims according to any social, occupational, or ethnic pattern.

Shipman's use of morphine-based drugs to kill was masked. As a physician, he legitimately used such drugs. Shipman subverted death certification procedures, sometimes harshly dismissing concerns of relatives. When suspicions were eventually raised, police officers involved in the inquiry lacked experience, and the advising doctor seemed naive. Speculation about why Shipman committed his crimes include a warped sense of doing society a service by reducing the burden on the health system, or that taking on the role of arbiter of life and death gave him satisfaction. His modus operandi was in his terms highly successful and as time passed he likely became more confident and skilled in judging when and how he could get away with killing.

[P2] Dr. Michael Swango, US

Sentenced 2000

The Case

Born in 1954 and raised in Quincy, Illinois, US, Michael Swango attended Quincy University, then studied at the Southern Illinois University School of Medicine. Just before graduation, authorities discovered that he had faked check-ups during his clinical clerkship. Given a second chance, he graduated a year later.

Dr. Swango gained a year's surgical internship at Ohio State University Medical Center in 1983. Concerned over Swango's sloppy work, the university withdrew a post-internship residency in neurosurgery. Five of Swango's assigned patients seemingly died in suspicious circumstances. In 1984, Swango worked in Quincy as an ambulance corps emergency medical technician. Paramedics fell ill when Swango prepared them food, and police arresting Swango found arsenic on him. In 1985, he was convicted of aggravated battery for poisoning co-workers and imprisoned for four years.

He next worked as a counsellor in Newport Virginia, then as a laboratory technician. At Riverside Hospital, Swango met and got engaged to nurse Kristen Kinney. In 1991, he legally changed his name to Daniel Adams and in 1992 began working at Sanford Medical Centre, South Dakota, forging legal documents to do so. When he attempted to join the American Medical Association, a background check uncovered Swango's poisoning conviction and he was fired. Kristen Kinney returned to Virginia soon after.

Swango joined a psychiatric residency programme at the Stoney Brook School of Medicine, doing a rotation in 1993 at the Veterans Affairs Medical Center, Northport, New York. His patients began dying unaccountably. Soon after, Swango's former fiancé Kristin Kinney committed suicide and arsenic was found in her body. Circuitously, Stoney Brook became aware Swango's poison conviction and he was fired.

The FBI discovered in 1994 that Swango was working as a company chemist and informed the company who, finding that Swango had fabricated his job application, fired him. Furthermore, the FBI gained a warrant charging Swango for forging credentials to get a job at the Veterans Affairs Hospital. However, Swango had already left the US.

In November 1994, using forged documents, Swango obtained a hospital post in Zimbabwe, but was suspended following suspicious patient deaths. Swango was renting a room in Bulawayo where his landlady fell sick after eating a meal he prepared. She consulted a local physician, Michael Cotton who suspected arsenic poisoning and had hair samples analysed confirming this. The FBI heard of the laboratory reports and had agents visit Zimbabwe to interview Cotton and others. Swango moved to Namibia doing temporary medical work and was charged in his absence with the poisonings.

Using a false resume, Swango applied for medical post in Saudi Arabia in March 1997. Meanwhile, FBI staff contacted the Veterans Affairs Office to discuss holding Swango. This led Swango's arrest in June 1997 at Chicago Airport bound for Saudi Arabia. In 1998, pleading guilty to defrauding the government, Swango was sentenced to imprisonment.

In July 2000, just prior to his release from prison, federal prosecutors charged Swango on three counts of murder, while Zimbabwean authorities charged him with murder. In September 2000, Swango pleaded guilty to three murders at the Veterans Hospital in Northport, New York. The victims, all patients who died of lethal injections, were: Thomas Sammarco, 73, George Siano, 60, and Aldo Serini. Prosecutors read passages from Swango's notebook describing the pleasure he felt while committing the crimes. Swango was incarcerated for three consecutive life terms.

References

Leduff, C. (2000, September 6). Man to Admit to Murdering Three L. I. Patients. *New York Times*. www.nytimes.com/2000/09/06/nyregion/man-to-admit-to-murdering-3-li-patients.

Stewart, J. B. (1999). *Blind Eye: How the Medical Establishment Let a Doctor Get Away with Murder*. New York: Simon and Schuster.

Points of Special Interest

Serial murderers need continuing strategies to avoid detection. For Swango these included (legally) changing his name, forging documents enabling him to work despite his criminal record, and moving from the US to Zimbabwe. Before any suspicions of murder, Swango had broken regulations by faking check-ups during his clinical clerkship.

It is unclear what was Swango's earliest murder. Stewart (1999) suggests that if one includes the unaccountable deaths at Ohio State University Medical Center in 1983, circumstantial evidence links Swango with 35 suspicious deaths. Alternatively, Swango's first involvement with poisons may have been in 1985, when convicted of aggravated battery of co-workers. Following his imprisonment, this escalated into poison murder during Swango's 1993 rotation at the Veterans Affairs Medical Center in Northport. He was found guilty of three murders there and may have committed more. Evidence also pointed to Swango murdering while in Zimbabwe.

[P3] Elfriede Blauensteiner, Austria

Sentenced 1997 and 2001

The Case

Elfriede Blauensteiner, was born in Vienna in January 1931. It appears she had an impoverished childhood and in later life aspired to be wealthy. She married several times.

Reports do not give the name of her first husband, when they married and what happened afterwards. It is speculated that her first killing may have been in 1981 and the victim may have been Erwin Niedermeyer the janitor of a building where she lived. Elfriede's second husband was Rudolph Blauensteiner who died in August 1992. Her third spouse was a retired man Friedrick Doecker who died in 1995 aged 64.

In 1995, Elfriede Blauensteiner met Alois Pichler aged 77 through a newspaper personal column advertisement where she presented herself as a caring companion. He died soon after. Autopsy showed fatal levels of the antidepressant Anafrinil and traces of euglucon a medication used to lower blood sugar levels in diabetes. Elfriede was arrested in January 1996 and charged with Alois Pichler's murder. Her former lawyer Harald Schmidt was charged with being an accomplice to grievous bodily harm and for forging Pichler's will.

In March 1997, at the court in Krems 30 miles from Vienna, Elfriede Blauensteiner seemed to bask in the attention, posing before the press holding up a golden crucifix. State prosecutor Friederich Kutschera affirmed that Elfriede had put numerous doses of euglucon in the deceased's milk to lower his blood sugar levels. Convicted of murder, the accused was given a life prison sentence in the Schwarzau am Steinfelde prison in Vienna. Her former lawyer was found guilty and imprisoned for colluding with Blauensteiner in forging the victim's will in her favour.

Following Elfriede's conviction, the bodies of two more suspected victims, former neighbour Franziska Koeberl and third husband Friedrick Doecker were exhumed. Evidence of euglucon was detected in the bodies. Neighbour Franziska Koeberl (aged 84) had given Blauensteiner her savings book in 1992. She died soon after with low blood sugar levels. Friedrick Doecker had died in 1995 soon after he had transferred the ownership of his house to Elfriede. Cause of death had been given at the time as cardiovascular failure and pneumonia. In 2001, Blauensteiner was charged and convicted of murder in connection with these two further deaths.

Police suspected that the accused may have committed more murders. It is believed that she committed her crimes to enable her to finance an obsessive gambling habit. She would frequent the roulette tables at Baden. Still serving her sentence, Elfriede Blauensteiner died in a Vienna hospital of a brain tumour in 2003 aged 72 years.

References

Bridge, A. (1996, January 21). Fatal Games of the 'Black Widow'. *Independent.* www.independent.co.uk/news/world/fatal-games-of-the-black-widow-1325010.

Leidig, M. (2001, April 21). The Black Widow is Guilty of Two More Murders. *The Telegraph.* www.telegraph.co.uk/news/worldnews/europe/austria/1316893/The-Black-Widow-is-guilty-of-two-more-murders.

Points of Special Interest

The two dates of sentencing of 1997 and 2001 reflect the fact that Elfriede Blauensteiner was originally found guilty of a single murder. Further investigations, while the prisoner was serving her sentence for this, revealed further killings, for which she was tried and found guilty. Blauensteiner counts as one of the older perpetrators of poisoning. If she did kill janitor Erwin Niedermeyer she would have been 50-years-old at the time. If her first murder was that of former neighbour Franziska Koeberl in 1992, Blauensteiner would have been 61-years-old. When first convicted the perpetrator was 66 years old.

The motive for these crimes is generally agreed to be financial gain to feed a gambling habit and a good lifestyle. Her victims and alleged victims were all men with the single exception of her former neighbour Franziska Koeberl. With Koeberl the motive was financial gain but through having the victim transfer her savings to Elfriede Blauensteiner before her death. If it is true that an early victim was Erwin Niedermeyer the janitor of a building in which she lived, it is unclear what the motive was and whether it involved financial gain. By some reports, Blauensteiner is supposed to have said that she killed him because he mistreated his family.

[P4] Sukhwinder Singh Dhillon, Canada

Sentenced 2001

The Case

In the province of Ontario, Canada, Stoney Creek is a community on south shore of Lake Ontario. It lies just east of Hamilton and in 2001 was amalgamated with that city. Sukhwinder Singh Dhillon, of Sikh origin, was a car salesman in Stoney Creek and lived in the Riverdale neighbourhood where Hamilton meets Stoney Creek.

On 3 February 1995, in Hamilton, Sukhwinder Singh Dhillon poisoned his 36-year-old wife Parvesh Kaur Dhillon with strychnine for insurance money. He collected $300,000. Her death was believed to be from natural causes. Following that murder, Sukhwinder returned to his native Punjab an area covering part of eastern Pakistan and part of northern India. (He had been born in Ludhiana in the North-Eastern part of India.) In Punjab, he married three women and collected their dowries. Police believed that Sukhwinder had two sons by one of those wives Sarabjit Kaur Brar and killed both infants at the age of 12 days. They also believed that he poisoned another of these wives, Kushwinderpreet Kaur Toor. Back in Canada, on 23 June 1996, Sukhwinder poisoned Ranjit Singh Khela, his friend and business associate and fellow resident of the Riverdale neighbourhood. Khela aged 25 was poisoned with strychnine for insurance money. Death was thought to be from natural causes. Sukhwinder put in a claim for $200,000.

At this point, given that Sukhwinder was a beneficiary in both the policies of Parvesh Kaur Dhillon and of Ranjit Singh Khela, the insurance company began investigations. Claims investigator Cliff Elliot contacted the police. This led to Hamilton detectives Warren Korol and Kevin Dhinsa (a native of India) visiting Ludhiana and various remote villages in the Punjab. Forensic investigations indicated that the poison used by Dhillon was strychnine that he may have bought as kulcha seeds in a Punjabi market and brought back to Canada.

In October 1997, Dhillon was arrested. A year later a mistrial was declared when it emerged that witnesses from India were imposters. However, in July 2001, he was convicted of the murder of his wife Parvesh Kaur Dhillon. In December, he was convicted of the murder of his business associate Ranjit Singh Khela.

He was given a twenty-year sentence and imprisoned in Warkworth Institution, Ontario. He became ill apparently with cancer and was transferred to Kingston Hospital, Toronto, where he died in May 2013 aged 54 years.

References

Metroland News Service. (2013, November 22). Hamilton Serial Killer Sukhwinder Dies in Prison. *Toronto Metro*.

Wells, J. (2009). *Poison: From Steeltown to the Punjab—The True Story of a Serial Killer*. Ontario, Canada: Wiley.

Points of Special Interest

Sukhwinder Singh Dhillon was convicted of two murders that took place in Canada and was suspected of perpetrating other murders in the Punjab. If the suspected murders did take place they reflect the adjustment of an offender to the social values of different settings. Accepting that Dhillon's motive was financial gain, he used the vehicle of life insurance in Canada and the source of the traditional dowry in the Punjab.

Conversant with the tendency that homicide is perpetrated intraracially Dhillon murdered members of his own ethnic group, his wife and a business associate and possibly a Punjabi wife and new-born infants. A cultural aspect also facilitated his being able to acquire poison. If Dhillon bought the strychnine as seeds in a market on a visit to the Punjab as it is believed, he avoided the possibility of the purchase being traced in the same was that it might have been if he had tried to purchase strychnine in Canada. In a similar way and for similar reasons Indian Lakvir Singh who killed her lover Lakhvinder 'Lucky' Cheema in London, UK with aconite had travelled to India to procure it (Farrell 2017, pp. 19–21).

The Hamilton Spectator newspaper published a series of articles about the case which led to a book *Poison* by Jon Wells.

[P5] Kristen Gilbert, US

Sentenced 2000

The Case

Kristen Gilbert (nee Stickland) was born in 1967 in Fall River, Massachusetts, US. In her teenage years and subsequently, she had a history of making violent threats to others and other problems. Graduating high school at 16, she attended Greenfield Community College, Massachusetts where she gained a nursing diploma and became a registered nurse in 1988. That same year, she married Glen Gilbert and began working at the Veteran Affairs Medical Centre, Northampton, Mass. where she appeared to fit in well.

She gave birth to a son in 1990 and returned to work, on the evening and night shift. In 1993, she gave birth to a second son. In 1996, colleagues noticed that there was a shortage of the heart stimulant epinephrine (synthetic adrenaline) and reported their concerns about the increase in patients' deaths owing to cardiac arrest. An investigation was initiated. During the investigation and apparently to distract it, Gilbert telephoned the hospital with a fake bomb threat. She left the hospital while the investigation was continuing and checked herself into a sequence of psychiatric hospitals for short periods. In January 1996, she stood trial for making the bomb threat and was convicted in April.

In 1998, Kristen Gilbert was charged with murder. Patients whom Kristen Gilbert killed were Stanley Jagodowski (65), Henry Hudon (35), Kenneth Cutting (41), Edward Skwira (69). Prosecutor William Walsh stated that Gilbert used emergency situations to get the attention of James Perrault who worked for hospital security and who at the time or later became her boyfriend. (It was a rule of the hospital that hospital police be present at an emergency.) James Perrault testified against Kirsten Gilbert and stated that she had admitted one of the murders to him by telephone while being treated in a psychiatric hospital. For the defence, David Hoose pointed to the lack of direct evidence. In March 2001, she was convicted on three counts of first degree murder, one count of second degree murder, and two counts of attempted murder. There were calls for the death penalty to be handed down including from prosecution lawyers and some relatives of victims. In the event, Kristen Gilbert was sentenced to life imprisonment and is incarcerated in the Federal Medical Center, Fort Worth, Texas.

References

Farragher, T. (2000, October 8). Death on Ward C: Caregiver or Killer. *The Boston Globe Online.* http://cache.boston.com/globe/metro/packages/nurse/part1.htm.

Reporter. (1999, May 16). Death Penalty Sought in Patients' Deaths. *Los Angeles Times*.

Points of Special Interest

Evidence of Gilbert's past disturbed behaviour was apparent for some time before the killings took place. A vivid example during the investigation was her attempt to distract the investigation by making a bomb threat to the hospital where she had worked. Eventually, the number of deaths that took place during her shifts attracted attention and at trial the evidence of James Perrault that she had admitted to at least one murder contributed to the case against Gilbert.

Defence lawyer David Hoose raised the issue of the lack of direct evidence. This needs to be taken into consideration by the court as direct evidence can be the more compelling. However, it is sometimes the case in poison killings that circumstantial evidence is more forthcoming. This is partly because when poison killing is perpetrated potential witnesses may not realise that a crime is being perpetrated. Some co-workers are said to speculate that Gilbert was responsible for many more deaths than those for which she was convicted and was implicated in many more medical emergencies.

Regarding sentencing the state of Massachusetts does not have capital punishment. However, there are exceptions for crimes committed on federal property which they were in Kirsten Gilbert's case. In fact, the jury recommended imprisonment.

[P6] Efren Saldivar, US

Sentenced 2002

The Case

Efren Saldivar, was born in 1969, in Brownsville, Texas where his parents had moved from Mexico. The family later moved to Los Angeles.

In high school, his grades deteriorated and he failed to graduate. He worked in a supermarket from which it is said he stole items. Having a friend who attended the College of Medical and Dental Careers in North Hollywood, Saldivar decided to follow similar studies. He took and passed the high school equivalency test and duly enrolled in the College from which he graduated following a year's course in 1988 at the age of 19.

He was a respiratory therapist at Glendale Adventist Medical Center for ten years. Substantial suspicions arose in 1997 when co-workers broke into his locker a part of a practical joke and discovered drugs including morphine, suxamethonium chloride, and Panuronium (Pavulon) (used to arrest a patient's respiration when they are about to be put on a ventilator). Saldivar was not entitled to be in possession of these. A year later this information had leaked and come to the attention of Grant Brossus a man with a criminal record. He attempted to blackmail the hospital by threatening to publicise the facts. In response, the hospital informed the police and held their own investigation.

Questioned by police, Saldivar confessed to perpetrating 50 murders, stating that the first was a patient with terminal cancer murdered in 1988 when Saldivar was 19 years old. He later retracted the confessions. Finding no drugs in Saldivar's home police released him without charge. In March 1998, based on their own enquiries the hospital terminated Salvidar's medical employment. Police arranged for the exhumation of 20 bodies of patients who had died under Salvidar's care and had been buried, seeking higher than expected levels of Pavulon. Six bodies indicated that lethal levels of the drug had been present. The victims were: Salbi Asatryan aged 75 (December 1996); Eleanora Schlegel, 77, Jose Alfaro, 82 and Luina Schidlowski, 87 all in January 1997; and Balbino Castro, 87 and Myrtle Brower, 84 both in August 1997.

By January 2001 police had a case against Saldivar. In March 2002, Salvidar entered a plea of guilty to these six counts of murder. Receiving six consecutive life sentences without the possibility of parole, Salvidar is incarcerated in Salinas Valley State Prison, California. There is speculation that the number of deaths caused by Salvidar could be much higher than the six for which he was convicted.

Working night shift where fewer staff were on duty than during the day, Salvidar killed patients by injecting them with a drug which caused respiratory arrest or cardiac failure. Panuronium (Pavulon) was one of these drugs. It is suspected that Salvidar may have also used morphine and suxamethonium chloride. His victims tended to be unconscious and close to death so that it was not possible to clearly discern an increase in death when he was on duty. Detecting such a pattern provides one indication that there may be malpractice.

Reference

Lieberman, P. (2002, April 18). Hospital 'Angle of Death' Gets Life Without Parole. *Los Angeles Times*. http://articles.latimes.com/2002/apr/18/news/mn-38536.

Points of Special Interest

The evasions or safeguards that Salvidar used included his working on night shift where fewer staff were on duty and he would calculate that there was less chance of being detected. He seems to have chosen patients who were close to death so that the death rates when he was on duty would not be markedly different from other times. He chose drugs with which he was familiar through his training and experience and which would cause respiratory and heart failure which would be put down as expected death.

The forensic checking for Pavulon rather than for other drugs that might have been used relates to the fact that it can be detected in remains for a longer period after death.

Although it is prudent to be careful about the numbers of murders claimed by an offender and others without clear evidence, there are indications that is Saldivar's case the numbers may have been higher than the six for which he was convicted. If it is correct that Saldivar committed his first murder in 1988, it is possible he committed murders in the intervening period. The bodies that were exhumed and contained evidence Pavulon were ones where indications of a drug could be found and pointed to several killings in the months of January and August 1997.

[P7] Lê Thanh Vân, Vietnam

Sentenced 2003

The Case

Born in 1956, in Vietnam, Lê Thanh Vân married a businessman and they subsequently had two children. She did a year of training in the army medical corps which gave her some knowledge of poisons. In 1993, Vân was arrested and jailed for fraud. In July 2000, she was again arrested on suspicion of the poison murder of a married couple to steal their minivan but no evidence of poisoning was found in the bodies.

It was eight years later, in August 2001, Lê Thanh Vân was arrested and charged with murder. She confessed to 13 killings. Between January 1998 and August 2001 police alleged that she murdered these people by administering cyanide to them in food and drinks. She often took victims to hospital after poisoning them to try to cover up her involvement.

Victims included her mother in law, brother in law, foster mother, lovers, and acquaintances. After the victims died, she forged their wills and other documents to steal their possessions. She is also said to have stolen goods from victims such as a motorcycle and told families after the victim died that she had bought the item from them previously. In this way, she appropriated Vietnamese Dong to the value of about $15,000 as well as items of electronic equipment. Victims came from Ho Chi Minh City, and the provinces of Binh Duong, Binh Phuoc, and Dong Nai. Vân identified wealthy people and gained their confidence until she could persuade them to accept food and drinks containing cyanide. She also murdered relatives. She is said to have poisoned her mother in law and her brother in law because of family conflicts.

Lê Thanh Vân was tried in August 2003 at the People's Court at the southern province Binh Duong on charges of murder, robbery, and the illegal possession of toxic chemicals. Found guilty, following the eight-day trial, Van was given the death penalty. Her 31-year-old 'husband without a licence' was found guilty of the murder of a motor bike taxi driver and jailed for 21 years. In September 2004, an appeal against the death sentence failed. The People's Supreme Court in Ho Chi Minh City upheld the earlier verdict.

References

ABC News. (2004, August 23). *Vietnam to Try Alleged Serial Killer.* http://www.abc.net.au/news/2004-08-23/vietnam-to-try-alleged-woman-serial-killer/2031066.

BBC News. (2004, August). *Vietnamese Serial Killer on Trial.* http://news.bbc.co.uk/1/hi/world/asia-pacific/3597358.stm.

Points of Special Interest

Details are limited for this case and what is available tends to repeat the same information. It would be useful to have further evidence from local sources, but even with the small amount of detail available a few tentative points arise. The range of people reported to be poisoned is wide and include relatives and acquaintances. The same modus operandi appears to emerge of poisoning a victim, apparently seeking to help them by taking them to hospital, and forging papers to gain valuables.

If this is so, there must have been a risk that hospital authorities would have noticed the repeated appearance of Lê Thanh Vân with ill people. The motive of financial gain also appears consistent across the different victims which also might have arouse suspicion earlier. However, it seems that Vân murdered people in different geographical areas which might have decreased chances of the authorities joining the dots if they did not communicate the crime with each other. Lê Thanh

Vân is said to have forged will and related documents to gain financially from the deaths of victims but this seems to have been done after the victim had died so that there would be no obvious evidence of her gaining financially at the time of death.

[P8] Lynn Turner, US

Sentenced 2004 and 2007

The Case

Lynn Turner (née Womack) was born 1968, Texas, US. In her early twenties, as a 911 dispatcher for Cobb County, Georgia, Lynn married police officer Glenn Turner. Lynn quit her job and spent freely, Glenn taking on extra jobs to compensate. As the marriage deteriorated, Lynn began a relationship with firefighter Randy Thompson.

By 1995, Glenn planned to move out and seek divorce. However, he fell ill, visiting the emergency room of Kennestone Hospital. Following treatment, he returned home, where according to his wife his condition deteriorated. Waking in the early hours hallucinating, he went to the basement and tried to drink gasoline. Lynn helped him back upstairs and by morning he seemed better. Lynn did some errands but on returning found Glenn dead. His death was certified as owing to 'natural causes'.

Lynn moved in with Randy and collected her husband's life insurance, but by 2000 their relationship problems led Randy to move out. In January 2001, Randy visited hospital with vomiting and stomach ache, and was treated and discharged. Next day the 32-year-old was found dead in his apartment. Lynn again collected life insurance. However, tests indicated ethylene glycol-based antifreeze in Thompson's blood. Now Glenn Turner's body was exhumed and revealed antifreeze poisoning.

Put on trial in 2004, Lynn was found guilty. The prosecution had permission to refer to the circumstances of Randy Thompson's death. A former insurance agent attested that Lynn persuaded Glenn to make her his death beneficiary. Samantha Gilleland stated that Lynn had visited her animal shelter establishing that antifreeze would poison cats. Dr. Freeman, who treated Glenn Turner the day before he died, testified that his symptoms suggested the chronic ingestion of small amounts of ethylene glycol. Medical examiner Dr. Frist, autopsied Glenn Turner in 1995 giving cause of death as heart failure, despite detecting calcium oxalate crystals. On hearing of Randy Thompson's death, Frist ordered Turner's exhumation reassessing that the crystals indicated ethylene glycol toxicity. A crime laboratory analyst stated that lethal levels of ethylene glycol were initially missed in Randy's body, but when the medical examiner found calcium oxalate crystals in the kidneys, further tests were conducted.

For the defence, Lynn Turner's mother testified that on the day of Glenn Turner's death, Lynn was, 'crying hysterically'. Lynn's apparent coldness at her spouses' funerals was because she concealed 'her feelings and emotions.' Toxicologist Dr. Palmer suggested that the calcium oxalate crystals found in Turner's corpse could be from embalming fluids or flowers decomposing inside the coffin. Also, the crystals in Glenn Turner's kidneys were unexpectedly absent from other organs.

In 2007, Lynn Turner was convicted of Randy Thompson's murder, and sentenced to life imprisonment. In 2010, she was found dead in a shared cell at Metro State Prison. She may have committed suicide by accumulating medication and taking a lethal overdose.

Reference

Martinez, E. (2010, August 31). Antifreeze Killer Lynn Turner Dies in Prison. *CBS News*. www.cbsnews.com/news/antifreeze-killer-lynn-turner-dies-in-prison.

Points of Special Interest

In this case, the perpetrator had committed murder undetected and was only caught years later trying the same modus operandi. Otherwise, it is unlikely that she would have been apprehended. Lynn Turner's timing of her first husband's murder prevented his filing for divorce, and she murdered her boyfriend before their deteriorating relationship jeopardised the prospect of financial gain. Both circumstance suggests monetary motivation.

So, what was the likely scenario of the first murder? Once married to police officer Glenn Turner, Lynn left her job and spent lavishly. When Glenn started plans to move out Lynn was already having a secret affair with Thompson. She saw the prospect of insurance money if Glenn died, and the chance of joining her lover, but she had to act Glenn left and filed for divorce.

Poison appealed because it was secret and might evade detection. Lynn researched ethylene glycol-based antifreeze at the local animal shelter. There was a legitimate supply in the couple's garage. Ethylene glycol antifreeze (1,2 ethanol) is odourless and highly soluble in water but sweet tasting making it unlikely to be detected in food and drink. Lynn would be able to easily determine a good time and place for poisoning, being familiar with her husband's habits and routines. Symptoms might look like natural causes (heart problems). Distancing herself from the killing, Lynn arranged to be out of the house when Glenn died. On her return, she made it appear that she immediately did the right thing when she found Glenn and called for help.

[P9] Benjamin Geen, UK

Sentenced 2004

The Case

Born in 1979, Benjamin Geen worked initially as a care assistant and later as a nurse. He was also a lieutenant in the Territorial Army. In 2004, Geen was convicted of murdering two patients and causing grievous bodily harm to others while working at Horton General Hospital, Banbury, Oxfordshire.

Seven patients experienced respiratory arrests between December 2003 and February 2004 while Ben Geen was a nurse on duty. Five of the patients recovered but two died in January 2004. They were Anthony Bateman (66) of Banbury, Oxfordshire who died on the 6 January and David Onley (77) of Deddington, Oxfordshire who died on the 21st.

The hospital carried out an internal investigation which ultimately identified 18 cases of different kinds that may have been suspicious and that could have involved Geen. When he next arrived at work on 9 February 2004 Geen was wearing nursing scrubs and a jacket. Arresting officers found a syringe in his pocket. Geen's explanation was that he had inadvertently taken the syringe home in his pocket following a busy day working in the emergency department and was planning to return it. Searching Geen's apartment, police found prescription medicines that were traced back to the hospital. Police cautioned Geen for theft.

Later, Geen was charged with administering unauthorised drugs that caused respiratory arrest or hypoglycaemic arrest (hypoglycaemia refers to low blood sugar levels) in 18 cases. He was tried at Oxford Crown Court. It was stated in court that Geen intentionally used potentially lethal doses of drugs to arrest patients' breathing because he liked the thrill of resuscitating them. Michael Austin Smith QC prosecuting said that Geen was satisfying his perverse needs. Found guilty in April 2006, Geen was given 17 life sentences, the trial judge recommending that Geen spend at least 30 years in prison before being considered for parole. Geen was acquitted in one of these cases which was found to be owing to natural causes.

References

BBC News. (2006, April 18). Nurse Guilty of Killing Patients (Updated).

Vinter, P. (2006, November 24). Killer Nurse—The Full Story. *Oxford Mail*.

Points of Special Interest

Following the trial, questions continued to be raised about some of the evidence including the interpretation of statistics relating to patterns of patients' illness, and the symptoms of the patients in relation to the drugs Geen was said to have administered. An appeal against the guilty verdict was lodged in 2009. The conviction was upheld (R. v. Geen [2009] EWCA Crim 2609). In 2013, Geen's case was submitted to the Criminal Case Review Commission.

The Commission state that in October 2015, they decided not to refer the case for appeal. Geen sought a judicial review of the decision not to review the case. The CCRC then conceded the matter before the need for a full judicial hearing and agreed to open a fresh investigation. That investigation was still ongoing as of September 2017 (Private communication, CCRC, September 2017).

The case attracted a campaign to argue that Geen is innocent (www.bengeen.wordpress.com). This included questioning the interpretation of statistics relating to patterns of patients' illness, and the symptoms of the patients regarding the drugs Geen was said to have administered. Following the case of Harold Shipman, it is understandable that hospitals and community physician surgeries are vigilant about the possibility of misconduct by their staff. The Geen case and related issues perhaps reflect the tension that arises between appropriate vigilance and the possibility that someone who may be innocent could come under suspicion.

[P10] Francisca Ballesteros, Valencia

Sentenced 2005

Born in Valencia in 1969, Francisca Ballesteros later moved to Melilla in North Africa. She was married Antonio González Barribino apparently a civil servant from Melilla in 1987. Two years later, their daughter Sandra was born followed by daughter Florinda in 1990, and son Antonio two years later. Florinda died aged only six months.

It is reported that in 2003, with her marriage floundering, Francesca made online contact with a man whom she then in November of that year visited in Tenerife. On 12 January 2004, her husband (aged 42) died apparently from myocardial infarction ('heart attack'). During 2003 and 2004, son Antonio (aged 12) became ill and is admitted to hospital on several occasions. On 4 June 2004, Francisca's daughter Sandra (aged 14) died. Autopsy revealed poison in her body. On 7 June 2004, police arrest Francisca Ballesteros and shortly after she was remanded in prison.

In 2005 Francisca Ballesteros stood trial at the Provincial Court of Malaga in Melilla. The prosecution case was that Francisca's first murder was that of daughter Florinda whom she poisoned between June and August 1990. Calcium cyanamide an inorganic compound used as a fertilizer also known as nitrolime was administered in food and drink. It can lead to liver problems relating to obstructions within the liver (intrahepatic) causing bile salts and other substances to accumulate in the bloodstream instead of being eliminated (intrahepatic cholestasis). It can also bring about ketoacidosis a pathological metabolic state which can be fatal. Florinda died of liver failure on 4 August 1990.

There was then a thirteen-year gap before the next killing. It was stated that Francisca began administering calcium cyanamide in August 2003 to her husband and remaining children Sandra and Antonio in their food and drink. Antonio González died on 12 January 2004 owing to multiple organ failure conversant with poisoning. Sandra was administered calcium cyanamide and the sedative Zolpidem for months as she grew weaker, dying on 4 June 2004 aged 15 years. Over a similar period, Francisca was administering the poison to her son Antonio along with sedatives Zolpidem and Bromazepam causing a deterioration in his health that required him to be admitted to hospital several times. His life was saved because at the death of his sister, he was promptly readmitted to hospital.

On her own confession, Francesca was found guilty of the murder of her daughters Florinda (in 1990) and Sandra (in 2004) and her husband (in 2004). She was also found guilty of the attempted poison murder of her son Antonio who survived after his hospital treatment.

Taking account of the cumulative sentences for the crimes, Francesca was given an 84 years prison term.

References

'Adegüello' Reporter. (2006). La envenadora de Melilla confiesa tres asesinatos. *Adegüello Crítica de Crímenes.* www.adeguello.net/ade04julio6.htm#veneno.

20 Minutes. (2005, September 21). La 'envenadora' se contradice sobre la muerte de su marido y dice que no quiso matar a sus hijas. http://www.20minutos.es/noticia/49407/0/envenenadora/juicio/melilla/.

Ramos, T. (2005, September 24). La fiscal eleva la pena para la 'envenenadora de Melilla' a 84 años' *El País.* https://elpais.com/diario/2005/09/24/espana/1127512820_850215.html.

Points of Special Interest

The motive for the 2004 murders and attempted murder seem to be rid of her whole family to enable Francesca to meet or live with a man whom she had met over the internet. One scenario was for her to move to Tenerife. But the motive for killing her daughter Florinda fourteen years earlier is unclear. By one account, in her initial confession to police Francesca admitted poisoning members of her family and said she planned to then commit suicide but denied having killed Florinda. Several days later, she changed her confession and said that she had murdered Florinda.

If Francesca did indeed kill daughter Florinda it is unconvincing that she did so with the intention of getting rid of her family, then waited 14 years to complete this plan. Possibly another there was another motive by which Florinda was an obstacle for Francisca, but this is speculative. Whatever the motive for killing Florinda, it may be that when years later, when presented with an opportunity for a new life, Francisca turned again to poisoning having eluded suspicion once.

[P11] Charles Cullen, US

Sentenced 2006

The Case

Charles Cullen was born 1960 in West Orange, New Jersey, US. He graduated as a registered nurse in 1967. Throughout his life he made several suicide attempts. In 1978 he enlisted in the navy from which he received a medical discharge in 1984. He studied at nursing school in New Jersey from 1984 graduating in 1987.

On graduating, Cullen took a post at the burns unit of St. Barnabas Medical Center, Livingston, New Jersey. Here he confessed later that he had killed several patients including John Yengo Sr. (a judge) whom he killed with an overdose of intravenous medication. In early 1992, as the hospital began investigating who might have contaminated intravenous bags, Cullen left.

He moved to Warren Hospital, Phillipsburg, New Jersey. There he murdered three elderly women patients with overdoses of digitoxin. He and his wife divorced and he moved to an apartment in Phillipsburg. He began stalking a female co-worker and was eventually arrested and given one year's probation. Following his arrest, he attempted suicide and was treated for depression. In late 1993, Cullen left his job at Warren Hospital.

From 1993 to 1996 he worked at the intensive care unit of Hunterdon Medical Center, Flemington. He later admitted killing five patients there with overdoses of digitoxin. After a brief spell at Morristown Memorial Hospital, Morristown, New Jersey, Cullen was unemployed for several months and was briefly admitted to a psychiatric facility.

In early 1998, Cullen worked at the Liberty Nursing Home and Rehabilitation Center, Allentown, Pennsylvania. Accused of giving patients drugs at unscheduled times, he was eventually fired. While at liberty, it appears he killed several patients. He moved to Easton Hospital, Easton, Pennsylvania from November 1998 to March 1999. While there he murdered a patient with digitoxin. There was suspicion and an internal investigation, but nothing was found to link Cullen firmly to the death.

He then left Easton for Lehigh Valley Hospital, Allentown where he killed a patient. In April 1999, Cullen moved to St. Luke's Hospital in Bethlehem, Pennsylvania. There he killed five patients In August 2000, a co-worker saw Cullen concealing medication in bins used for needles. The hospital reported Cullen to Pennsylvania State Police who investigated but inconclusively. In September 2002, Cullen worked at the Somerset Medical Center, Somerville, New Jersey. There he killed eight patients using digitoxin, and other drugs.

In mid-2003, Somerset Medical Center began investigating irregularities. For example, Cullen was accessing the records of patients to whom he was not assigned and his requests for patient drugs was erratic. In October 2003, a patient died from low blood sugar and the Center alerted state authorities. An investigation of Cullen's employment history showed suspicions about his involvement in past deaths. The Medical Centre fired Cullen and police kept him under observation until there enquiries were completed.

In December 2003, in Somerset, New Jersey detectives arrested Cullen for the murder of a patient at the Somerset Medical Center. Two days later Cullen confessed to killing, over sixteen-years, over thirty patients. In April 2004, Cullen pleaded guilty in a New Jersey court to killing 13 patients and other crimes while at Somerset. Soon after, he pleaded guilty to the killing of three more patients in New Jersey. In November of that year, he pleaded guilty before a court in Allentown Pennsylvania to killing six patients and other crimes. In 2006, he was sentenced in New Jersey and shortly after in Lehigh County. Serving multiple life sentences Cullen is incarcerated at New Jersey State Prison, Trenton, New Jersey.

Reference

Daily Mail Reporter. (2013, April 29). 'Angel of Death' Nurse Who Murdered at Least 40 Patients to Become One of America's Worst Serial Killers Speaks from Prison for the First Time to Chillingly Claim: 'I Thought I Was Helping'. *Mail Online*.

Points of Special Interest

The Cullen cases highlighted weaknesses in the communication of concerns between hospitals and across states. Largely because of the case, Pennsylvania, New Jersey, and many other states adopted new laws encouraging frank appraisals of employers' performance. These provided immunity to employers when providing truthful appraisals.

[P12] Vickie Dawn Jackson, US

Sentenced 2006

The Case

Vickie Dawn Jackson was born 1967 and brought up in Nocona, Montague County, Texas, US. Vickie wed and divorced (husband not known) while still in her teens. In 1984, she married her second husband Leroy Carson and the couple subsequently had a son and a daughter (Jennifer) but divorced in 1996. Vickie wed her third husband Kirk Jackson, but this failed. In 2000 Vickie faced a difficult year. A close relative died. Vickie lost custody of her two children who were allegedly being ill-treated by Jackson and they went to live with their father Leroy Carson. She had a miscarriage after fighting with Kirk and became depressed.

Having long had a vocation to be a nurse, in the early 1980s when married to Leroy Carson, Vickie attended night school, qualifying as a licenced vocational nurse. She then worked at several nursing homes and hospitals. One of these was Nocona General Hospital a small 40–45 bed facility. There between December 2000 and January 2001 (a period of eight days) unusually eight patients died during the night shift when Vickie Dawn Jackson was working. On other shifts during the same period there was a single death. Known victims, all of whom died of respiratory arrest were: Donnie Jennings (100) died 11 December; Elgie Hutson (87) died 20 December; Sanford Mitchell (62) died 20 December; Barbara Atteberry (50) died 24 December; Boyd Burnett

(87) died 24 December 2000. Other unusual patient deaths were also suspected including the death of her third husband's grandfather.

By 30 January hospital authorities had established that a vial of Mivacurium chloride had been taken from the crash carts on the night shift of 30 and 31 January 2001. This is drug which may be injected during procedures where it is necessary to insert a breathing tube into a patient. An internal investigation was started. In February 2001, the hospital pharmacist alerted the State Board of Pharmacy that at least ten vials of Mivacurium chloride were missing. An investigation was instituted and during this, traces of the drug were found in Vickie Dawn Jackson's trash. Vickie was obliged to leave her job. In June 2001, the bodies of ten of her patients were exhumed. All showed traces of the drug.

Inquiries continued and by June 2002 police were ready to make an arrest. By this time Vickie was living in Ringgold and working in a grocery store delicatessen in Bowie. There, she was arrested and charged with murder relating to the ten deaths.

In February 2005, a pretrial hearing was held in Archer County Court House, Archer City, Texas. In October 2006 a week before her trial was scheduled to begin, although she did not confess or admit guilt, Vickie Dawn Jackson entered a no contest plea. An FBI special agent David Burns speculated that Jackson may have been angered towards patients, who because of their anxiety could sometimes be demanding, when other nurses were compassionate towards them. Jackson was sentenced to life imprisonment. She is held in the Crain Unit, Gatesville, Texas.

References

Associated Press. (2006, October 3). Life Term for Ex-nurse in Patient killings. *NBC News.* http://www.nbcnews.com/id/15119953/ns/us_news-crime_and_courts/t/life-term-ex-nurse-patient-killings/#.WgwGcWi0OM8.

Henderson, J. (2002, July 18). Nocona Seeks Pattern Linking Nurse to Deaths. *Houston Chronicle.*

Points of Special Interest

The case raises the issue of someone gradually changing from being an apparently caring person with a vocation for nursing to becoming a serial killer. If this is a correct picture the reasons for such a change may be speculated upon, possible factors being Vickie Dawn Jackson's life problems. The year in which the killings took place Vickie had faced the death of a close relative, had lost custody of her two children, and had a miscarriage after fighting with Kirk, and had become depressed. Another scenario is that she was never the caring person that she depicted so that the question of change does not arise. Relatedly it is unclear what the motive was for the killings. Mercy killing appears to be implausible because several patients who were killed were being treated for relatively minor ailments.

Regarding the drug that Vickie Dawn Jackson used, mivacurium chloride (Mivacron) temporarily causes paralysis and is used during emergency procedures where it stops natural breathing so that a breathing tube can be inserted.

[P13] Mohan Kumar, India

Sentenced 2016

The Case

Between 2003 and 2009, some 20 women were found dead across six towns in five districts of southern Karnataka (south-west India). Eight bodies were recovered from a bus stand in Mysore; and another five from a bus station in Bangalore. Police assigned all 20 cases to 'unnatural deaths' and 'suspected suicides' in files of 10 police stations.

This changed with the disappearance of Anita Barimar (22) from Bantwal (east of Mangalore), who disappeared on June 16, 2009. Her community alleged that she had run away with a Muslim man and pressured Bantwal police to trace her. Police investigations of Anita's landline telephone call records eventually led to Mohan Kumar.

Born in 1963 Mohan Kumar worked as a teacher from 1980 to 2003. He met his first wife Mary, when she was a student at the Shiradi Primary School in a rural area of Mangalore where he taught but they were later divorced. He married a second and a third time. Mohan was dismissed from teaching after being accused of trying to drown a woman in the river Netravathi (south of Mangalore) although he was acquitted.

Investigations of the bus stand deaths revealed that Mohan purchased cyanide from a chemical dealer who testified in court that he sold the poison to Mohan thinking he was a jeweller. Investigating Officer Nanjunde Gowda said Mohan planned carefully and used a very similar modus operandi for each murder.

On September 22, 2016, Mohan attended a Special Trial Court in Mangalore, to be tried separately for 20 murders for which investigating teams had gathered evidence and witnesses. Having initially admitted murders, Mohan claimed that all 20 women committed suicide by consuming cyanide because he refused to marry them.

The trial for three murders was concluded in December 2016. The victims were Anitha Barimar (22) from Barimaru in Bantwaltaluk; Lilavati Mistry (age unrecorded); Leela, (32) from Kodambettu in Belthangady Taluk; and Sunanda Pujari (32) of Peruvaje in Bellare village of Sullia Taluk.

Typical is the murder of Sunanda Pujari. She left home on 11 February 2008, saying that she was going to a nearby temple. That night, her body was found at a state bus stand in Mysore. Apparently, Kumar met Sunanda several times using a false name. On 11 February he took her to a lodge in Mysore, poisoned her that evening at the bus stand and stole her gold jewellery which he later pawned.

Mohan was sentenced to death for these three murders but escaped and fled to Australia. He was arrested at Bali airport, Indonesia by officials tipped off by Australian police. He was later tried for other murders.

Reference

Siddiqui, I. (2016, October 9). Prof Mohan Kumar, the Man Who Killed 20 Women with 'Anti-pregnancy Pills'. *Bangalore Mirror*. www.bangaloremirror.indiatimes.com/bangalore/cover-story//articleshow/54758093.cms.

Points of Special Interest

It appears that police missed common features of the deaths of the victims that might have led earlier to the suspicion that a serial poisoner might be responsible. The victims were all women in their mid-20s or early-30s; all 20 bodies were found in restrooms of bus stands; and all 20 victims were dressed in what appeared to be their wedding sarees minus jewellery. None it seems were identified nor their families traced. While postmortems in all 20 cases revealed poisoning, blood samples of only two victims were forensically tested. These showed the presence of cyanide, which is not easily available and used rarely in suicides.

These indications of a pattern were seemingly reflected in the planning and repeated modus operandi of the killer. According to Investigating Officer Gowda, Mohan would typically pose as a government employee with a stable job. He would identify women from poor background, desperate to marry. Mohan even calculated their fertility cycles so that they would willingly take the supposed contraceptive pill. Hotels he chose for the last night before killing his victims were always near a bus stand. After having sex, he would ask the women to take a walk with him, ensuring that they left all their valuables in the hotel room. Escorting them to the bus station he would ask them to take the pill in the washroom in case it made them feel sick. Then he would return to the hotel room, collect their valuables and decamp. He always planned these last nights in towns far from the victim's place of residence.

[P14] Stephan Letter, Germany

Sentenced 2006

The Case

Stephan Letter was born in 1978, in Germany. He worked for the Red Cross and studied nursing at a college in Ludwigsburg. On qualifying, he took a post at a hospital in Sonthofen, Bavaria where there were many elderly patients.

Officials found that quantities of drugs normally in the hospital were unaccounted for. They included lysthenon, a muscle relaxant. An investigation was put underway and as part of this, the dates when the drugs had gone missing was compared with staff duty rotas. It was eventually judged that Letter was responsible for the drugs being missing. When questioned, Letter admitted taking away the drugs. When arrested by police, in 2004, Letter stated that he had killed 12 patients with lethal injections. He has worked mainly on the night shift.

Police arranged for the exhumation of the bodies of over 40 people who had died at the clinic during Letter's tenure of 17 months between January 2003 and July 2004. Autopsies were carried out. Following this Letter was charged with the deaths of 29 patients (17 women and 12 men). It is thought that this was the largest number of homicidal killings since World War II.

In court, he retracted the statements and did not say how many deaths he was responsible for. Prosecutors told the Bavarian State Court in Kempten that investigators had found vials of drugs at Letter's home. They contained sufficient medications to kill 10 individuals.

Letter was arrested in 2004. Accused of stealing medication, he admitted it and stated that he had killed patients.

Brought to trial in 2006, he was accused of the deaths of 29 patients. The trial lasted 9 months. There were 16 counts of murder, and 12 counts of manslaughter and one count of killing on request. Most of the patients were elderly but the youngest was 40. The oldest victim was

94-years-old. The defence lawyer Juergen Fischer presented the cases that Letter had acted out of sympathy for patients who were suffering. However, this was not supported by the fact that several patients were in stable condition and due to be released from hospital. Also, Letter had contact with some patients only briefly and prosecutors argued that he had acted out of malice. Letter was found guilty of the killings and sentenced to life imprisonment. Judge Harry Rechner pronounced Letter guilty of 12 cases of murder, and 15 cases of manslaughter as well as other crimes. Letter is incarcerated in the prison of Straubing in Southern Bavaria.

References

BBC News. (2006, February 7). *German Male Nurse Admits Killings.* http://news.bbc.co.uk/1/hi/4689006.stm.

Cleaver, H. (2006, February 8). Angel of Death 'Driven by Kindness'. *The Telegraph.*

Points of Special Interest

A series of indicators pointed to possible wrongdoing which are typical of some healthcare poisoning cases. Medication that could cause deaths when given as overdoses were found to be missing from hospital supplies. Drugs were found in Letter's apartment for the possession of which he had no reasonable explanation. Letter admitted to carrying out some of the killings. The question of motive was therefore important.

During investigation and trial, Letter's claimed motive was challenged. The challenge had two compelling parts. The defendant had stated that he had acted out of sympathy for patients who were suffering. However, prosecutors pointed to the brevity of some of the contact with patients, arguing that no bonds of sympathy could have formed in that limited time. Also, prosecution showed that in some instances patients were in a stable condition and ready to be released from hospital.

[P15] Viacheslav Soloviev, Russia

Sentenced 2008

The Case

Viacheslav Soloviev was born in 1970 in Russia. He married a high school sweetheart Olga and lived in Yaroslavl in central Russia. In the early 2000s, he appears to have developed an obsessive interest in poisons which extended to his buying several different toxic metal salts including thallium sulphate.

His first victim was his wife Olga to whom he had been married for 14 years. She died in December 2003 apparently of a heart attack. Soloviev himself called the ambulance when she became ill to try to avert any suspicion. Next was Nastya (14) his daughter who died after a protracted illness. By some reports this death was unintended, and the proposed target was a neighbour. Other interpretations are that the killing was both purposely protracted and intended.

Against the trend of killing relatives, Soloviev poisoned Valery Shcherbakov a police investigator who was looking into a brawl in a local café in which Soloviev was been involved. It is said that Soloviev added poison to a glass of water that his interrogator was drinking during questioning. In May 2005, Soloviev's common law wife Irina Astakhov died in hospital where doctors found she had damage to her liver and kidneys. In late 2006, Soloviev went to live with Oksana Gurieva a gymnastics coach and poisoned her grandmother Taisiya. Finally, he attempted to kill his sister Oksana and her husband and succeeded in killing their one-year-old child. By this time, suspicions were aroused, and police investigated.

Viacheslav Soloviev was arrested in March 2008. His lawyer Sultan Umarov admitted that the defendant could not explain his behaviour. It appears that Soloviev administered thallium sulphate in the form of rat poison in his victims in food. The motive seems to be sadistic or at least killing for pleasure but is not established and remains puzzling. Soloviev's explanations for the killings were varied and included that he killed the police inspector because the officer was rude to him. He supposedly killed his wife Olga because he was bored with her.

As the trial was approaching and scheduled at Yaroslavl Regional. Soloviev attempted suicide by slitting his wrists. He was referred to hospital. On his recovery the trial took place. Found guilty of six murders, Soloviev was sentenced to life imprisonment. On 2 December 2008, he was found dead in his cell at the detention centre where he was incarcerated. It is believed that his death was brought about by his experimenting on himself with poisons over a period.

References

Reuters / Sydney Morning Herald. (2008, April 10). Poisoner Killed Family for Fun. *Sydney Morning Herald.* http://www.smh.com.au/news/world/poisoner-killed-family-for-fun/2008/04/10/1207420526584.html.

RIA Novosti. (2008, April 9). Trial of Rat Poison Killer Suspended in Central Russia. *Sputnik International.* https://sputniknews.com/russia/20080409104192288/.

Points of Special Interest

Soloviev's obsessive interest in poisons, and the apparent pleasure in killing, echoes the case of Graham Young the UK serial poisoner who murdered work colleagues also using thallium. The poison administered in tiny doses kills slowly as the victim gradually weakens so that cause of death can appear to arise from an unspecified or unclear illness.

Most of Soloviev's victims were related by blood or marriage and ranged in age from infant (1-year-old) to adults. The exception to the killing of relatives was the murder of police investigator Valery Shcherbakov which appears opportunistic and barely credible.

Indeed, the whole case has an air of unreality. The unclear motive, the sequence of killings that apparently went unsuspected including the murder of a police officer while under interrogation, Soloviev's dramatic attempt to take his own life, and his ironic death supposedly from the effects of chronic poisoning taken together seem fictional.

[P16] Colin Norris (Now Colin Campbell), Scotland

Sentenced 2008

The Case

Born 12 February 1976, in Milton, Glasgow, Scotland, Colin Norris originally worked in the travel business. He later trained in nursing where he appeared to be a hard-working student. After qualifying from 2001, he worked at Leeds General Infirmary, and at St. James Hospital, Leeds, England. In 2002 following the death of several patients between 2001 and 2002 while Norris was on duty, suspicions began to be aroused.

Police questioned Norris about these deaths and investigated 72 cases in total. Charges were brought for the killing four patients during the period July to October 2002. Three were killed at the Leeds General Infirmary. These were Bridget Bourke (86) who died 22 July, Doris Ludlam (80) a former teacher died 27 June, and Ethel Hall (86) a retired shopkeeper, died 20 November. Irene Crookes (79) was killed on 22 October at St. James Hospital, Leeds.

Norris was charged and tried at Newcastle Crown Court, Judge Griffith presiding. He was convicted on a majority jury verdict on 3 March 2008 of murdering the four women patients and the attempted murder of a fifth. The method was injecting high levels of insulin into the patients. Norris was sentenced to a minimum of 30 years imprisonment. The judge Justice Williams rejected the idea that Norris was practicing euthanasia because none of the patients was terminally ill but admitted to not being able to figure out a motive. Justice Williams suggested a possible motive of having the power over life and death, telling Norris 'I suspect you enjoyed the power that ending life gave you'. The judge added, 'You are an arrogant and manipulative man with a real dislike for elderly patients'. Norris is incarcerated in the high security Frankland Prison, County Durham, England.

In 2011 new concerns were raised about Norris's conviction. Vincent Marks, Emeritus Professor of clinical biochemistry, Surrey University,

UK questioned some of the evidence. He stated that the jury had inadvertently been led to mistakenly believe that there was something sinister in a cluster of hypoglycaemic episodes (involving low blood sugar levels) appearing in people who were not diabetic. Studies since Norris's conviction indicated that other factors could have created a risk of the episodes such as infection or malnutrition.

In May 2013, the Criminal Cases Review Commission agreed to re-examine the case in the context of new evidence. In 2017, the commission confirmed that the case was still under review (Personal communication 19 September 2017).

References

Burns, J. (2008, March 4). Death Spree of Serial Killer Nurse Colin Norris. *Daily Record*.

Campbell, D. (2011, October 4). 'Angel of Death' Colin Norris Could Be Cleared of Insulin Murders. *The Guardian*.

Points of Special Interest

It is reported that Norris carried out the murders while he was on night shift or at weekends when senior staff and specialists would tend not to be on duty. He is said to have injected patients with morphine to make them drowsy and then injected insulin into their stomach using a long syringe. Suspicions began to crystallise at the death of Ethel Hall at the Leeds Infirmary. She had been admitted for a routine hip operation and had been recovering well. When her condition suddenly declined, a specialist ordered tests to be carried out which revealed high levels of insulin.

The case as indicated was referred to the Criminal Cases Review Commission an independent organisation which investigates suspected miscarriages of justice in England, Wales and Northern Ireland. Its commissioners decide whether to send a case back to the courts for a fresh appeal (http://ccrc.gov.uk/about-us/).

[P17] K. D. Kempanna, India

Sentenced Various Dates Including 2012

K. D. Kempanna, born in 1965, killed six women worshipers between 1999 and 2007 at remote temple sites where she had lured them. Typically, Kempanna poisoned the victims with cyanide, then robbed them. Her death sentence in 2012, was commuted to life imprisonment.

Married to a tailor, Kempanna had a son and two daughters. In 1998, she was abandoned by her husband having suffered large losses running a chit fund savings scheme. She killed her first victim in 1999 when 34-years-old. In 2001, working as a maid in Bangalore, Kempanna was arrested for attempting to steal jewellery from an employer's home and jailed for several months. She murdered a further 5 victims in 2007.

Her modus operandi was at temple sites, posing as a pious woman knowledgeable about temple rituals. Kempanna would befriend wealthy worshipers and lure them to other temples remote from their home where she would poison and rob them. Cyanide would be administered in holy water or in a prasad (food given as a religious offering). Arrested in 2007 for trying to dispose stolen jewellery, Kempanna admitted a series of murders.

Details of victims are sketchy and media reports conflicting. On 19 October 1999 Kempanna killed 30-year-old Mamatha Rajan at her home outside Bangalore. Following a long gap, Kempanna perpetrated 5 murders between 10 October and 18 December 2007. Muniyama (60) of Chikka Bommasandra was murdered at Yediyur Siddalingshwara temple, Kunigal. Elizabeth (52 or 61) of Banaswadi, was lured by Kempanna promising rituals to aid the return of her missing grandson. Regarding Yashodamma (60) of Yelahanka, Kempanna offered rituals to cure her asthma. Pillamma (50 or 60) of Hebbal was murdered on 17 December 2007. At a Bangalore temple, Mallika befriended Pillamma who was seeking a tower design for a temple that she and her husband were building. Mallika suggested visiting Vaidyanathapura to study its tower. The woman rented a room there and on 17 December Mallika poisoned Pillamma with cyanide in supposed holy water, strangled, and robbed her. **Nagaven**i, a housewife (30) from Allalasandra, was killed in a temple in Doddaballapur on 18 December 2007. Kempanna offering to help Nagaveni in desire for a male child by performing a special puja (Hindu prayer ritual), administered cyanide in supposed holy water. For these crimes, Kempanna was sentenced on different occasions in 2010, March 2012 and October 2013.

Reference

Abraham, B. (2017, February 18). Meet Cyanide Mallika India's First Woman Serial Killer…. *Times of India.* www.indiatimes.com/news/india/meet-cyanide-mallika-india-s-first-woman-serial-killer.

Points of Special Interest

Location was important for this series of murders. Sites where victims were recruited helped to ensure that they were religious devotees. Based on this, Kempanna lured them to other temples remote from the victim's home where she could more safely commit her crimes. Different locations were chosen because there was no attempt to pass the killings off as owing to natural causes nor disguise the robberies. Poison was used, not to deceive police, but to ensure a quick death and perpetrate robbery.

Trust was likely built by victims thinking Kempanna was a fellow devotee. All her victims being female suggests they were more likely agree to Kempanna meeting them on a remote site than if she were a man. Gender and apparent interest and knowledge helped to promote trust. Kempanna was similar in age to several victims being 34 at the time of the first murder and 42 at the time of the remaining five murders.

Kempanna's occupations had included that of domestic help during which she had taken the opportunity to steal and been charged for doing so. Stealing continued as the motive for the later murders with the refinement that Kempanna could arrange a venue that would not be directly connected to her as could her employment in a household. The service aspect of her domestic work was continued in a criminal way as she pretended to be eager to help devotees achieve their goals. Kempanna reportedly stole cyanide from a goldsmith for whom she worked as a domestic help, or bought it from a gold polishing shop.

The apparent gap between the murder of 1999 and the subsequent five killings in late 2007 is puzzling. The impact of her arrest in 2001 may have curbed her tendencies to stealing for some time. But the long gap and perhaps more importantly the trigger for the spate of murders in late 2007 remains unexplained.

[P18] Kimberley Clark Saenz, US

Sentenced 2012

The Case

Kimberley Clark Saenz (neé Fowler) was born on 11 November 1973 at Fall River, Massachusetts, US. She trained as a licenced practical/vocational nurse.

Married to Mark Saenz she had two children. Kimberley worked at Woodland Heights Hospital, Lufkin, Texas about 125 miles northeast of Houston. She was fired from the hospital for stealing pethidine/meperidine (as Demerol), an opioid painkiller.

In 2007 Mark Saenz filed for divorce. From September 2007, Kimberley worked at a dialysis Clinic in Lufkin, run by Denver-based healthcare company DaVita. She had worked there for eight months when concerns began to be raised. In April 2008, an official wrote an anonymous letter requesting that the state health department inspectors investigate the clinic's high number of emergency calls for paramedics. Within a few days investigations, began and it was noted that emergency crews had been called many more times than expected that month. Four people had died.

Two dialysis patients, on 28 April 2008, reported that they saw Saenz using syringes of sodium hypochlorite (bleach) from a cleaning bucket and injecting it into the dialysis lines of patients who later died. A dialysis line, sometimes called an IV or intravenous line, is a central venous catheter used for haemodialysis treatment. It comprises a soft plastic tube inserted into a large vein. The tube is connected to a dialysis machine to enable blood to be circulated to the machine and back to the patient's body. Saenz was fired, the clinic was closed-down for two months. Saenz was sent home and was fired the next day. Police were called in and the clinic was temporarily closed for patient safety.

Saenz was charged a year later. She pleaded not guilty and was freed on bail. Saenz was put on trial in 2012 for the 2008 murders of 5 patients: Clara Strange, Thelma Metcalf, Garlin Kelley, Cora Bryant, and Opal Few. Defence lawyer Ryan Deaton argued that Saenz and others at the clinic used syringes for bleach to make sure exact amounts were used when mixing the solutions used to disinfect the plastic lines. However, investigators testified that internet searches on Saenz' computer showed searches for bleach poisoning and whether bleach could be detected in dialysis lines.

Although Saenz had previously sworn an affidavit that she had no previous felony record, it emerged that there were allegations that she had overused prescription drugs, had problems with addiction and substance abuse, had put false information on a job application, and had been fired several times from healthcare jobs.

Saenz was tried and found guilty in Texas District Court of these and other offences. Prosecutor Clyde Herrington believed that there were more victims. Saenz was sentenced to life imprisonment without the possibility of parole. She is serving the sentence in the Dr. Lane Murray Unit.

References

Daily Mail Reporter. (2012, March 31). Nurse Faces Death Penalty After Being Found Guilty of Killing Five Patients by Injecting IV Lines with Bleach. *Mail Online.* http://www.dailymail.co.uk/news/article-

2123252/Nurse-Kimberly-Saenz-faces-death-penalty-murdering-patients-bleach.html.

Fox News. (2012, March 31). *Texas Nurse Convicted in Blech Deaths Case.* http://www.foxnews.com/us/2012/03/31/texas-nurse-convicted-in-bleach-deaths-case.html.

Graczyk, M. / Associated Press. (2015, November 14). *Nurse's Bleach Injection Deaths Trial Begins.* KIMATV. http://kimatv.com/news/nation-world/nurses-bleach-injection-deaths-trial-begins-11-14-2015-230029540.

Points of Special Interest

As well as the testimony of patients who reported seeing Saenz introducing bleach into the IV lines, statistical evidence was presented to the court about the increase in the number of deaths that had occurred at the clinic during Saenz tenure there. As with some other healthcare serial murder cases, there was debate about the meaning of statistics connected with the allegations. A review of clinical records found that Saenz was on duty for 84% of the cases where patients experienced chest pains or cardiac arrest. However, the defence lawyers pointed to other clinic staff who were present even more often.

[P19] Victorino Chua, UK

Sentenced 2015

Born in the Philippines in 1956, Victorino Chua, worked as a nurse at Stepping Hill Hospital in Stockport, England where in June and July 2011 he was responsible for poisoning patients Tracey Arden 44, and Derek Weaver 83, for which he was sentenced in 2015. Chua injected insulin into saline bags and ampules which were unwittingly used by other nurses and delivered a fatal insulin overdose. The motive was likely sadistic.

Following the suspicious deaths of several patients at Stepping Hill Hospital, an investigation indicated that saline ampules and saline drips had been contaminated with insulin. In July 2011, Greater Manchester Police announced that they were conducting a murder enquiry into how the saline solutions had come to be contaminated. One nurse was arrested but eventually not charged. In January 2012, following claims that he had altered prescription charts so that dangerously high levels of medication would be administered to patients, another nurse was arrested, 46-year-old Victorino Chua. Following questioning Chua was placed on police bail which was renewed several times. A letter found at Chua's home and written by him referred to his being 'an angel turned into an evil person'.

Chua was charged in March 2014, with the murders of Tracy Arden, Arnold Lancaster and Alfred Derek Weaver. He was further charged with other offenses including grievous bodily harm and attempted poisoning. In May of that year, he was found guilty of the murders of Tracy Arden and Alfred Derek Weaver but not guilty of the murder of Arnold Lancaster. He was also found guilty of many offences of grievous bodily harm and other offenses relating to poisoning. At Manchester Crown Court, Chua received multiple life sentences and was told that he would be ineligible for parole for 35 years. Judge Openshaw pointed out that Chua did not personally administer the insulin to most of his patients so that it was unpredictable which would receive the fatally doctored solutions. The judge referred to this as 'strikingly sinister and truly wicked'.

Reference

Scheerhout, J. (2015, May 18). Did Killer Nurse Victorina Chua Pay Someone to Pass His Nursing Exam? *Manchester Evening News* (Updated).

Points of Special Interest

Working as a nurse gave Chua access to patients and drugs. The crimes appear to have been restricted to patients within the hospital wards where Chua worked. In this setting, Chua would know the routines and procedures that typify work in hospital wards. He used this knowledge over time to carry out his crimes, subverting the routines so that instead of them being beneficial they became harmful.

With each occasion where he could tamper with equipment or records undetected, there was the opportunity to learn from his actions and improve the chances of his not being caught in the act. The main modus operandi was to use drugs having a legitimate use but to either administer them or arrange that others inadvertently administered them in dangerous quantities.

As well as the experience of administering the drugs directly it appears that Chua was also motivated by the experience of knowing that others were doing harm arranged by him. The number of instances including murder as well as grievous bodily harm suggests a compulsion to carry out the acts. It also suggests that Chua did not necessarily have a grievance against particular patients but wished to do harm to patients generally.

Related to this is the distance the perpetrator removed himself from the killing. Poisoning is unlike most violent confrontational killing in that it done not require physical face to face conflict. The murdered person is unlikely to know he is a victim until it is too late, Yet, in Chua's case the distancing went even further. He did not even necessarily administer the poison but acted as an intermediary for others to do so suggesting even more a generalising of victims rather than a specific grievance against particular patients.

[P20] Niels Högel, Germany

Sentenced 2008

The Case

Born in 1975, in Germany, Niels Högel trained as a nurse and worked in various clinics, a home for the elderly, and for the emergency medical services.

On 22 June 2005, a colleague saw Högel administering an unauthorised injection of ajmaline to a patient at a clinic in Delmenhorst. The patient died the following day. It is reported that the hospital management did not call police or raise the matter directly with Högel unto two days later. By this time the nurse had killed another patient on the evening of 24 June.

Tried and convicted of attempted murder, Högel was given a jail sentence in 2008 of seven and a half years. Following the 2008 trial further investigations were conducted during which Högel is said to have admitted administering around 90 unauthorised injections to patients following which 60 were resuscitated and 30 patients died. In February 2015, Högel was tried and convicted and given a life jail sentence for the murder of two intensive care patients and the attempted murder of three others. Prosecutors said that he acted out of boredom and a desire to show off his resuscitation skills. He would inject patients with a drug that induced heart failure and then attempt to 'rescue' the patient with artificial respiration. In court, Högel stated that he felt elated when his resuscitation attempts succeeded and downcast when they failed.

It was reported in October 2017, that investigators revealed that the bodies of 99 patients had been exhumed. In 33 instances analysis indicated that death was caused by lethal injections. Police believe that Högel committed his first murder in February 2000 while employed at the Oldenburg Clinic in Lower Saxony near the border with the Netherlands and subsequently carried out 35 more murders there. In 2002, he moved to Delmenhorst near Bremen where it is suspected that he killed a further 48 patients.

Högel used various drugs which when administered as an overdose can cause cardiac arrhythmia and lowered blood pressure which can be fatal. The drugs included ajmaline, (Gilurytmal), sotalol (Sotalex), lidocaine/ xylocaine, amiodarone (Cordarex), and potassium chloride.

Oldenburg Police Chief Johann Kuehme spoke of the special investigative team 'Kardio' Having detected 84 killings, while accepting that the likely actual number is much higher. He criticised hospital delays in alerting the proper authorities (See Olterman 2017 for video speech).

Reference

Oltermann, P. (2017, August 28). German Nurse Suspected of Murdering at Least 90 Patients. *The Guardian*. www.theguardian.com/world/2017/aug/28/german-nurse-niels-hoegel-suspected-murdering-90-patients.

Points of Special Interest

The estimates of the number of patients killed are based on exhumations of bodies that were previously buried. Where patients were cremated, it cannot be established whether they died by lethal injection.

Possible prevention opportunities appear to have been missed. The death rate at the intensive care facility at the clinic in Delmenhorst almost doubled during Högel's tenure there. Even towards the end of his killings delays in acting when Högel was seen illicitly injecting a patient were delayed and another killing took place in the interim. He was given a clean reference when he moved to Delmenhorst Hospital although it is said that people in Oldenburg knew of his abnormalities.

In trying to explain possible motive, Högel is reported to have referred in court to seeking thrills and the excitement of what would happen next. He said he felt elated when able to resuscitate a patient and dejected when he could not. Each time a patient died he would vow never to repeat the game, but his intentions faded each time.

The case echoes that of the German nurse Stephan Letter who was sentenced in 2006 to life imprisonment for administering lethal injections to 28 mainly elderly patients.

[P21] Elizabeth Wettlaufer, Canada

Sentenced 2017

Canadian Elizabeth Wettlaufer (nee Parker) was born 10 June 1967. Raised in Woodstock, Ontario, she attended Huron Park Secondary

School. Wettlaufer gained a degree in religious education counselling from London Baptist Bible College before training as a nurse at Conestoga College in southwestern Ontario.

Working as a registered nurse at Caressant Care long-term care home in Woodstock, she began improperly injecting some of the patients with insulin in the second half of 2007. Later she confessed to two counts of aggravated assault regarding this. It appears that the first occasion on which she injected sufficient insulin into a patient to kill them was August 2007. The victim was patient James Silcox aged 84 and who had dementia. During March 2014, Wettlaufer is said to have murdered six other patients at Caressant Care: Maurice Granat (84), Gladys Millard (87), Helen Matheson (95), Mary Zurawinski (96), Helen Young (90), and Maureen Pickering (79). She attempted to murder two other patients.

That same year, Wettlaufer left the employment of Caressant Care and worked part-time in other institutions and in patients' homes. She killed a further patient Arpad Horvath (75) at Meadow Park facility, London, Ontario, and injected two other patients with insulin at other venues with intent to murder them. Between 2007 and 2014 she had murdered eight patients and attempted to murder a further six.

In September 2016, Elizabeth Wettlaufer entered an inpatient drug rehabilitation program in a Toronto psychiatric hospital. There she confessed to hospital staff that she had kill and attempted to kill her patients. It is speculated that she was driven by guilt to confess her crimes. Staff passed her confession to Toronto police and informed the College of Nurses, Toronto. Wettlaufer subsequently provided police with a full confession. She was charged with the eight murders on 25 October 2016 and following further investigations was charged with four counts of attempted murder and two counts of aggravated assault on 13 January 2017. She confessed to all charges in court on 1 June 2017. Later that month she was sentenced to eight concurrent life terms in prison without the possibility of parole for 25 years.

References

Associated Press, Woodstock, Ontario. (2017, June 26). Former Nurse Who killed Eight Elderly People in Her Care Gets Life in Prison. *The Guardian*. www.theguardian.com/world/2017/jun/26/canada-nurse-deaths-elizabeth-wettlaufer-prison-life.

McQuigge, M. (2017, June 2). If You Ever Do This Again, We'll Turn You in Pastor Tell killer Nurse. *The Canadian Press*. www.thestar.com/news/canada/2017/06/02/if-you-ever-do-this-again-well-turn-you-in-pastor-told-killer-nurse.html.

Points of Special Interest

A judge led public inquiry was set up in August 2017 by the provincial government owing to the case. It was to consider 'The Safety and Security of Residents in the Long-term Care System'.

The modus operandi appears to have stayed the same in the murders and other offences, presumably because the offender did not arouse suspicion that might have led to varying the MO. If the timeline for the murders and attempted murders is correct, it is unclear why there were several killings and attempted killings in 2007 and then an apparent gap of seven years before any further murders. Possible motive remains obscure although it has been speculated that it might relate to feelings of power over life and death. In taped records of her confession to police Wettlaufer speaks in one section of a 'red surging' that she identified as God telling her, 'This is how you work for me'.

Wettlaufer stated that she had confessed to various people in the several years prior to 2017 that she had killed patients, but this led to no one acting. She stated that she had told a priest, a lawyer, and a sponsor of a charity. She stated that she admitted herself into psychiatric care so that her confessions would be heard and acted upon.

[P22] Chisako Kakehi, Japan

Sentenced 2017

The Case

Chisako Kakehi, was born 1947 in Japan. She married aged 24 and founded a fabric printing company with her husband in the Osaka Prefecture. Her husband died in 1994. The business failed and Kakehi got into debt. Later, she registered with a dating service through which she married or was associated with several men from whom she inherited money. She continued to be in debt owing to activities on the stock market. In November 2013 she married but her husband died a month later at their home in Muko, Kyoto Prefecture. A year later, in December 2014 she was charged with killing her husband. She was later charged with the killing of two other men. The victims were her husband Isao Kakehi (75); Masanori Honda (71) a common law partner; and Minoru Hioki (75), The murders were said to have been committed between 2007 and 2013. Kakehi was also charged with the attempted murder of an acquaintance. She had administered cyanide in drinks purporting to be health cocktails. The motive was financial gain from inheritance to pay off debts. When police raided the suspect's home in Kyoto, it was said that they found traces of cyanide in rubbish as well as instruments for administering drugs and medical books.

The trial took place in 2017 at Kyoto District Court where Kakehi pleaded not guilty. Prosecution lawyers stated that the crimes had been planned, including convincing the victims that the cyanide drink they were given was a health cocktail and the preparation of notary documents. Defence counsel cited lack of physical evidence. Also, it was suggested that the victims may have died of natural causes or from other drugs. Defence claimed that the defendant then aged 70 years could not be held responsible because of early onset of dementia when the murders took place. It was claimed that Kakehi had been diagnosed with mild dementia in December 2016 and that this had progressed so that at the trial she was unable to comprehend proceedings. However, the physician who made the diagnosis stated that Kakehi could be held responsible for any crimes committed at that time. The accused was found guilty in November 2017 and Judge Ayako Nakagawa passed down the death penalty stating that the motive was greed. An appeal was lodged by defence lawyers.

Reference

Reporter. (2017, November 7). Japan's 'Black Widow' Serial Killer Gets Death Sentence. *The Japan Times*.

Points of Special Interest

The evidence of motive seems strong given that Chisako Kakehi who had once had a successful business fell on hard times and sought out wealthy elderly partners who subsequently died leaving large amount of money. The same modus operandi of administering cyanide in supposed health cocktails appears to have been used as it was successful several times. Further evidence was that Kakehi had prepared notary documents in advance of the deaths of her partners.

Given the defendants not guilty plea, the defence put forward several propositions at the trial.

Lack of physical evidence was cited although the prosecution in poison cases often have to face this challenge given the secretive nature of poisoning. It was suggested that the victims may have died of natural causes or from other drugs. The defendant was claimed not to be responsible because of early onset of dementia when the murders took place. Strong contrary evidence was provided by the prosecution who called the physician who diagnosed dementia but who at the trial stated that Kakehi could be held responsible for any crimes committed at the time of the killings.

Index

A

Aconite 15, 47, 60, 77, 119, 126, 160, 198
Acute poisoning 38, 61
Age
    of poisoner 13, 17, 25, 131
    of victim 16, 26, 121
Ajmaline 25, 53, 54, 98, 232
American Psychiatric Association 28, 29, 37, 86, 104, 152
Amiodarone 26, 53, 54, 98, 232
Anafrinil 128, 194
Angelo, Richard 54, 85, 96, 103, 173
Animal poisons 15, 50, 66
Antimony 47, 60, 77, 87, 95, 119, 126, 130, 161
Arsenic 14, 15, 33, 38, 39, 51, 58–60, 62, 65, 76, 84, 87, 89, 95–97, 105, 120, 126, 127, 130, 134, 160–162, 164, 165, 169, 170, 175, 192
Autopsy 138, 145, 148, 166, 171, 194, 210

B

Bacterial poisons 15, 50, 66
Ballesteros, Francisca 65, 73, 122, 127, 132, 178, 209, 210
Becker, Marie Alexandrine 46, 73, 77, 128, 166
Belladonna 46, 47, 98, 102
Biological factors 28, 30

Blauensteiner, Elfriede 57, 73, 121, 128, 194
Britland, Mary Ann 48, 76, 84, 128

C
Calcium cyanamide 65, 127, 210
Case logic 17, 137, 141, 156
Chronic poisoning 14, 21, 38, 39, 62, 222
Chua, Victorino 26, 57, 73, 75, 85, 98, 102, 120, 230
Control theory 21, 30, 34, 35, 38, 39, 140
Conviction (for crime) 8, 70, 99, 100, 116, 118, 119, 155, 178, 192, 195, 209, 223
Copper sulphate 45, 60, 77, 126, 132, 161
Court 5, 99, 118, 146, 189, 195, 200, 204, 208, 210, 213, 215, 217, 219, 223, 224, 228–230, 232, 233, 236
Cream, Dr Neill 24, 48, 79, 95, 130, 131, 149
Criminology 1, 2, 5–7, 17
Cullen, Charles 35, 51, 86, 97, 104, 119, 120, 212–214
Cyanide 10, 25–27, 32, 33, 38, 49, 50, 61, 65, 75–77, 81, 84, 95, 97, 98, 100, 104, 120, 121, 125, 127, 129, 130, 132, 149, 167, 180, 181, 183, 203, 217, 225–227, 236, 237
Cyanide injections 98, 100, 167

D
Data
 Federal Bureau of Investigation (FBI) 115
 Hickey 9, 69, 70, 72, 74, 76, 78, 80, 82, 88, 89, 94, 116, 119, 121, 123, 125, 131, 134, 142–144
 Holmes and Holmes 9, 22–24, 27–30, 37, 38, 40, 70, 72, 78, 80, 89, 101, 102, 110, 116, 152
 Trestrail 2, 12, 13, 25–27, 63, 71, 72, 117, 142
Demographics 17, 18, 69, 99, 112, 133, 135, 156
Dhillon, Sukhwinder Singh 48, 73, 76, 77, 129, 155, 176, 196, 198
Diaz, Robert Rubane 73, 85, 101
Differential reinforcement theory 21, 30, 33, 34, 38, 39, 139
Digitalis 46, 51, 77, 128, 166
Digitoxin 35, 51, 97, 104, 119, 212, 213
Diphtheria germs 84, 126
Doss, Nannie 10, 12, 17, 24, 31, 59, 76, 82, 83, 123, 127, 131, 133, 142, 144–146
Drugs as poisons 66
Dudley-Terrell, Bobby Sue 57, 96, 111, 121, 173

E
E605 15, 61, 62, 86, 87, 120, 124, 128, 129, 171
Elements

their compounds 15, 58, 66
their derivatives 15, 58, 66
Epinephrine 52, 53, 97, 102, 103, 121, 199
Ethnicity
  of poisoner 13, 17, 66
  of victim 16
Ethylene glycol anti-freeze 63, 64, 127, 155
Explanation 14, 18, 21, 22, 28, 30, 37, 39, 110, 138, 141, 144, 156, 208, 220, 221

F

Fletcher, Yvonne 63, 73, 76, 77, 84, 127

G

Geen, Benjamin 55, 73, 85, 97, 103, 120, 207
Gender
  of poisoner 5, 15, 90, 119, 120, 150
  of victim 6, 15, 16, 119, 120
Gibbs, Janie Lou 59, 127, 170
Gifford, Bertha 59, 87, 165
Gilbert, Kristen 53, 85, 97, 103, 176, 198, 199
Glyburide (as euglucon) 57, 176
Grills, Caroline 63, 79, 87, 128, 168
Grinder, Martha 60, 87, 130, 160

H

Harvey, Donald 50, 86, 97, 104, 142–144

Healthcare serial poisoner 16, 27, 73, 84, 85, 87, 100, 101, 107, 126, 133, 151, 152, 154, 159
Högel, Niels 2, 13, 25, 54, 85, 98, 103, 120, 182, 231–233
Homicide
  corporate 3, 8
  legal frameworks for 7, 17
  mass 9, 18, 22
  multiple 9, 17, 18, 22
  scale of 1, 11, 17, 18
  serial 1, 2, 9, 11, 12, 14, 17, 18, 22, 78, 81, 86, 94, 115, 116, 118, 122, 125
Hospital 26, 35, 50–52, 55–57, 63, 74, 80, 82, 86, 87, 94, 96–98, 104–110, 112, 117, 119–122, 133, 134, 148, 151–155, 170–172, 189, 192, 193, 195, 199–201, 203, 205, 208–210, 212, 214, 219–223, 229, 230, 232, 234

I

Insanity 59, 87, 100, 105
Insulin 15, 25, 26, 50, 56, 57, 96, 98, 102, 105, 111, 121, 223, 224, 229, 230, 234
Insulin injections 25, 57, 97, 98, 102, 105
Investigation 2, 3, 5, 11, 16–18, 64, 108, 111, 136–138, 140, 153, 155, 190, 197, 199, 200, 208, 213, 215, 217, 220, 227, 229, 234

Index

J

Jackson, Vickie Dawn 31, 54, 84, 97, 101, 142, 143, 214–216
Jeanneret, Marie 11, 47, 73, 85, 98, 102, 161
Jégado, Héléna 14, 33, 59, 76, 84, 130, 132, 160
Jones, Genene 55, 86, 96, 104, 121, 172

K

Kakehi, Chisako 10, 25, 50, 73, 75, 76, 80, 121, 127, 183, 236, 237
Kempanna, K.D. (Mallika) 24, 32, 50, 75, 83, 120, 123, 132, 149, 225–227
Kumar, Mohan 25, 65, 73, 75, 77, 81, 119, 123, 131, 132, 134, 180, 217

L

Labelling theory 14, 21, 30, 35, 36, 38, 39, 141
Lehmann, Christa 73, 87, 120, 124, 129, 168
Letter, Stephan 35, 55, 73, 86, 98, 104, 219, 233
Lidocaine 15, 26, 51, 54, 96, 98, 102, 182, 232
Location of poisoning 82
Lylles, Anjette 59, 127, 169

M

Majors, Orville Lynn 52, 102, 121, 175
Malèvre, Christine 35, 52, 73, 86, 98, 104, 177
Manslaughter 7, 8, 11, 219, 220
Marek, Martha 62, 128, 167
Methods of killing 15, 88, 90
Mivacurium chloride (Mivacron) 54, 97, 101, 102, 215, 216
Modus operandi 17, 34, 35, 39, 81, 99, 131, 140, 145, 147, 148, 155, 191, 204, 206, 217, 218, 225, 231, 235, 237
Moral reasoning theory 14, 21, 30, 38, 39, 139
Moreau, Pierre Désiré 73, 77, 84, 119, 126, 132
Morphine 10, 15, 48, 52, 55, 56, 77, 98, 104, 120, 130, 164, 167, 177, 190, 191, 202, 224
Mors, Frederick 65, 87, 97, 98, 105
Motive
    claimed mercy killing 38, 86, 154
    factitious disorder imposed on another 83, 100, 103, 112
    financial gain 13, 14, 26, 84, 95, 100, 124, 125, 131, 142, 144, 145, 154, 196, 198
    jealousy 13, 33, 83, 84, 100, 101, 112
    revenge 26, 84, 100, 101, 112
    thrill/excitement 24
Murano, Yiya 33, 73, 82, 84, 120, 130, 132, 172

N

Nesset, Arnfinn 10, 12, 55, 73, 82, 85, 98, 102, 121, 171
Nickell, Stella 26, 49, 79, 81, 83, 125, 129, 172
Norris, Colin (Campbell, Colin) 57, 85, 98, 102, 112, 181, 223, 224

O

Occupation
  of poisoner 120
  of victim 15, 16, 123, 124
Opportunity 31, 32, 39, 101, 105–107, 124, 139, 140, 152, 154, 211, 231, 233

P

Pancuroneum 54, 103
Patient (role) 78, 153
Perpetrator-patient role 105
Personal history
  of poisoner 15, 79, 90, 150
Pethidine (as Demerol) 56, 102, 227
Petiot, Dr Marcel 49, 73, 95, 98, 100, 167
Phosphorus 15, 61, 127
Planning
  quick 25–27, 83
  slow 25–27
Plant poisons 15, 50, 66
Point of entry for investigation 137
Police 2, 10–12, 17, 31, 64, 82, 111, 117, 118, 123, 124, 136, 144, 149, 155, 156, 164, 166, 178, 190–192, 195, 197, 199, 201, 203, 207, 208, 211, 213, 216, 217, 219, 221–223, 226, 230, 232, 234–236
Popova, Madame 59, 73, 84, 120, 130, 164
Potassium 26, 35, 49, 52, 54, 58, 60, 62, 98, 102, 104, 121, 175, 177, 182, 232
Potassium chloride 26, 52, 54, 98, 102, 121, 175, 182, 232
Preventative measures 108, 112
Pritchard, Dr Edward 47, 60, 77, 86, 95, 119, 126, 160
Profiling 17, 137, 147–149, 156
Psychological factors 14, 21, 28, 30
Puente, Dorothea 56, 79, 97, 174

R

Rational choice theory 14, 21, 30, 32, 38, 140
Red flags 107, 108, 152
Rosenfeld, Brian 56, 85, 97, 102, 174
Routines
  of victim 16, 107, 122

S

Saenz, Kimberley Clark 63, 87, 97, 105, 181, 227
Saldivar, Efren 54, 75, 79, 87, 97, 122, 177, 201, 202
Serial homicide 2, 9, 11, 12, 17, 18, 22, 37, 72, 78, 81, 86, 94, 115, 116, 118, 122, 125
Serial killers

hedonistic 22–24, 31, 40, 70, 102, 152
missionary 22–24
power/control 22–24, 40, 70, 100, 101
visionary 22, 24, 29, 70
Shipman, Dr Harold 10, 12, 49, 71, 79, 80, 85, 97, 101, 105, 118, 122, 155, 189–191, 209
Social background
of poisoner 15, 76, 90, 124
of victim 16, 124, 154
Sodium hypochlorite (bleach) 97, 105, 181, 228
Soloviev, Viacheslav 10, 36, 63, 73, 80, 121, 129, 221, 222
Sorenson, Della 73, 87, 121, 128, 165
Sotalol (Sotalex) 26, 98, 182, 232
Strain theory 21, 30, 32, 33, 38, 39, 139
Strychnine 38, 45, 47, 48, 65, 76, 77, 79, 84, 95, 128–130, 155, 162, 163, 196–198
Succinylcholine chloride (as lysthenon) 10, 35, 56, 104, 180
Succinylcholine chloride 10, 35, 54–56, 98, 102–104, 171, 173, 180
Suicide 3, 8, 10, 33, 89, 138, 175, 178, 181, 189, 192, 206, 211, 212, 216–218, 222
Suxamethonium chloride 55, 97, 177, 201, 202
Swanenberg, Maria 59, 73, 76, 84, 130, 161
Swango, Dr Michael 59, 81, 87, 96, 105, 111, 131, 175, 191–194

T
Team serial killers 9, 87, 134
Team serial poisoners 88, 134
Thallium 10, 14, 36, 38, 62, 63, 74, 76, 79, 84, 85, 87, 121, 127–130, 155, 167, 168, 170, 180, 221, 222
Theory 6, 7, 14, 18, 21, 28, 30, 32–36, 39, 40, 90, 137–139, 141, 156
Toppan, Jane 48, 73, 85, 96, 98, 102, 163
Trial 11, 17, 90, 102, 118, 145, 160, 173, 181, 190, 199, 200, 204, 205, 208–210, 215, 217, 219, 220, 222, 228, 232, 236, 237
Tuberculosis germs 84, 126, 165
Turner, Lynn 207
Tylenol 27, 56, 79, 97, 130
Typologies 14, 16, 21, 22, 24, 25, 27, 29, 39, 40, 70, 101–103, 152

V
Vân, Lê Thanh 50, 73, 76, 77, 129, 203, 204
Velten, Maria 62, 86, 128, 171
Victim
random 23, 25–27
specific 23, 25, 27

W
Waddingham, Dorothea 48, 73, 84, 97, 101, 120, 166
Waite, Dr Arthur 51, 73, 84, 120, 126, 132, 165

Wettlaufer, Elizabeth 25, 57, 73, 87, 97, 98, 105, 182, 233–235
Whiteling, Sarah 59, 84, 127, 162
Wiese, Elisabeth 48, 77, 84, 119, 121, 130, 132
Wilson, Mary 61, 74, 108, 119, 125, 127, 132, 152, 169, 175

Y

Young, Graham 14, 38, 63, 73, 74, 76, 79, 85, 120, 124, 130, 132, 155, 170

Printed by Printforce, the Netherlands